Antifundamentalism in Modern America

Antifundamentalism in Modern America

David Harrington Watt

Cornell University Press
Ithaca and London

First published 2017 by Cornell University Press

Printed in the United States of America

Library of Congress Cataloging-in-Publication Data

Names: Watt, David Harrington, author.
Title: Antifundamentalism in modern America / David Harrington Watt.
Description: Ithaca ; London : Cornell University Press, 2017. | Includes bibliographical references and index.
Identifiers: LCCN 2016048570 (print) | LCCN 2016049371 (ebook) | ISBN 9780801448270 (cloth : alk. paper) | ISBN 9781501708534 (pdf) | ISBN 9781501708541 (epub/mobi)
Subjects: LCSH: Religious fundamentalism—History. | Religious fundamentalism—United States—History. | Religion and politics—United States.
Classification: LCC BL238 .W38 2017 (print) | LCC BL238 (ebook) | DDC 200.973/09051—dc23
LC record available at https://lccn.loc.gov/2016048570

Cornell University Press strives to use environmentally responsible suppliers and materials to the fullest extent possible in the publishing of its books. Such materials include vegetable-based, low-VOC inks and acid-free papers that are recycled, totally chlorine-free, or partly composed of nonwood fibers. For further information, visit our website at www.cornellpress.cornell.edu.

For D. M. S., D. V. S., and W. R. H.

Contents

Preface

What is fundamentalism? What do fundamentalists believe? What do they do? What can we do to keep fundamentalists from obstructing human progress?

Americans have been discussing these questions since 1920—the year in which the word "fundamentalist" first entered the English language. Their attempts to answer them are the focus of this book. *Antifundamentalism* traces how the meaning of fundamentalism has changed over time and explores how the label "fundamentalists" came to be assigned to a great many people who were sure that they were not, in fact, fundamentalists. It explores Americans' fears about the destructive power of religion and their efforts to distinguish "good" religious practices from "dangerous" ones.

In July 2006, Salim Chowdhury and I hired a cycle rickshaw to take us from the University of Dhaka to the headquarters of Jamaat-e-Islami, at that time part of the coalition that governed Bangladesh.[1] Members of Jamaat-e-Islami played an important role in the deliberations of Parliament, and the party held two posts in the cabinet.[2]

The building that served as the party's headquarters was not in an exclusive neighborhood and it was not especially large; it seemed to consist of only eight or nine rooms. The file cabinets, desks, chairs, and couches with which the office was furnished were not at all flashy: they looked like the sort of furniture one might find in a middle-class home or in a history department of a university that did not have a great deal of money. The posters that served as decorations for the walls carried slogans that were meant to be inspirational. Some of the posters were slightly tattered. To me, the headquarters of Jamaat-e-Islami seemed quite modest. It was an attractive enough place, but it certainly was not majestic or awe-inspiring. Given that Jamaat-e-Islami was, in the summer of 2006, one of the more powerful political parties in one of the most populous nations in the world, its offices were remarkably unpretentious.

Chowdhury, who taught in the University of Dhaka's Department of World Religions, introduced himself to the dozen or so men who were working in the front offices of the building. Then he introduced me and told them that I was in Bangladesh to deliver some lectures. The men all seemed genuinely happy to see Chowdhury and me, and they all seemed eager to make sure that we felt like welcome guests. We exchanged pleasantries and then made the ritualistic exchange of business cards that seems to be a part of all meetings in Bangladesh. After the exchange of cards, Chowdhury and I were ushered into the study of one of the most powerful and learned of Jamaat-e-Islami's leaders, a man named Bashir Khan.[3] After a few minutes, Khan entered the room, greeted Chowdhury and me warmly, and arranged to have us brought water to drink and slices of mango to eat.

Khan was a handsome man with a pleasing voice. His manners were impeccable. And he was also remarkably intelligent—a good deal more intelligent than most of the American politicians I have met. Khan knew a great deal about many topics and he was a wonderful conversationalist. He talked to Chowdhury for a while in Bangla about matters that did not concern me and then politely asked why I had wanted to meet with him. I told him that between giving my lectures, I was trying to learn as much as I could about Bangladeshi religion and politics and that I had been repeatedly struck by the fact that many people I had met during my travels had very strong views concerning Jamaat-e-Islami.

That was actually something of an understatement. Jamaat-e-Islami is strongly committed to refashioning Bangladeshi culture and society so that they will conform more closely to Muslim ideals, and it actively works toward Bangladesh's transformation into "an Islamic Republic" whose laws are based solely on the Qur'an and Sunnah.[4] That is a controversial goal; many of the Muslims and Hindus who live in Bangladesh believe that Bangladesh ought to be a secular society—secular not in the sense of irreligious but in the sense of having a polity in which religion and politics are completely separate. In the eyes of many Bangladeshis, Jamaat-e-Islami's program is objectionable: many Bangladeshis believe that it combines religious commitments and political activity in a way that is illegitimate. Indeed, some of the Bangladeshis I met told me that they believed that the leadership of Jamaat-e-Islami included a number of thugs whose behavior during Bangladesh's War of Independence had literally been criminal. (Some of the leaders of Jamaat-e-Islami are thought to have helped Pakistani soldiers round up and massacre innocent Bangladeshi civilians.) In the eyes of some of its critics, Jamaat-e-Islami is a Bangladeshi analog to the Taliban.[5]

During the course of our meeting, Khan explained why so many of the leaders of Jamaat-e-Islami had fought against the creation of an independent Bangladesh. He also told Chowdhury and me about what would happen to the millions of Hindus who live in Bangladesh if Jamaat-e-Islami succeeded in putting the policies it advocated into effect; he claimed that Jamaat-e-Islami was deeply committed to making sure that Hindus were treated with respect. Khan, Chowdhury, and I also talked about socialism, about the American political scientist Samuel Huntington, and about the doctrine of the trinity. (Khan was pleased to learn that I was not a Trinitarian.) We also talked about what gets lost when the Qur'an is translated from Arabic into English and about the ideas of Sayyid Qutb, the Egyptian intellectual from whom Osama bin Laden derived some of his ideas. Everything that Khan had to say about these various topics was interesting to me. But there was one point in the conversation in which Khan's remarks took me entirely by surprise. That came when Khan warned me that it would be a terrible mistake for me to think that the members of Jamaat-e-Islami are fundamentalists. They are nothing of the sort, he asserted. If one began one's analysis of Jamaat-e-Islami by labeling it as an expression of fundamentalism, Khan said, one could never begin to grasp the true nature of the movement.

In point of fact, it never would have occurred to me to describe Jamaat-e-Islami as a fundamentalist organization. Of course, I knew that there were many people in the world who had fallen into the habit of speaking about "Islamic fundamentalism" and that the hallmarks of that phenomenon were sometimes said to be a hostility to feminism, democracy, and modernity. And I knew that some social scientists had said that fundamentalism is "a discernible pattern of religious militance by which self-styled 'true believers' attempt to arrest the erosion of religious identity, fortify the borders of the religious community, and create viable alternatives to secular institutions and behaviors."[6] But my understanding of fundamentalism is quite close to the definition to be found in the second edition of Webster's *New International Dictionary*, which defines it as a movement made up of American Protestants who were opposed to theological modernism and who were determined to emphasize the importance of some of the tenets of traditional Christianity: the virgin birth and Christ's physical resurrection, for instance.[7] The members of Jamaat-e-Islami do not embrace that set of doctrines, they are not Protestants, and they are not Americans. Nor have they been influenced, in any direct way, by American fundamentalists. Given all that, it seemed clear to me that it would be wildly anachronistic to assign the fundamentalist label to that organization. Khan obviously thought so too. Nevertheless, he seemed to think that there was a good chance that I was going to assume that he and the other members of Jamaat-e-Islami were fundamentalists, and he wanted to make sure that I did not make that erroneous assumption.

Khan's suspicion was well founded: nearly all Americans believe that fundamentalism is noxious. But most of us do not have a clear understanding of what fundamentalism actually is. When we are asked precisely what we mean when we are talking about fundamentalism, we have a difficult time giving a coherent response. When asked that question, Americans have a tendency to say something about extremism or a hostility to feminism or a rejection of the modern world and then go on to declare that although it is difficult to define fundamentalism with any exactitude, it is not at all hard to have a *general* sense of what it is and of the threats it poses to people "like us." Nearly all Americans believe, as Barack Obama asserted in 2004, that "the embrace of fundamentalism . . . dooms us all."[8]

Obama's assertion can be seen as an example of a phenomenon that is referred to as "antifundamentalism" in the pages of this book. As I understand it, antifundamentalism is a set of conversations (literal and metaphorical) that began in the 1920s and that have continued to the present. People who have engaged in those conversations are asking the four questions with which this preface began. They were trying to figure out what fundamentalism is and what fundamentalists do. But they were doing more than that. They were also trying to assess the threats that fundamentalists pose to human progress, and they were attempting to determine the best ways to respond to those threats.

To avoid any possible misunderstandings, I need to emphasize from the outset that antifundamentalism as it is used in the pages of this book is *not* a stable concept. Far from it. It is rather a set of shifting heterogeneous conversations.

Antifundamentalism as it presently exists—the form that is directed at Muslims, Jews, Sikhs, and Hindus, as well as at Protestant Christians—is a relatively recent phenomenon; it did not arise until the early 1980s. But the roots of this kind of antifundamentalism go back to the fundamentalist-modernist controversies that took place in the early decades of the twentieth century. Antifundamentalism was invented in the 1920s and was refined and propagated in the 1930s, 1940s, 1950s, 1960s, and 1970s. The concept of fundamentalism was never intended to be neutral or value free. From the very beginning, people who invoked the concept were making evaluative judgments. When someone like Curtis Lee Laws—the man who coined the word "fundamentalists"—said that a particular group of Protestants was composed of fundamentalists, he was making an implicit comparison to nonfundamentalists, whom he viewed as inferior. In Laws's view, fundamentalists were people who were loyal to the fundamentals of the Christian faith and who were willing to stand up for what was right. Nonfundamentalists, in contrast, had never accepted the fundamentals of the faith, had drifted away from them, or had not defended them with as much conviction as they should have. From the perspective of a man like Laws, it was quite clear that fundamentalists were doing the work of God and that nonfundamentalists were not living their lives in accord with God's will. Fundamentalists had correctly perceived the nature of the universe; nonfundamentalists had failed to do so.

That was not, of course, the only way the relationship between fundamentalists and nonfundamentalists could be understood. One could also use the binary of fundamentalists and nonfundamentalists as a way of dividing the world into people who were backward, intolerant, regressive, and unenlightened (fundamentalists) and people who were modern, tolerant, progressive, and enlightened (nonfundamentalists). According to this scheme—which was developed by liberal polemicists such as Harry Emerson Fosdick and Kirsopp Lake—fundamentalists were the people who had failed to grasp the nature of the universe, stubbornly old-fashioned Protestants determined to stand in the way of progress and modernity. The nonfundamentalists were people who had jettisoned outworn dogmas and embraced new truths.

This view was no less tendentious than the one fundamentalists such as Laws presented; it was a concoction used by people on one side of a cultural and political struggle to advance their cause and belittle their adversaries. But the interpretation of fundamentalism that progressive Protestants such as Fosdick and Lake advanced was adopted by scholars such as H. Richard Niebuhr and Talcott Parsons and presented as though it were simply a straightforward description of social reality. In 1931, Niebuhr said that fundamentalism was a form of religion that was practiced in the less-developed regions of the United States. All rational men, Parsons confidently declared in 1940, could see that history was on the side of the nonfundamentalists. At best, fundamentalism was an understandable but misguided response to the challenges of modernity; at worst, it was an embodiment of irrational atavism.

In the 1950s and 1960s, historians such as Norman F. Furniss and Richard Hofstadter and filmmakers such as Stanley Kramer vividly presented the dangers of fundamentalism. In the 1970s, most Americans came to think that fundamentalism was linked to anti-intellectualism, obscurantism, zealotry, religious extremism, fanaticism, and narrow-mindedness. Fundamentalists were seen as people who were fighting modernity, a foe they could not possibly defeat.

The late 1970s and early 1980s marked the crucial turning point in the history of antifundamentalism. During those years the concept of fundamentalism was reinvented as it was turned into a way of talking about Hindus, Sikhs, Jews, and Muslims. In 1980, in "Fundamentalism Reborn," Martin Marty drew on the ideas of Parsons to create one of the first—and one of the most compelling—denunciations of global fundamentalism.

Within a few years of the publication of Marty's article, men and women closely associated with the U.S. government began to worry about the threats Islamic fundamentalism posed to world peace. One might even go so far as to say that in the 1980s and early 1990s, "threats posed by Islamic fundamentalism" became a quasi-official governmental category. In 1990, Vice President Dan Quayle, speaking to an audience at the U.S. Naval Academy at Annapolis, likened Islamic fundamentalism to communism and Nazism. The threat it posed to the world, he asserted, was one of the primary reasons the United States was obliged to maintain well-trained and well-equipped armed forces.[9] A 1993 congressional report included warnings from foreign affairs experts about the threats to the United States fundamentalist movements in the Muslim world posed. The United States, one expert said, should try to undercut and thwart such movements wherever it had the power to do so.[10] In 1994, the Federal Bureau of Investigation went so far as to establish a surveillance unit that monitored people associated with "radical fundamentalism." The next year, the speaker of the U.S. House of Representatives remarked that he had come to suspect that Islamic fundamentalism was "probably the largest single threat to civilized behavior in the next decade anywhere on the planet."[11] That same year, while speaking in Paris, President Bill Clinton told reporters that he was gravely concerned about "the rise of militant fundamentalism in Islamic states."[12]

Governmental officials spoke about the threats associated with the varieties of fundamentalism rooted in Christianity, Judaism, Hinduism, and Buddhism far less frequently than they talked about those associated with Islamic fundamentalism. But in the years after the publication of Marty's essay, Muslims were not the only kind of fundamentalists that attracted attention. Many Americans came to assume that fundamentalists were creating turmoil all over the world. The actions of Jewish fundamentalists in Israel, Hindu fundamentalists in India, Buddhist fundamentalists in Sri Lanka, and Christian fundamentalists in the United States and Latin America were also decried. In the late twentieth and early twenty-first centuries, the concept of fundamentalism—which had earlier been thought of as a problem that was chiefly limited to the United States—became a way of reflecting on problems that seemed to have cropped up all over the world. The story of how fundamentalism came to be seen as a global menace—rather than simply an American one—is at the heart of this book.

My understanding of the histories of fundamentalism and antifundamentalism developed as I was exploring a set of sermons, speeches, memos, articles, and books published in the United States between 1920 and the present. The great preponderance of those texts were written by people who were living in or visiting the United States at the time they wrote them. The procedures I used to identify the texts were fairly straightforward. I began by looking for relevant materials in the collections of the libraries of Temple University and Harvard University, and I found that those collections contained a vast amount of material that was germane to this project. Later on, I made a series of systematic searches through the collections—both physical and electronic—of several other libraries located in Pennsylvania, New Jersey, New York, and New Hampshire.

Another of this book's limitations should be noted at the outset. While the way historians who were working in the 1940s, 1950s, 1960s, and 1970s thought about Protestant fundamentalism receives a good deal of attention in the pages of this book, I have made no attempt to give a detailed chronological account of the evolution of historians' views of Protestant fundamentalism since the 1980s. Instead, my account of antifundamentalism in the years from 1980 to the present focuses on writers' approaches to global fundamentalism—not on Protestant fundamentalism in North America. Historians' views of Protestant fundamentalism have shifted dramatically in the past four decades, and it is difficult to overstate the significance of those changes. I am deeply indebted to the work of more recent historians of fundamentalism, and chapter three of this book draws heavily on their articles and books.

But for all its significance, the work of those scholars lies outside the boundaries of antifundamentalism proper. The more nuanced interpretations of Protestant fundamentalism that they have produced in recent decades are not, as a general rule, aimed at alerting readers to the dangers of fundamentalism or at telling those readers what they ought to do to fight back against fundamentalists. In recent years, historians seem to have been less interested in denouncing Protestant fundamentalists than in understanding them. I hope that other scholars will turn their attention to the recent historiography of Christian (Protestant) fundamentalism. A thorough explanation of how and why historians' understanding of Protestant fundamentalism in the United States has shifted so dramatically between the 1970s and the present would be enormously useful.

As the pages that follow suggest, the history of antifundamentalism in the United States is a rich and interesting one. It contains a good deal of conflict, and there are many twists and turns. However, I did not write this book solely because I wanted to chronicle the history of antifundamentalism. What I wanted to do, rather, was to tell that story in a way that sheds fresh light on a set of crucial questions that are of great interest to a good many thoughtful Americans. What is the relationship between analyses of religious movements and attempts to regulate such movements? To what degree is it possible to relegate religion to the private sphere and seal it off from the realm of government and politics? In what ways, if any, have the events of the past century forced us to revise our notions about modernization, secularization, and the ideals of the European Enlightenment? Those basic questions surface time and time again in the history of antifundamentalism. Those questions—and the various ways people living in the United States have tried to answer them—are explored in this book.

People who read it will, I hope, reach four principal conclusions. First, a good many of the most influential analyses of fundamentalism were created by men and women who had not spent much time investigating the beliefs and practices of actual fundamentalists. Second, fundamentalism is a concept that has been used at least as often to express certain moral commitments—that human beings have a duty to accept and affirm the universal truths discovered by the European Enlightenment, for example—as it has been used to make an honest effort to comprehend the beliefs and practices of religious people. Third, using the term "fundamentalism" to describe the beliefs and practices of conservative Protestants such as Bob Jones Sr. and Jerry Falwell makes a great deal of sense; it does not make much sense at all, however, to use that concept to analyze the beliefs and practices of Jews, Muslims, and Hindus. As a general rule, assigning the fundamentalist label to people who do not think of themselves as fundamentalists tends to produce skewed analyses of the world in which we live. Trying to use a concept that is firmly rooted in the polemical battles waged by American Protestants in the 1920s and 1930s to understand the beliefs and practices of contemporary Muslims, Jews, Hindus, and Buddhists seldom accomplishes much. Trying to decide, for example, which Muslims are fundamentalists and which are not makes no more sense than trying to figure out which Christians are Sunnis and which are Shiites. Fourth, not all of the people who focus their energies on bringing an end to the fundamentalist threat are full of virtue and not all of the people who get called fundamentalists are thoroughly evil. The world is more complicated than that. The people who embrace the beliefs and practices that are associated with what we call fundamentalism sometimes do and say terrible things. So do people who are dyed-in-the-wool antifundamentalists.

I don't expect all—or even most—readers to reach those conclusions. Controversies have swirled around fundamentalism since the year that it was invented. This book will not end them. I do hope, however, that it will encourage readers to spend some time reflecting on the many peculiarities connected to fundamentalism and on how relying on that concept can hinder our attempts to make sense of the role religion plays in shaping world events. At the present moment, it seems clear that millions of men and women are deeply attached to religious practices and beliefs that other human beings see as primitive and outmoded. Those attachments are unlikely to fade away anytime soon. It is possible that those attachments—and the need to make sense of them—will persist long after fundamentalism has become obsolete.

Acknowledgments

The people who work in the libraries of Temple University, Palmer Theological Seminary, Westminster Theological Seminary, the University of Pennsylvania, Princeton University, Princeton Seminary, Columbia University, Union Theological Seminary, Dartmouth College, and Harvard University have given me a huge amount of assistance on this project; time and time again I have been struck by their professionalism and kindness. I would especially like to express my gratitude to Larry Alford, Jennifer Lee Baldwin, Steven Bell, Fred Burchsted, Ruth Tonkiss Cameron, Karla Grafton, Penelope Myers, Grace Mullen, David Murray, Fran O'Donnell, and Fred Rowland.

Temple University has been generous in its support of this project. It has given me time off from my teaching responsibilities to focus on research and writing and it has awarded me several research grants to defray costs associated with my research. My colleagues in the History Department, the Department of Religion, the General Education Program, and the Center for the Humanities at Temple have gone out of their way to be helpful.

Temple University, Lehigh University, New York University, Monash University, Princeton University, and Yale University were kind enough to let me try out some of my ideas about fundamentalism before highly intelligent, skeptical, and extremely generous audiences. Similar audiences at conferences sponsored by the American Historical Association and the American Academy of Religion also helped me refine my ideas about fundamentalism. Courtney Bender kindly invited me to present material from this book to Columbia University's Seminar on Religion in America. Columbia's Schoff Fund provided funds to support this book's publication. Portions of this book appeared in a somewhat different form in *Fides et Historia*, the *Journal of Religion & Society*, and in *Fundamentalism: Perspectives on a Contested History* (an anthology that I, together with Simon A. Wood, edited for the University of South Carolina Press). Permission to reprint that material is greatly appreciated.

While writing this book I received advice from Alison Anderson, Julie Byrne, Cecelia Cancellaro, Joel Carpenter, Steven Conn, Rosemary Corbett, Jerilyn Famighetti, Petra Goedde, Janet Jakobsen, Kathryn Lofton, Harvey Neptune, Ann Pellegrini, Marian Ronan, Leigh Schmidt, J. Terry Todd, Theodore Trost, Thomas Tweed, Daniel Vaca, Elise Watt, and Simon A. Wood. I'm deeply grateful to them for their generosity.

The research assistance I received from Richard Kent Evans was invaluable. Working with him was a joy. On several occasions, Martin Marty took time out from his very busy schedule to talk to me about how he and other scholars think about religious fundamentalism. Marty's views on fundamentalism and antifundamentalism are very different from mine, but I have certainly profited from his advice, and I greatly admire his generosity of spirit. Laura Levitt's support of this project has been unflagging. But that is by no means the primary reason that I am grateful to her. After all these years, Laura still surprises, inspires, and amazes.

Antifundamentalism in Modern America

Introduction

Putting Fundamentalism to Work

At 8:46 on the morning of September 11, 2001, hijackers flew a Boeing 767 into the north tower of the World Trade Center in New York City. Seventeen minutes later, another airliner was flown into the south tower. At 9:37 a plane slammed into the Pentagon, outside Washington, DC. A fourth plane crashed near Shanksville, Pennsylvania, less than a half-hour after that. It soon became clear that the men who carried out the attacks of 9/11—unlike those associated with the attack on the federal building in Oklahoma City that had occurred in 1995—were Muslims. While Americans were still reeling, the editors of *GQ*, a monthly men's magazine whose editorial offices were located in Midtown Manhattan, asked Karen Armstrong to write an article that explained the causes and consequences of the attacks of 9/11. Armstrong was a well-known journalist who was well versed in the history of Judaism, Christianity, and Islam. In 2000, she had written a book, *The Battle for God*, about conservative religious movements, that had received a number of positive reviews. Seven years before that, she had published a book on the history of monotheism that had become, somewhat improbably, a *New York Times* bestseller.[1]

The article Armstrong produced for *GQ* was called "Is a Holy War Inevitable?"[2] It appeared in December 2001, a month after the last Taliban soldiers fled Kabul and a month before the first prisoners were sent to Guantanamo Bay. In that article Armstrong gave her readers a primer on who fundamentalists were and how they viewed the universe. She told them that fundamentalists were defined by their hostility to the modern world. If I am not mistaken, I ran across "Is a Holy War Inevitable?" in a barbershop. It caught my eye in part because I was already familiar with Armstrong's work and in part because it was accompanied by a remarkable full-page image of a dark-skinned Muslim man draped in black from head to foot and carrying an AK-47. The man in the photograph looked both dashing and sinister; he resembled the models whose photographs accompanied the various fashion articles in *GQ*.

Armstrong's article gives me a convenient starting point for thinking about what happens when we talk about the nature of fundamentalism and how its adherents are different from other human beings. After looking at Armstrong's article, I examine the analyses of fundamentalism that were produced by a group of scholars associated with the highly influential Fundamentalism Project, which was sponsored by the American Academy of Arts and Science and housed at the University of Chicago in the late 1980s and early 1990s. These analyses are among the most sophisticated interpretations of fundamentalism that have ever been presented. Armstrong relied on them heavily as she was formulating her ideas about fundamentalism, as have many other writers and scholars. The influence the Fundamentalism Project has exerted on the way Americans think about fundamentalism is almost impossible to exaggerate. But for all its influence, the Fundamentalism Project was an odd enterprise in several important respects. Reflecting on those oddities will enable us to get a better sense of what is at stake in the debates over the usefulness of the term "fundamentalism."

Holy War

In her article for *GQ*, Armstrong assured her readers that America did not have to get embroiled in a holy war and that the attacks of 9/11 were not a sign that Islam had declared war on the West. Islamic civilization, she said, was not an adversary that had to be defeated. The civilization Muslims had created was a great one worthy of our admiration and respect. Islam was a religion that helped its adherents to live decent, meaningful lives. It taught them the importance of treating the poorest members of the community with kindness and generosity. According to Armstrong, Islam was a religion whose adherents were obliged to eschew bigotry and hatred and to embrace tolerance and compassion. It was a religion that exhorted its followers to regard violence as "abhorrent and evil" and to do all that they could to promote compassion and peace.

Armstrong's glowing description of the Muslim religion must have left some of her readers scratching their heads. If Islam was as meritorious as Armstrong said it was, then how in the world could a group of Muslims carry out the attacks of 9/11? How could such a religion give rise to such heinous acts? "Is a Holy War Inevitable?" suggested that in order to answer those questions we had to stop thinking of the hijackers as Muslims per se and begin thinking of them as Islamic fundamentalists—as people who had, in other words, failed to embrace authentic Islam and instead chosen to adhere to a debased form of that religion. The fundamentalists who had carried out the attacks of 9/11 were angry men who had distorted the faith they claimed to defend. Armstrong told her readers that moderate Muslims were appalled by what had occurred on 9/11. They were sympathetic to the West and wished to ally themselves with it. Fundamentalists, on the other hand, saw the West as the enemy. Not all fundamentalists were evil, Armstrong said. The vast majority of them were good people who were simply trying to live religious lives in a world that seemed to be becoming more and more secular. And only a tiny portion of the fundamentalists in the world were willing to use terrorism to accomplish their goals. But some fundamentalists were brutal men who were full of nihilistic rage. Those fundamentalists posed a grave threat to world peace.

According to Armstrong, fundamentalists' anger was rooted in part in their conviction that the United States was hypocritical: it claimed to be devoted to principles of morality and justice but often treated other societies with callous disdain. It was impossible, the fundamentalists believed, to reconcile U.S. foreign policy with the most basic notions of fairness and decency. But fundamentalists' rage, Armstrong told her readers, was not directed primarily at the foreign policies of the United States.

Fundamentalists were enraged by—and also frightened of—modernity itself. Their hostility to the modern world was what set Islamic fundamentalists apart from their moderate coreligionists. A determination to fight modernity was, Armstrong said, the defining characteristic of fundamentalism. Although Armstrong clearly believed that the fundamentalists' struggle against modernity would inevitably end in defeat, she did not portray that struggle as completely irrational. The ideas propagated by people such as Sayyid Qutb and the Ayatollah Khomeini were impractical, but they were not preposterous or deranged. Fundamentalists' way of life really was inimical to modernity. Modern civilization and fundamentalism were polar opposites. From some points of view, it made sense for the fundamentalists to try to strike back.

Nowhere in "Is a Holy War Inevitable?" did Armstrong give her readers a clear definition of modernity. But she suggested that modernity was associated with capitalism, technological sophistication, freedom, and individualism and then went on to observe that people who rejected modernity often had good reasons to reject it. The coming of modernity was a traumatic process that was accompanied by a great deal of bloodshed and suffering. Even in the West, where the gifts that modernity can bestow were most evident, the transition from traditional societies to modern ones had given rise to exploitation, persecution, genocide, environmental degradation, and "spiritual disorientation." And in the Muslim world modernization had been an especially painful process. Muslims experienced modernization not as an organic development of their own societies but rather as a by-product of having been subjugated. For them, modernization was deeply intertwined with colonization, violence, and compulsion. Devout Muslim men and women had been compelled to abandon traditional styles of dress and adopt Western styles. Some Muslims who opposed the policies of modernizers such as Muhammad Reza Shah had been imprisoned, tortured, and killed.

Armstrong told her readers that the coercive measures that had been used against the fundamentalists had only rarely led them to abandon their religious commitments. Attempts to suppress fundamentalism actually made it more virulent. Given that fact, the United States' response to the attacks of 9/11 ought not to be limited to a series of military engagements. The response should also include two campaigns, both of which were entirely nonviolent. The first campaign Armstrong called for was in large part concerned with public relations: it would try to change how Muslims thought about the United States. Many Muslims—moderates as well as fundamentalists—believed that the United States was a thoroughly secular nation in which immorality and greed were allowed free rein. Americans, Armstrong suggested, ought to make a determined effort to set the record straight. They ought to let the Muslim world know that the United States was, in fact, an unusually religious nation, many of whose citizens were deeply concerned with questions of morality. Americans ought to devote a great deal of energy to helping Muslims see that on many important matters connected to religion and morality, Americans and Muslims were in complete agreement. The second campaign Armstrong directed her readers' attention to had to do with matters of foreign policy. It would involve taking a hard look at the policies the United States had embraced and jettisoning those that were not in line with the nation's highest ideals. The United States should minimize the coercive and exploitative aspects of its relations with the Muslim world and ensure that it was treating the world's Muslims with the respect that they deserved.

"Is a Holy War Inevitable?" was more useful than a great many articles that were published in the immediate aftermath of 9/11. Armstrong wrote at a time when some people were saying that the attacks of 9/11 had been planned and executed by a network of evil fundamentalists and that all the Muslims involved in the conspiracy ought to be thought of as "rabid dogs" who needed to be hunted down and killed off with great dispatch.[3] When compared to those sorts of analyses, Armstrong's article seems calm, sensible, and remarkably humane. In sharp contrast to some of the texts that were published in the aftermath of the attacks, "Is a Holy War Inevitable?" portrayed fundamentalists as human beings who were wrestling with serious problems, not as crazy brutes. "Is a Holy War Inevitable?" was also full of praise for Islam. By emphasizing Islam's admirable characteristics, Armstrong made it more difficult for her readers to think of Muslims as evil incarnate; she also made it difficult for them to believe that everything associated with the West was good and everything associated with Islam was bad.

But in order to encourage her readers to reject one simpleminded comparative proposition—Islam is bad and the West is good—Armstrong exhorted them to accept another proposition—that Muslims who embrace fundamentalism are dangerous and those who reject it are trustworthy—that was not much more sophisticated than the first one. Armstrong described fundamentalism in ways that made it clear that she believed that it was, at base, a problem that had to be solved. It was clear to her that fundamentalists had misperceived the true nature of the universe and that compared to their moderate coreligionists and to people who were a part of Western civilization, they were somewhat backward. Fundamentalists were still struggling to adjust to modernity. They were still grappling with issues that Westerners had dealt with long, long ago.[4]

Militant Opposition to Modernity

None of the observations in "Is a Holy War Inevitable?" were novel or idiosyncratic: the article was, in large part, simply a popularization of other writers' ideas. The writers who had the greatest influence on Armstrong's understanding of fundamentalism were, it seems clear, a group of scholars associated with the Fundamentalism Project. "Influential" is one of the adjectives that is most frequently attached to that project, and for good reason: the role the project played in shaping how journalists, politicians, and scholars think about global fundamentalism is hard to exaggerate. In 1987, when the project was launched, the notion that fundamentalism was something that could be found in most of the world's religions was really nothing more than a speculative hypothesis. By the time the project came to an end, in 1995, global fundamentalism had come to be thought of, at least in the minds of many, as an established fact.[5]

The Fundamentalism Project was directed by R. Scott Appleby, a church historian who had received his PhD from the University of Chicago in 1985 and who would later go on to teach at Notre Dame, and by Martin E. Marty. The senior partner in the relationship was clearly Marty, an indefatigable writer who had been writing about the dangers of global fundamentalism since 1980.[6] Marty was also one of the most famous church historians in the world. A devout Lutheran and an ordained minister, he was particularly well known in church circles, but his scholarly explorations of modern church history had earned him fame well beyond the ecclesiastical realm. He held an endowed chair at the University of Chicago and in 1987 was elected to the presidency of the American

Academy of Religion. Ten years later, President Bill Clinton awarded him the National Humanities Medal.

The Fundamentalism Project was the result of an extraordinarily generous grant the John D. and Catherine T. MacArthur Foundation awarded to the American Academy of Arts and Sciences in the mid-1980s. The grant was meant to help the Academy, one of the most prestigious learned societies in the world, establish a program in public policy. The grant had relatively few strings attached to it; its terms allowed the Academy to investigate a topic of its own choosing. However, the terms of the grant required the Academy to launch an investigation that was "interdisciplinary, cross-cultural, and dedicated to the study of a subject of enduring relevance to public policy makers." The leaders of the Academy engaged in lengthy discussions about what subject ought to be investigated. They considered a wide range of possible topics, including AIDS and teen pregnancy.[7]

By the fall of 1987, the leaders of the Academy had decided to use the MacArthur money to fund an ambitious long-term exploration of global fundamentalism, named a steering committee to oversee the project, and asked Marty to serve as that committee's chair. Of course, Marty was not himself a fundamentalist, and he was convinced that global fundamentalism was a troublesome phenomenon. But as the project was being launched, the leaders of the Academy emphasized the importance of looking at the positive sides of fundamentalism and made it clear that scholars who were fundamentalists would be asked to make contributions to the project. Scholars who were fundamentalists would, it was hoped, help shape the project's overall design and conduct a portion of the research the project commissioned.[8]

The working assumptions on which the Fundamentalism Project rested were carefully spelled out in Marty's "Fundamentalism as a Social Phenomenon," an article that appeared in the *Bulletin of the American Academy of Arts and Sciences* in the fall of 1988. Marty said that the project was not meant to deplore, denounce, or deride fundamentalism. The goal was to understand fundamentalism, not to condemn it. Marty noted that although scholars who investigated fundamentalism might well discover things that made them want to laugh or cry, smirks or tears were not helpful. Cool, dispassionate analysis was what was needed.[9]

In order to understand what fundamentalism was, Marty asserted, one had to realize that it no longer made any sense to think of fundamentalism as a form of religion that could be found only among Protestant Christians. It was true, of course, that fundamentalism was created as a way of identifying a group of American Protestants who were deeply committed to a particular set of beliefs. But the older, restrictive definition of fundamentalism was now outdated. Nowadays, fundamentalism was a concept that was used to describe a variety of religious movements that were scattered all over the globe. And though some academics had originally hoped that the new broader meaning of fundamentalism would not take root, scholars were now increasingly inclined to accept the term's new meaning and to adopt it to their own ends. Global fundamentalism was here to stay, Marty predicted.

One of the best ways of getting at the new meaning of fundamentalism, Marty said, was to proceed "phenomenologically." He "had read widely in the comparative fundamentalism field" and paid careful attention to what the types of movements people thought of as being a part of fundamentalism had in common. On the basis of his reading, Marty offered a set of observations about how people think about fundamentalism. Those observations did not allow him to present a crystal-clear definition of fundamentalism and they did not enable him to present a simple procedure whereby one could separate fundamentalists from nonfundamentalists. But Marty's observations did allow him to create a list of tendencies that could, he thought, be used to begin to understand what global fundamentalism was.[10]

Fundamentalist movements were, Marty said, "absolutist." Often they were authoritarian. Fundamentalist movements were characterized by a "selective" retrieval of religious traditions; fundamentalists deemphasized certain elements of their traditions and singled out others as essential. Fundamentalists saw themselves as agents of a "sacred force, power, or person" and believed that they knew what the purpose of history was and the general direction history was moving in. Fundamentalists saw the world in terms of good and evil; their view of the world was "Manichean." Marty believed that fundamentalists were "reactive": they were trying to respond to a perceived threat. In short, fundamentalists had rejected conventional norms of secular rationality and were "antievolutionary," "antipermissive," and "antihermeneutical."[11]

A tendency to define fundamentalists in terms of what they opposed rather than in terms of what they supported became a hallmark of the project that Marty directed. When the American Academy of Arts and

Sciences wanted to explain to the public what the Fundamentalism Project was up to, it said it was investigating "militant religious movements" that were "anti-modernist and anti-secular." During the seven years in which it was in existence, the Fundamentalism Project sponsored ten major scholarly conferences.[12] A total of 220 scholars ended up contributing, in one way or another, to the project's work.[13] A great many of the scholars who participated in the Fundamentalism Project taught at universities in Israel and in the United States. But the project also drew on the expertise of scholars who were affiliated with institutions in Europe, South Asia, and Africa. A few of the scholars—Wayne Booth, Stanley Tambiah, and William H. McNeill, for example—were academics who possessed truly astounding intellectual gifts, and nearly all of the women and men who participated were scholars with very fine academic credentials. A fair proportion worked in the humanistic disciplines; many more worked in the social sciences.[14] Sociologists and political scientists seem to have played a particularly important role in shaping the work of the Fundamentalism Project.

The Fundamentalism Project sponsored a remarkably wide range of activities. It helped produce a series of television programs on global fundamentalism and created a companion volume to the series, called *The Power and the Glory*. (That book, by Martin Marty and R. Scott Appleby, presented the work of the project to a popular audience.)[15] The project also published an anthology of essays that explored the role of fundamentalism in shaping the Gulf Crisis of 1990–1991.[16] The Fundamentalism Project's activities received a good deal of attention in the press; journalists were understandably impressed by a project that had received the blessing of the University of Chicago, the American Academy of Arts and Sciences, and the MacArthur Foundation. Some government officials were also quite taken by the Fundamentalism Project and turned to R. Scott Appleby and other participants for advice on how to best respond to the rise of global fundamentalism.[17] A good many of the reviews of the various publications that grew out of the project were quite warm; some of the books that grew out of the project received awards for scholarly excellence.[18]

It is generally agreed that the most important publications to come out of the project were five books the University of Chicago Press published in the period 1991 to 1995. *Fundamentalisms Observed*, the first of those five volumes, contains fourteen essays that describe specific religious movements. The authors of those essays generally do not try to make comparisons between various forms of fundamentalism. Instead, they simply present clear analyses of, for example, Protestant fundamentalism in North America, Islamic fundamentalism in South Asia, and Jewish fundamentalism in Israel. *Fundamentalisms and Society*, the second volume in the series, explores how fundamentalism influences women's rights, education, and scientific research. Fundamentalism's effect on politics, economic systems, and state security is explored in the third book, *Fundamentalisms and the State*. The fourth, *Accounting for Fundamentalisms*, examines how fundamentalist movements are organized, how they recruit adherents, and how they change over time. The essays in the final volume in the series, *Fundamentalisms Comprehended*, consider how people in fundamentalist movements behave toward outsiders. They also reflect on a number of matters connected to defining what fundamentalism is and explaining why it arose.

The slimmest of the five books, *Fundamentalisms Comprehended*, was more than 500 pages long. The longest of them, *Fundamentalisms Observed*, is nearly 900 pages. Taken together, the books in the series contain 3,556 pages and weigh over seventeen pounds. The volumes present a wealth of empirical information about religious revitalization movements and constitute something akin to an encyclopedia of global fundamentalism. If you want to find out more about Jerry Falwell's theological positions, there is an article in *Accounting for Fundamentalisms* that can tell you exactly what you need to know. If you want to learn more about the history of Jamaat-e-Islami, there is an essay in *Fundamentalisms Observed* that you can consult. If you want to understand how marriage works among Mormon fundamentalists, you can turn to a wonderful essay on that topic in *Fundamentalisms and Society*. The quality of the empirical data presented in the five volumes is extraordinarily high. Overall, the publications that grew out of the Fundamentalism Project embody the study of global fundamentalism at its very best.[19]

Anomalies

None of the investigations of global fundamentalism that preceded the Fundamentalism Project were as comprehensive and sophisticated, and no subsequent investigation of global fundamentalism has surpassed the standard of scholarly excellence that the project established. Nevertheless, the Fundamentalism Project was in some respects an unusual endeavor. Several of those oddities are worth noting. For one thing, the conclusions to which the investigations sponsored by the project pointed are not especially impressive. One of those conclusions is that fundamentalists are committed to patriarchal values. A second conclusion is that many fundamentalists are very good at making use of mass media. A third conclusion is that there is some reason to believe that Muslim fundamentalists might be better positioned than Christian fundamentalists to bring about profound social change. Given the amount of time, energy, and money that were poured into the project, the conclusions seem surprisingly modest.[20]

Another anomaly concerns how little substantive analysis of fundamentalists' religious beliefs, practices, and experiences emerged from the Fundamentalism Project. Many of the texts that grew out of the project don't focus much attention at all on religion qua religion. If we are willing to assume that religion does not play a significant role in creating and animating the movements that get labeled as fundamentalist, then that is not a problem. But religious beliefs, practices, and experiences may lie at the very heart of most of the movements that are labeled as fundamentalist. If so, then accounts of global fundamentalism are explorations of religious phenomena, and if they consistently fail to take religion seriously, then they are, almost by definition, profoundly inadequate.

There is also something anomalous about the assumptions upon which the project rested. By the time the books that grew out of the Fundamentalism Project made their way into print, scholars had been talking about postmodernism, poststructuralism, and postcolonialism for more than two decades. And when one reads through the pages of books that grew out of the project, one sometimes encounters statements that suggest that the assumptions of "the West" have somehow been called into doubt. But the questions intellectuals such as Jacques Derrida, Jean-François Lyotard, and Edward Said asked had surprisingly little direct effect on how the scholars associated with the Fundamentalism Project approached their topics. When one reads through texts that grew out of the Fundamentalism Project, it sometimes seems hard to believe that they were really published in the 1990s. Huge chunks of them could have been produced in the 1970s, 1960s, or 1950s. They seem to have been written in a world in which Michel Foucault does not exist and one in which the ideas of men such as Max Weber and Talcott Parsons have never been contested.

And one also seems to be entering a world in which fundamentalists are unable to say anything about themselves. For reasons they did not fully explain, Marty and Appleby had difficulty finding fundamentalists who were willing to participate in the Fundamentalism Project. By 1991, Marty and Appleby had decided that the five volumes published by the University of Chicago would not include even a single essay written by a fundamentalist. The absence of such an essay exposed the project to the charges that its treatment of fundamentalism was somewhat one-sided. A five-volume set of anthologies on the nature of Judaism that did not include any texts whatsoever written by Jews would strike many readers as odd. So would a set of anthologies on liberalism that did not include any texts written by a liberal. Wasn't there something fishy, a reader might wonder, about producing five mammoth anthologies on fundamentalism that did not include even a single essay in which fundamentalism was analyzed by an actual fundamentalist?[21]

Another anomaly has to do with the question of whether global fundamentalism is a valid concept. The Fundamentalism Project was, of course, based on a wager that the concept was valid and helpful. However, a great many of the essays that grew out of the project were written by people who had concluded that the idea of global fundamentalism obscured more than it illuminated. A number of the essays include frank admissions that the concept of global fundamentalism does not illuminate the topic they discuss.[22] The number of such declarations in the publications the Fundamentalism Project sponsored is really quite extraordinary.[23] Marty and Appleby were not alarmed by the choruses of "for what I study, this just doesn't work." Instead, they soldiered on. They continuously tweaked their definitions of global fundamentalism and they consistently asserted that they believed that the concept might well prove to be useful.

However, in their introduction to *Fundamentalisms Comprehended* (the fifth and final volume in the Chicago series), Marty and Appleby frankly noted that there really are some quite legitimate arguments against accepting the validity of global fundamentalism. The doubts that surfaced in the early days of the project about the usefulness of the concept of global fundamentalism by no means disappeared as the project went on. The scholarly debates about whether the concept was valid, Marty and

Appleby predicted, would probably continue for the foreseeable future. They also said that they believed that there might come a time when the term "fundamentalism" might disappear from the scholarly lexicon.[24] A careful reader of the texts that grew out of the Fundamentalism Project might possibly conclude that she or he was reading about a phenomenon whose very existence was still in doubt.

Such a reader might also have been left with a clear impression, however, that, if fundamentalism really did exist, then its existence created a set of problems that needed to be solved. To be sure, most of the work that grew out of the Fundamentalism Project was not overtly polemical, and the directors took pride in presenting a set of texts that they thought of as evenhanded and fair. But the Fundamentalism Project included a number of scholars who had strong personal convictions about the dangers associated with antimodern religious movements.

Marty expressed his views on such movements in his final report on the accomplishments of the Fundamentalism Project. That report, titled "Too Bad We Are So Relevant," appeared in the *Bulletin of the American Academy of Arts and Sciences* in 1996. In his report, Marty declared that "anyone who is not a member of a fundamentalist movement" could clearly see that fundamentalism is a dangerous phenomenon. It was undeniably true, Marty said, that a good deal of what went on in fundamentalism was "threatening—or even devastating—to other kinds of fundamentalists, to more moderate co-religionists in the complexes out of which particular fundamentalisms grow, to their neighbors and rivals, to governments, and to the idea of civil society." It looked as though fundamentalist movements were going to have the power to shape world events for the foreseeable future. In a way, Marty implied, that was a good thing: it meant that the Academy's decision to pour millions of dollars into studying fundamentalism had been money well spent. But in the final analysis, Marty asserted, the continuing strength of religious fundamentalism was most unfortunate. It would be best for the human race if fundamentalism had less power and if the people who opposed it had more.[25]

A similar point of view was expressed by Egyptian scholar Abdel Azim Ramadan, who wrote an essay for the Fundamentalism Project on the history of Egyptian fundamentalism. Ramadan's narrative of that history was workmanlike, calm, and perhaps a little dull. But writing in an Egyptian publication called *Uktubar*, Ramadan gave his readers a passion-filled account of how his participation in the Fundamentalism Project had transformed his understanding of fundamentalism. Before he became involved in the project, Ramadan said, he had believed that "the fundamentalist phenomenon was confined to Egypt and the Islamic world." But participating in the project—a project that included, Ramadan was careful to note, scholars from schools such as Harvard, Chicago, and Stanford—had taught him that fundamentalism actually "encompassed the entire surface of the globe, including all revealed and natural religions."[26]

Fundamentalists throughout the world, Ramadan had learned, rejected existing political structures. Their attempts to overthrow those structures endangered societies. For that reason—and others, too—fundamentalism ought to be understood as a "disease." In the past, scientists had studied many other diseases in order to determine how they could be dealt with and (one hoped) eradicated. That was the spirit in which fundamentalism ought to be investigated. "As is the case for any new disease," Ramadan said,

> scientists start to study [fundamentalism] for the purpose of dealing with it and eliminating it. All the political systems in the world today regard fundamentalist movements as a new disease; they must study it, and understand it thoroughly, so that they can eliminate it with ease.[27]

Ramadan's position was clear: participating in the Fundamentalism Project had taught him that fundamentalism had much in common with a disease and that the point of studying it was to learn how it could be eradicated. Ramadan's observations underscored one of the most conspicuous anomalies connected to the Fundamentalism Project: on some occasions the project was presented as an attempt to stamp out a plague and on others it was presented as an open-ended, bias-free investigation of an intriguing phenomenon that scholars ought neither to praise nor to condemn.

The various anomalies of the Fundamentalism Project shed some light on the question to which I turn in the next chapter: why has global fundamentalism aroused such fierce resistance? Before taking up that topic, it might be useful to make three preliminary observations about what happens when people talk about global fundamentalism. Talking about global fundamentalism gives people a way of trying to make sense of the role religion has played in shaping the world in the twentieth and the twenty-first centuries. It opens up the possibility of using the fundamentalist movement that arose among American Protestants in the 1920s, a movement with which many Americans are somewhat familiar, as the starting point for analyzing other religious movements about which they know less and that arose in other places and at other times. Second, when people talk about global fundamentalism, they sometimes have a hard time explaining precisely what they mean; some of the definitions of global fundamentalism they present are quite confusing. Third, when people talk about global fundamentalism, they sometimes invoke sets of sharp binaries: progressives/fundamentalists; the West/the rest of the world; accepting modernity/rejecting it; and religious practices that are normal/those that are dangerous. Whether or not those sorts of binaries are helpful is one of the issues that is at stake in the debates over the validity of global fundamentalism. Those debates are explored in the next two chapters.

1

Skeptics

In spite of all its achievements, the Fundamentalism Project failed to conclusively demonstrate that global fundamentalism is a useful concept. When the project began, Marty presented it as an exploration of a hypothesis: it was possible that global fundamentalism might prove helpful to students of religion in the modern world. From the outset, there were doubts about that hypothesis. As the project progressed, those doubts did not disappear. Instead, they deepened. By the time the project came to an end, it was clear that global fundamentalism made many people exceedingly uneasy. This uneasiness has only grown in the years since the project ended in 1995. Many people—who, for the sake of convenience, I am going to refer to as skeptics—have concluded that global fundamentalism is often used in ways that impede rather than advance our attempts to understand the world in which we live.[1] Questions about the usefulness of global fundamentalism came from many different quarters—including from people who wrote ill-tempered letters to newspaper editors that simply asserted that they objected to global fundamentalism without explaining why. In this chapter, I focus largely on the arguments advanced by scholars who were leery of global fundamentalism.

Some of these skeptical scholars say that when it is used with great care, the concept of global fundamentalism can be—on occasion at least—a helpful idea. Others maintain that even if the term is used carefully, speaking of global fundamentalism adds nothing to the discussion about world religions. To this second group of skeptics, the concept is fatally flawed. Some go so far as to say that talking about global fundamentalism is a great deal like talking about primitive religion or unicorns. In other words, global fundamentalism provides people with a way of talking about something that does not exist.

Scholars began asking questions about the usefulness of global fundamentalism in the mid-1990s. These questions have not subsided. Although scholars who work in the humanities generally view global fundamentalism with somewhat more skepticism than do those who work in the social sciences, there is no single discipline in which scholars find global fundamentalism questionable. Economists (Laurence Iannaccone), sociologists (John Simpson), philosophers (Alvin Plantinga), anthropologists (Saba Mahmood), literary critics (Edward Said), and religious studies scholars (Khalid Blankinship) have all expressed doubts about global fundamentalism.

Not surprisingly, given the range of perspectives from which global fundamentalism has been interrogated, the questions that have been asked about it concern a diverse group of issues. Five of these issues have been the focus of much concern. What is the significance of the fact that most people who get called fundamentalists do not think of themselves as fundamentalists? Does global fundamentalism lump together a set of movements that do not have all that much in common with one another? Is it possible to craft a coherent and convincing definition of global fundamentalism? Do accounts of global fundamentalism delegitimize fundamentalists? Do they use the West as a yardstick by which to judge the rest of the world? Exploring these questions gives us a better sense of what might be lost and what might be gained when global fundamentalism is invoked.

Fundamentalists' Self-Perceptions

Most of the people who are called fundamentalists don't think of themselves as fundamentalists. To be sure, a few of the conservative Protestant evangelicals who get labeled as fundamentalist do call themselves fundamentalists. And so do some followers of Joseph Smith (the ones who continue to practice plural marriage). But it is clear that the overwhelming majority of Christians who are labeled fundamentalist do not use that term to describe themselves. And virtually none of the Buddhists, Hindus, Jews, or Muslims in the world think of themselves as fundamentalists. As Khalid Blankinship points out, the term "fundamentalist" is almost always used as a way of labeling others. It is almost never a way of defining oneself.[2]

Skeptics suggest that global fundamentalism is constructed in a way that does not do justice to fundamentalists' understanding of who they are and what they believe. Heretics do not think of themselves as heretics, apostates do not think of themselves as apostates, and fundamentalists don't think of themselves as fundamentalists. There might be a simple explanation for that. These categories all condemn the people to whom they refer. There is no such thing as a good heretic or apostate. Similarly, a good fundamentalist is (in most contexts) a contradiction in terms.

A good many of the people who are called fundamentalist find the label deeply offensive. Alvin Plantinga is a case in point. Plantinga, the great philosopher who taught at Notre Dame for many years, argued that the term "fundamentalist" is simply a pejorative word for a group of people thought to be surly, obtuse, and reactionary. A writer who labels a man a fundamentalist is simply saying, Plantinga asserted, that the man is a stupid son of a bitch whose theological views are farther to the right than those of the writer. Liberal theologians applied the label to people such as Thomas Aquinas, Martin Luther, John Calvin, and Karl Barth; secular thinkers such as Richard Dawkins and Daniel Dennett applied it to people who believed in a personal God. Plantinga adopted a jocular tone when he discussed what he believed to be the real meaning of fundamentalism, but his observations suggest that he found the label deeply offensive.[3]

One could argue, of course, that Plantinga was wrong to say that the people who get labeled as fundamentalists are simply people who are regarded as mean sons of bitches. One can argue that all the people who get labeled as fundamentalists are, in fact, people who practice forms of religion that are thought of as "overly authoritarian."[4] There is probably a grain of truth in that observation. But of course there is no general agreement about precisely what it is that constitutes being overly authoritarian.

A religious movement that one person might think of as authoritarian—the Jesuits, for example—might be seen as well ordered by someone else. And if all that we mean by fundamentalism is religious authoritarianism, it is hard to see why we need the concept at all. Why not simply use "religious authoritarianism" instead? In any case, the basic point that skeptics make is clear enough. "Fundamentalist" is, for better or worse, a word that we use to describe other people—not ourselves. And that, to many skeptics, is suspect.

Differences between and within Fundamentalist Movements

The concept of global fundamentalism is quite expansive: there are hundreds and possibly thousands of different movements to which it is applied. In "Fundamentalism Reborn," Martin Marty described a quite remarkable range of movements that he saw as expressions of fundamentalism. Preachers associated with the New Christian Right and conservative Roman Catholics who insisted on "clinging to the Latin Mass" were fundamentalists. Some Russian Pentecostals were fundamentalists. So were Russians—such as Alexander Solzhenitsyn—who were devoted to a "rigid Eastern Orthodox outlook." Some of the "Hindu fanatics" in India were fundamentalists; so were some of the orthodox Jews who lived in Israel and in settlements on the West Bank. Some of the Muslims in Saudi Arabia—those, for example, who wanted to overthrow the Saudi regime and replace it with one that better accorded with traditionally Muslim ideals—were fundamentalists. The members of some of Japan's "Buddhist sects" were also fundamentalist.[5]

There are, of course, a number of commonalities among all the people described in Marty's article. How could there not be? By definition, all religious human beings have something in common with all other religious human beings. Indeed, all humans have something in common with all other humans, whether they are religious or not. But there are obviously a great many important differences to be found among the people Marty thought of as fundamentalists. Imagine, for example, a week-long conference at which representatives of all the groups Marty discussed came together to compare notes on their religious beliefs and practices. The representatives of the New Christian Right would be deeply committed monotheists who firmly embraced the doctrine of biblical inerrancy. Other attendees would find the claims that there is only one God and that the Christian Bible is an indispensable guide to his nature to be absurd. The conservative Catholics would insist that God teaches us that true religion doesn't have anything to do with refusing to eat pork or shellfish, and that would strike some of the Muslims and Jews who were there as ridiculous. And some of the claims made by the Hindus and Buddhists at the conference might be dismissed as "heathen nonsense" by some of the Christians in attendance. In many situations, those kinds of disagreements matter a great deal. There are in fact enormous differences among the movements from the various traditions that are said to constitute global fundamentalism. Skeptics suggest that accounts of global fundamentalism tend to systematically erase those differences—to treat them as though they are not worth taking seriously.[6] And this, they argue, seriously distorts the movements under discussion.

Even when we confine ourselves to looking at fundamentalists within a single religious tradition, we still find a number of important differences, some of them quite startling. There are, for example, enormous differences among the Jewish movements that get labeled as fundamentalist. The term is applied both to ultra-orthodox Jews living in the United States—a nation in which Jews make up only about 2 percent of the populace—and to Jews living in Israel—a nation in which they make up about 75 percent of the populace. Some of the so-called Jewish fundamentalists in Israel are deeply opposed to Zionism; indeed, the leaders of Netorei Karta have sometimes gone so far as to say that the Palestinian people and Israel's religious Jews are fellow sufferers under Zionist domination.[7] Other ultra-orthodox Jewish movements in Israel—Gush Emunim, for example—are deeply committed to Israel and the expansion of its borders.

When it is applied to Islamic movements, the concept of fundamentalism becomes even more expansive. When Ira M. Lapidus, a highly respected historian of Islam, examined the list of movements to which the fundamentalism label is routinely applied, he pointed out that some are "intolerant and exclusivist, some pluralistic; some favorable to science, some anti-scientific; some primarily devotional and some primarily political; some democratic, some authoritarian; some pacific, some violent."[8] Blankinship has noted, with some exasperation, that the fundamentalist label has been applied at one time or another to virtually *all* of the important Muslim movements that have arisen since the eighteenth century. How can such an all-encompassing concept be valuable? As Blankinship suggests, the category "Islamic fundamentalism" is completely void of any real specificity.[9]

Definitions of Fundamentalism

The many definitions of global fundamentalism display a great deal of heterogeneity. The hallmarks of fundamentalism have been said to include an obsession with controlling women's bodies, a tendency to sanctify a sacred text and to read it literally, an inclination to mix religion with politics and politics with religion, and a predilection to adopting an oppositional stance toward modernity. Skeptics sometimes suggest that the great variety of ways in which global fundamentalism is defined limits the concept's usefulness. If we can't agree on a definition of global fundamentalism, then how can the concept be useful at all?

Skeptics often find all of the definitions of global fundamentalism with which they are familiar to be inadequate. Sometimes they go even further, arguing that the circumstances under which global fundamentalism was created—including the tremendous hostility between the people who are labeled as fundamentalists and the people who use the term to define others—may make it impossible for us to ever come up with a useful definition of fundamentalism.[10] Although skeptics have not been able to prove that global fundamentalism can never be satisfactorily defined—it is difficult, after all, to prove a negative—they have certainly raised serious doubts about the existing definitions of the term.

Controlling Women's Bodies

Consider, for instance, the issue of controlling women's bodies. Skeptics do not deny that some of the people who are called fundamentalists have a deep interest in controlling women's bodies. However, problems arise if we try to make a deep interest in controlling women's bodies *the* hallmark of fundamentalism. For one thing, this can lead us to think that the movements that get labeled as fundamentalist are exclusively defined by the concerns of the men who join them. According to this line of thinking, fundamentalist movements are, in essence, male movements, movements that are fueled exclusively by the energies of the men. But a great deal of evidence suggests that women are wholehearted participants in some of these movements and that they play an important—one might even say crucial—role in shaping them.[11] In other words, it is not accurate to say that fundamentalists are all men with a particular interest in controlling women's bodies.

Moreover, it is not at all clear that the people who get labeled as fundamentalists are more interested in controlling women's bodies than their opponents are. British sociologist Bobby Sayyid has noted that the secular leaders of Iran and Turkey sometimes took a deep interest in controlling women's bodies. Reza Shah Pavlavi and Mustafa Kemal Atatürk both associated the veil with backwardness and did not want women to wear them, and both used the power of law to enforce their preferences. One could make the case that men who are willing to use the law to prevent women from wearing veils are just as interested in controlling women's bodies as men who want to use the law to compel them to wear them. Sayyid went on to say that he suspected that were we to affix the fundamentalist label to all of the governments in the world that strive to control women's bodies, we would make the concept so elastic as to lose all utility. One could argue that all nation-states have a stake in controlling women's bodies. If they didn't, they wouldn't try to control which women could and which women could not cross over their borders. Sayyid also said that there is a sense in which controlling women's bodies is a "function of governmentality itself."[12] Not everyone would accept that argument. But it does seem clear that a definition of fundamentalism that implies that fundamentalists are interested in controlling women's bodies and that nonfundamentalists are not is somewhat problematic. Patriarchal practices and beliefs are embedded in many movements and institutions that are generally not labeled as fundamentalist.

Reading Sacred Texts

Skeptics suggest that problems also arise when we try to define fundamentalism in terms of people's attitudes toward sacred texts. Some scholars who have compared the way people who are labeled as fundamentalists use the texts they regard as sacred have found that those people do not read sacred texts in similar ways. Historian Jay Harris has concluded that the world does not contain any Jews who read sacred texts the same way that Christian fundamentalists do. Jews assume—as the physical layout of the Talmud demonstrates—that to understand the meaning of the Bible one has to cherish multiple, conflicting interpretations of particular biblical passages. When Jews in orthodox communities read the Bible, they (like all Jews) use a set of techniques that would strike Protestant fundamentalists as bizarre. Jews, in turn, would find the procedures that Protestants use when they are reading the Bible exceedingly strange.[13]

It is often said that whatever differences there are between the various ways fundamentalists read, all fundamentalists have one thing in common: they read their sacred texts literally. There is a grain of truth in that observation. But there are problems connected to defining fundamentalism in terms of a predilection for literalism. For one thing, some of the people labeled as fundamentalist do not always interpret texts literally. A great many conservative Jews and Christians know that the Hebrew Bible contains many metaphors. When they explain the meaning of the twenty-third psalm, they do not say that we ought to think of ourselves as literal sheep or God as a literal shepherd. Moreover, saying that fundamentalists are people who believe that the scriptures are a literal record of God's word produces an odd result. The vast majority of Muslims believe that the Qur'an is a literal record of God's final revelation to humanity. Does that mean they are all fundamentalists? The usefulness of such a categorization is far from obvious. It raises the possibility that the phrase "Muslim fundamentalists" is redundant—akin, one supposes, to "Roman Catholics who regard the Pope as the leader of the Christian Church."[14] In short, it is not at all clear that defining fundamentalism in terms of scriptural literalism makes much sense.

Melding Religion and Politics

Skeptics also conclude that defining fundamentalism in terms of the conflation of two distinct spheres of life—the religious and the political—does not really work either. If we were to rely on such a definition, then we would have to classify the movement Gandhi led, which was clearly both religious and political, as fundamentalist.[15] It seems possible that one would also have to apply the fundamentalist label to the movements led by Martin Luther King Jr., Carrie Nation, William Lloyd Garrison, Tenskwatawa, John Calvin, Constantine, Mohammed, and Moses. All of those remarkable individuals led movements that were simultaneously religious and political, from some points of view. But few, if any, would really want to label those movements fundamentalist. If we do assign that label to those movements, then we have drifted very far away indeed from what most people have in mind when they talk about fundamentalism.

Skeptics suggest that this drift is emblematic of a deeper problem. Defining fundamentalism as a conflation of religion and politics works well only if we assume that a set of distinct practices exists that is naturally religious and another set that is naturally political. But that assumption, skeptics point out, might actually be quite dubious. It is entirely possible that "religious" and "political" are both unstable categories. What counts as religious and what counts as political might well change from place to place and from time to time. In any case, it is hard to see why we should assume that the religious and the political are naturally distinct. In many places and at many times religio-political movements have been the rule, not the exception. A definition of fundamentalism that is based on the assumption that religio-political movements are abnormal or unnatural is one that many people would find suspect.[16]

Resisting Modernity

Skeptics claim that difficulties also arise if we try to define fundamentalism in terms of "resisting modernity." Defining a phenomenon primarily in terms of what it is against, skeptics argue, is a questionable procedure. To be sure, analyzing a phenomenon in terms of what it opposes can sometimes be useful. When, for example, someone wants to explain what Lutheranism is, they might well want to talk about Lutherans' opposition to the papacy. But that person would also generally want to go on to say something about the doctrines—such as justification by faith alone—to which Lutherans are deeply attached. Defining Lutheranism solely in terms of what it opposes does not give us a complete understanding of it. The same might well be true of fundamentalism.

But even if we decide that defining fundamentalism primarily in terms of what it resists is a reasonable procedure, it is not immediately clear that modernity is what fundamentalism is resisting. Saba Mahmood, the Berkeley anthropologist, suggested that some fundamentalists were responding to Western intervention in Muslim societies or corrupt regimes that failed to meet the most basic needs of their subjects, rather than to modernity.[17] In a similar vein, Bobby Sayyid stated that the people who get labeled as Islamic fundamentalists might well be thought of as people who are protesting against the hegemony of consumerist values or the oppression of the poor.[18] This suggests that when we are trying to understand fundamentalist movements, we ought to pay careful attention to the specific problems they are responding to instead of focusing on their supposed hostility to modernity.

Defining fundamentalists as people who are resisting modernity is also not going to work if we cannot be clear about what we mean by modernity. Modernity is, skeptics say, a relative concept. They say that defining global fundamentalism as resistance to something as amorphous as modernity inevitably leads to confusion and imprecision.[19] There are hundreds of different definitions of modernity. There might also be hundreds of different definitions of what it means to resist it. Fundamentalism is a somewhat fuzzy concept. Modernity is, if anything, even fuzzier. Definitions of a fuzzy concept that rely on an even fuzzier one, skeptics note, are seldom very satisfying.

Delegitimizing Fundamentalism

Analysts of global fundamentalism sometimes argue—or simply assume—that fundamentalism ought to be understood as an irrational response to the social dislocation that results from the coming of modernity. They say that fundamentalists are people who have trouble adjusting to the stresses and strains of modernity. Skeptics argue that from some points of view at least, resisting modernity is an unreasonable thing to do. Defining fundamentalists as people who are trying to resist modernity can make it sound as though fundamentalists are trying to do something that just cannot be done. This analysis implies that their hopes are simply delusions, thus serving to delegitimize and critique the movement of which they are a part.

Henry Munson, an anthropologist with a strong interest in comparative religion, has noted that there is a sharp contrast between the way people analyze fundamentalist movements and the way they analyze political movements that oppose militarism, the subjugation of women, or the degradation of the environment. People are generally reluctant to say, Munson has observed, that the men and women who join the latter movements are "really trying to cope with stress engendered by rapid modernization." The arguments those activists make are usually treated with at least a modicum of respect. Fundamentalists' arguments are sometimes treated very differently: as symptoms of an inability to adjust to the changes produced by the coming of modernity. For that interpretation to be convincing, Munson said, analysts would have to show that there is good reason to believe that the stresses that fundamentalists have experienced are more severe and more distressing than those nonfundamentalists have experienced. Analysts have failed to demonstrate that. Munson actually had fewer doubts about the usefulness of global fundamentalism than many other writers; he had no admiration whatsoever for many of the people who are labeled fundamentalists. But to him, the claim that fundamentalists are simply people who have trouble adjusting to modernity seemed bizarre; it was nothing more than polemic masquerading as something else.[20]

Whether or not Munson was right about that particular point, it does seem clear that people who write about global fundamentalism tend to present fundamentalists as people who are discombobulated, confused, misguided, or ignorant. Skeptics say that people who rely on global fundamentalism inevitably produce skewed analyses of the movements they are writing about and that the resulting texts are often little more than crude antifundamentalist propaganda. To the skeptics, it seems clear that labeling someone as a fundamentalist nearly always has the effect of delegitimizing them.[21] "Global fundamentalism" is not, they believe, a neutral term. It actually censures the phenomenon it conjures up.

Mark Juergensmeyer, a scholar with a strong interest in religion and violence, made this point quite deftly. Juergensmeyer said that in popular discourse "global fundamentalism" is often wielded as a political weapon.

He said that people who seek to minimize the cultural authority and political power of religious movements use the term with great avidity and characterize their religious opponents as fundamentalists who are part of a mammoth fundamentalist conspiracy. Juergensmeyer said that fundamentalists are often portrayed as comrades in a network of weird peripheral movements that are linked together as a worldwide force that threatens the liberty and life of freedom-minded peoples everywhere. Civil rights can be denied, deportations can be justified, military coups can be explained, and ethnic cleansing can be excused (or at least made less repugnant) if one can claim that those actions are necessary in order to beat back the fundamentalist menace.[22]

In popular discourse, Juergensmeyer said, the term "fundamentalists" is used much as the term "communists" was used in the past. It marks off a group of outsiders who cannot be trusted, and it implies that those outsiders might not be human in the fullest sense of that term. Juergensmeyer focused his attention on how global fundamentalism works in popular discourse. But the term has implications for scholarly conversations, too. He warned that scholars should be aware of how popular polemics against global fundamentalism shape the way people think about it. Scholarly conversations cannot be completely sealed off from popular ones. They are, to some degree at least, tainted by the popular polemics against fundamentalists. Scholars should therefore think twice before using the label "global fundamentalism."

Juergensmeyer was not willing to say that scholarly conversations about fundamentalism are necessarily illegitimate. He believed that many scholars who write about global fundamentalism are not interested in delegitimizing it; some scholars who write about global fundamentalism are engaged in a disinterested search for the truth.[23] But a good many skeptics see things differently. They think that scholarly accounts of global fundamentalism, like popular ones, are deeply political and that many scholarly accounts of global fundamentalism, again like popular ones, serve to delegitimize global fundamentalism. Saba Mahmood argued that political concerns permeated every aspect of the Fundamentalism Project. For example, the project did not subject the monarchies of Saudi Arabia or Kuwait to close scrutiny. Both regimes, by Marty's and Appleby's standards, were clearly fundamentalist. The fact that both were allies of the U.S. government seemed to have led to their being given much less critical attention than, for example, the government of Iran. Mahmood also concluded that the Fundamentalism Project used a double standard when it looked at movements it saw as fundamentalist and when it looked at the secular regimes those movements challenged. The human rights abuses of the fundamentalists were highlighted; those of their secular opponents were consistently minimized.[24]

Other scholars express a similar view. In a review in the *Journal for the Scientific Study of Religion*, John Simpson argued that even scholarly accounts of global fundamentalism tend to portray fundamentalists as villains who stand in the way of progress. He also suggested that scholarly accounts of fundamentalism, no less than popular ones, are written in ways that imply that the ideas of fundamentalists are not worth taking seriously and that those accounts end up suggesting that the arguments fundamentalists advance are simply "beyond the pale of civil discourse."[25] Laurence Iannaccone, an economist with a deep interest in religion, also emphasized the links between popular discussions of fundamentalism that were clearly polemical and scholarly texts that appeared to present an evenhanded analysis. Iannaccone said that even in scholarly accounts, a group gets labeled as fundamentalist more because of "who it *scares*" than because of "what it *is*."[26] He said that scholars tend to talk about fundamentalism in ways that reinscribe rather than question the polemics written by "politicians, journalists, religious leaders and intellectuals" who find fundamentalism distasteful. He suggested that scholarly accounts of global fundamentalism are inevitably skewed.[27] They are written from the perspective of opposition rather than from a desire to carefully examine the beliefs and practices of fundamentalists. Scholarly accounts of global fundamentalism are skewed in much the same way that accounts of exotic religious cults, false religion, and primitive religions are.

Valorizing the West

Skeptics claim that accounts of global fundamentalism tend to treat Christianity, the West, and the European Enlightenment with too much deference. They view attempts to use fundamentalism—a category firmly anchored in Christian discourse—to make sense of Hindus, Jews, Buddhists, and Muslims with a good deal of suspicion. Why should Christianity be the starting point for investigations of all the world religions? Skeptics contend that trying to sort all of the religious people in the world into two categories—fundamentalists and nonfundamentalists—makes no more sense than trying to sort all the religious people in the world into Shiites and Sunnis. They argue that fundamentalism is an intensely parochial concept that does not have universal applicability. Using a concept that was created by Christians in order to talk about the Christian Church to analyze non-Christians, skeptics suggest, does not make much sense.

Skeptics also suggest that accounts of global fundamentalism present a distorted analysis of the relationships between "the West" and other regions of the world by assuming that the West is the protagonist of the story of human history and that all the other characters in the story are defined in terms of their relationships with it. They say that discussions of global fundamentalism rest on the assumption that world history is moving in a particular direction, that we know what that direction is, that the West is farther along that road than other societies, and that the rest of the world is bringing up the rear of the march toward progress. According to Bobby Sayyid's astute analysis, accounts of global fundamentalism are based on the assumption that Western cultural practices provide a set of norms that can be used to map, judge, and police all the other regions of the world.[28]

Skeptics assert that global fundamentalism discourse often rests on a set of assumptions that constitutes a kind of "Enlightenment fundamentalism"[29] that is predicated on a belief that the European Enlightenment revealed a set of truths that are eternal, universal, and incontrovertibly true. These accounts make it sound as if the first fundamentalists to appear on the scene were backward Christians who lived in the West but refused to embrace the great truths the Enlightenment revealed. This gives the impression that people in other parts of the world were subsequently brought into contact with Enlightenment truths and that non-Westerners who rejected those truths became fundamentalists, too. According to this story, fundamentalists are not distributed equally throughout the world. Some can still be found in the West, but they are especially numerous in the region that used to be called the Orient.[30]

Skeptics admit that this approach to human history has a long lineage. But they also know that this approach became controversial before scholars began relying heavily on global fundamentalism. *Orientalism*, Edward

Said's brilliant, controversial, and much-discussed analysis of Orientalist discourse, was published in 1978—nearly two decades before the Fundamentalism Project concluded its work. Skeptics suggest that it is no longer reasonable to assume that Western cultural practices provide a template for the rest of the world, and they question accounts of global fundamentalism that assume that everyone agrees that the West provides norms by which the rest of the world can be judged.[31]

Critics of global fundamentalism, including Said himself, have argued that the concept must be understood not as a description of what was actually happening in Asia, Africa, or Latin America but as a reflection of the anxieties in "intellectual factories" in metropolitan centers such as London and Washington.[32] Accounts of global fundamentalism create "an exotic, mysterious, and sometimes dangerous stranger."[33] That stranger was created, skeptics suggest, in order to support the dubious proposition that there is no rational alternative to embracing the norms that have taken root in post-Enlightenment Christendom.

Skeptics lamented the naturalization of the norms associated with post-Enlightenment Christendom. They knew that scholarly explorations of the humanities often help us realize that all social arrangements and all ways of looking and the world are specific, local, and parochial. Those explorations often denaturalize our own way of life and our own way of thinking. Accounts of global fundamentalism, skeptics suggest, nearly always fail to do that. Instead, they generally do the reverse; they assure their readers that they are advanced and that the people who are labeled as fundamentalists are backward.

Conclusion

In the eyes of skeptics, accounts of global fundamentalism are both dangerous and flawed. In their view, these discussions do not help us understand our world better but instead lead us down a set of blind alleys. Skeptics note that the people who get labeled as fundamentalists do not, as a general rule, think of themselves as fundamentalists, and this fact indicates that global fundamentalism is a problematic concept. Skeptics argue that accounts of global fundamentalism don't do justice to the differences among and within the various movements that are labeled fundamentalist.

Many, even those based on the best definition of fundamentalism as religious movements that seek to resist modernity, raise more questions than answers. Skeptics think that it is impossible to write an objective account of global fundamentalism, and they contend that the accounts that exist inevitably suggest that fundamentalists' ideas and practices are inferior to the ideas and practices of nonfundamentalists. In their opinion, accounts of global fundamentalism are based on a simplistic and outdated understanding of the relationship between the West and the rest of the world.

Of course, the concept of global fundamentalism has defenders as well as critics. The next chapter evaluates the arguments put forth in defense of global fundamentalism.

2

Defenders

Defenders of global fundamentalism sometimes act as if they are certain that the arguments skeptics present are not worth answering. For instance, Steve Bruce, a sociologist with a strong interest in religion and politics, told the readers of his book on fundamentalism that he was well aware that his approach to the topic would strike some as Orientalist, noting that a report submitted to a potential publisher had condemned his manuscript on precisely those grounds. Bruce also gave his readers a careful summary of Orientalism and of the reasons why some people find it so abhorrent. But he did not reply to the claim that his study of fundamentalism was Orientalist; he simply dismissed it. He said that he was not convinced that the concept of Orientalism was a helpful one and went on to talk about fundamentalism in ways that made it clear that the issues related to Orientalism were not worth more than a moment's thought.[1]

Bruce was by no means the only person to present a nonanswer to the criticisms of global fundamentalism. Near the beginning of *Between Warrior Brother and Veiled Sister*, Minoo Moallem noted that using fundamentalism to analyze Muslim beliefs and practices is highly problematic. But, she went on to say (without explaining why), this was exactly what she was going to do.[2] The editors of the *Encyclopedia of Fundamentalism*, which was published in 2001, told their readers that many people did not believe that fundamentalism can be legitimately applied to non-Christians and then declared they "have concluded that it can." They did not give readers any hints about how and why they reached that conclusion.[3] In a book-length study of Christian, Jewish, and Muslim fundamentalism called *The Battle for God*, Karen Armstrong responded to criticisms of global fundamentalism in a similarly dismissive fashion. She noted that many observers had concluded that the concept was not at all helpful but went on to say that other people believe that, like it or not, global fundamentalism is here to stay. Armstrong argued that the concept was imperfect but also useful. She did not explain precisely what it was that made it so useful.[4]

The tactic of noting the arguments against global fundamentalism without responding to them is one that champions of the concept rely on quite frequently, and it is somewhat risky. It gives some people the impression that the arguments' weaknesses are so obvious that it is a waste of time to answer them. We do not, after all, generally try to answer the arguments of people who say that gravity does not exist. But others reach a very different conclusion: that the defenders of the concept have no answers to give. This conclusion is not entirely justified. The arguments that support global fundamentalism are not, it seems to me, particularly strong. But they certainly are not ludicrous either. In this chapter, I examine the arguments the champions of global fundamentalism advance and look at how critics of global fundamentalism respond to those arguments. Analyzing the debates between the champions and the critics of global fundamentalism will help us get a sense of what is lost and gained when that concept is invoked.

Some Grains of Truth

Defenses of global fundamentalism often acknowledge that the arguments of skeptics contain more than a few grains of truth. Defenders are quite willing to admit, for example, that skeptics are right to say that the people who get labeled as fundamentalists differ from one another in a number of significant respects. Indeed, Marty was willing to assert—using all capital letters to emphasize his point—that on matters of substance, the world's fundamentalist movements "HAVE LITTLE OR NOTHING IN COMMON WITH ONE ANOTHER."[5] But champions of global fundamentalism also argue that it is easy to exaggerate the importance of the heterogeneity within fundamentalism. They say that if we focus our attention not on specific rituals, beliefs, or practices but on general patterns of thought and behavior, we can see that all fundamentalists share certain "family resemblances." For example, all fundamentalists rely on religion for a source of identity, they all set boundaries, and they all mythologize their enemies.[6] Champions of global fundamentalism argue that there are a great many more family resemblances than skeptics are willing to admit. They say that the concept, when used skillfully, does a splendid job of highlighting those commonalities.

Champions of global fundamentalism say that skeptics are right to warn that when used sloppily, the concept can produce inadequate analyses of the people to whom it is applied. Bruce Lawrence, one of the most thoughtful champions of global fundamentalism, acknowledged that people often talk about fundamentalists in ways that are shallow and tendentious. But Lawrence noted that observing that *some* descriptions of fundamentalists are inadequate does not force us to conclude that *all* of them are defective. He argued that when the concept of global fundamentalism is used correctly, it sheds light on a number of important questions having to do with religion and the modern world.[7] Appleby's defense of global fundamentalism also included an acknowledgment that skeptics' suspicions about the concept's usefulness are not groundless: it is undeniably true that some conversations about fundamentalism are sloppy and sensationalistic. But he and Marty, Appleby said, made a point of protesting the errors in such texts and encouraging scholars to use the concept carefully and soberly. It was unfair and illogical to hold the two of them responsible for other people's misuse of global fundamentalism. Appleby insisted that he, Marty, and the other scholars associated with the Fundamentalism Project had used the concept to produce nuanced and fair-minded analyses of the role of religion in the modern world. Their work did not caricature fundamentalists; instead, it demonstrated how much can be accomplished when scholars make a determined effort to avoid distorting the religious movements they study.[8]

People who champion global fundamentalism readily admit that the vast majority of the people they call fundamentalists do not apply that label to themselves. But they see no reason to let how fundamentalists see themselves determine which categories can and cannot be used to analyze them. They claim that it makes no sense to let other people's opinions about themselves govern our analyses of them. We routinely use the category "dictator" when analyzing people who would never call themselves that. Why should we be more scrupulously subjective in our use of "fundamentalist" than in our use of "dictator"?[9] To drive home this point, defenders sometimes draw a comparison between fundamentalists and crabs.

There are no crabs in the world, they observe, who think of themselves as crustaceans. But we all know that is exactly what crabs are. Champions of global fundamentalism say the classification of fundamentalists is similar to the classification of crabs. Only a tiny percentage of the world's fundamentalists classify themselves as such, and many of those who are so denominated take great umbrage at the classification. Nevertheless, that is exactly what they are.[10] Crabs like to think that they are sui generis. They do not like to be compared with other crustaceans; they do not like to be told that they actually have a great deal in common with lobsters, crayfish, and shrimp. Likewise, Islamic fundamentalists do not like it when writers point out how much they have in common with Jewish and Christian fundamentalists. But those commonalities are evident for all to see, and it makes no sense to pretend otherwise.[11]

Searching for a Definition

Defenders of the concept of global fundamentalism are willing to admit that it is extremely difficult to come up with a perfect definition of the term. But they insist that an inability to define it perfectly does not require that we abandon it. For one thing, if we abandon global fundamentalism, we cannot turn to another term whose meaning is any clearer. When we talk about fundamentalism, people have a general sense of what we are talking about. If we were to speak instead of "belligerent neo-radical proto-revolutionary extremist conservatism," we would not make it easier for people to understand what we are saying. We would make it more difficult.[12] In any case, defenders say, we do not have to come up with a flawless definition of fundamentalism; we need to construct one that is good enough to help us as we try to make sense of the religious movements we want to explore. Such a definition, they assert, is well within our grasp.

Lawrence, for example, accepted the fact that people could quibble with his definition of fundamentalism as "the affirmation of religious authority as holistic and absolute, admitting of neither criticism nor reduction." But he was sure that definition was more than adequate for the task at hand.[13] Moallem admitted that her definition—"a regime of truth based on discourses identified with or ordained by God (understood metaphorically or literally) which binds observers to it"—was far from perfect. But she also concluded that in spite of its faults, this definition gives us a useful tool for analyzing the relationships between gender and religion.[14] Marty and Appleby were as aware as anyone else of the complexities that arise when we try to define global fundamentalism. They did not believe, however, that those complexities posed an insurmountable barrier to constructing a definition that can do what we need it to do. They said that fundamentalism had appeared in the twentieth century as

> a tendency, a habit of mind, found within religious communities and paradigmatically embodied in certain representative individuals and movements, which manifests itself as a strategy, or set of strategies, by which beleaguered believers attempt to preserve their distinctive identity as a people or group. Feeling this identity to be at risk in the contemporary era, these believers fortify it by a selective retrieval of doctrines, beliefs, and practices from a sacred past. These retrieved "fundamentals" are refined, modified, and sanctioned in a spirit of shrewd pragmatism: they are to serve as a bulwark against the encroachment of outsiders who threaten to draw the believers into a syncretistic, areligious, or irreligious cultural milieu.[15]

It is worth noting that Marty and Appleby's definition of fundamentalism is scrupulously neutral. It is capacious enough to include benign movements as well as dangerous ones, and it is framed in a way that seems to make it useful to people who want to produce fair-minded analyses of fundamentalists rather than crude screeds against them. Marty and Appleby often made a point of their determination to be fair to fundamentalists, and they sometimes said there were aspects of fundamentalism that they found praiseworthy.[16] But champions of global fundamentalism rarely pour too much energy into answering the questions skeptics ask about the term's many negative connotations. Many of its defenders do not think that its negative connotations are problematic; fundamentalism is, they assume, a term that describes a phenomenon that all of us find distressing.[17] We do not spend much time brooding over the negative connotations attached to the term "extremism," for we know that extremism can have many unfortunate effects. For the same reason, it does not make sense to worry about fundamentalism's negative connotations.

Henry Munson made this point rather elegantly. He was quite willing to say that global fundamentalism is a concept that is often used quite sloppily. He acknowledged that categorizing a person as a fundamentalist often implies a certain amount of hostility toward that person. But Munson had little patience for people who argue that fundamentalism's negative connotations make it impossible to use the term in describing and analyzing religious movements. He said that people who get called fundamentalists are often "militant zealots who seek to take over governments and impose their religious beliefs on their fellow citizens." So it is not especially surprising that the term has a good many negative connotations. We are obliged to make every effort to understand how fundamentalists see the world and what it is they want to do, but attempting to understand fundamentalists does not oblige us to defend them. Many scholars, Munson said, have a difficult time grasping that basic point.[18]

Appleby advanced a slightly different but related argument about the nature of fundamentalism. He noted that many men and women have argued that fundamentalism is "less an objective set of phenomena" than a set of conversations rooted in Europe and the United States and decisively shaped by the desire of Westerners to "subordinate and control" people they see as frightening. That argument is, Appleby said, simply absurd. It is true that many people in the world want to restrain the power of fundamentalism. But that desire is in large part "a direct response to an objective set of phenomena" such as death threats against authors, abuse of unveiled women, and multifarious acts of terrorism. Appleby is a careful writer who made clear that he knew that not all fundamentalists are terrorists and not all terrorists are fundamentalists. But he was sure that fundamentalism was an observable phenomenon in the actual world, not a Western invention. It really did exist, and it posed real threats to flesh-and-blood human beings.[19]

Appleby, Marty, and the other scholars associated with the Fundamentalism Project did not try to conceal the fact that the project was firmly rooted in Western academia and that it was led by "white American Christian males." They also said that they were well aware of the fact that the texts that grew out of the Fundamentalism Project were shaped by the "prejudices and cultural background" of the people who wrote them. But the scholars associated with the project insisted that their explorations of fundamentalism were not motivated by a desire to discredit people who reject Western values. People who claimed that the Fundamentalism Project was associated with imperial enterprises were just wrong.[20] Global fundamentalism was a legitimate field of inquiry; it wasn't a concept that had been manufactured by apologists for the West.

Defenders of global fundamentalism say that the dangers associated with using Western concepts to analyze other regions of the world can easily be exaggerated. In scholarly conversations, they say, concepts rooted in the West are appropriated and adopted more readily than are other sorts of concepts. But champions of global fundamentalism insist that this state of affairs is not the result of "Western linguistic imperialism"; it is just the way things are.[21] In the contemporary world, all sorts of scholars make use of concepts that originated in the West to analyze other regions of the globe. Capitalism, conservatism, liberalism, nationalism, and socialism are all concepts rooted in the West that are now routinely used to analyze other regions of the world. So is fundamentalism. Describing a particular man who lives in Egypt as a fundamentalist is not, in principle, any different from describing him as a socialist. No one gets bent out of shape when we label an Egyptian a socialist. There is thus no reason for people to become agitated when the fundamentalist label is applied to an Egyptian. Undeniably, the first people to use the term "fundamentalists" were Christians who spoke English. But it can also be usefully applied to Muslims who speak Arabic. It is unreasonable to say otherwise.[22]

In the minds of some of the champions of global fundamentalism, the question of whether concepts rooted in the West should be used to analyze non-Western societies is closely connected to the thought of postmodernists such as Jacques Derrida and Jean-François Lyotard. Few of the defenders of global fundamentalism have much sympathy for those sorts of thinkers; many of them believe that postmodern ways of thinking need to be fiercely critiqued and steadfastly resisted. Haideh Moghissi, for instance, argued that postmodernist ideas make it difficult for us to correctly understand the nature of global fundamentalism. Moghissi said that when postmodernist thinkers analyze the way that fundamentalists treat women, they refuse to ground their arguments in concepts such as modernity, equality, and universal human rights.

Postmodernists, Moghissi declared, are so afraid of saying anything that might possibly be construed as Orientalist that they fail to critique fundamentalism with the necessary vigor. Instead, they ended up providing legitimation to the fundamentalist movements they ought to excoriate. He argued that postmodernists and fundamentalists have far more in common than is generally recognized. To be sure, postmodernists forthrightly reject the metanarratives and dogmas in which fundamentalists take solace. But postmodernists, just like fundamentalists, greatly undervalue the achievements of the European Enlightenment. And they, no less than their fundamentalist brethren, often refuse to conform to rules of logic and principles of sound reasoning. Postmodernism and fundamentalism are not polar opposites. Moghissi concluded that the fallacies on which they are based are quite comparable and the obstacles they pose to human progress are distressingly similar.[23]

The Outcome of the Debate

The arguments champions of global fundamentalism present are, I think, less compelling than those its critics present. To be sure, some of the skeptics' arguments are slightly off target and some of the champions' retorts are quite reasonable. But to me it seems clear that the champions of global fundamentalism have not won the debate over the concept's usefulness and that they did not even fight their opponents to a draw. They were, I believe, soundly defeated. I realize, of course, that my interpretation of the outcome is not definitive. I certainly have not read every text that defends the concept of global fundamentalism, and perhaps there is a text lurking in some library that would lay to rest all my doubts were I to encounter it. And although it seems clear to me that most of the people who have carefully followed the battles over global fundamentalism have concluded that the skeptics' arguments are stronger than those of their opponents, I also have to acknowledge that some very thoughtful people have reached the opposite conclusion. The concept of global fundamentalism still has a good many astute defenders. So in what follows I give my own slightly idiosyncratic analysis of the outcome of the debate. Other writers would present analyses that are somewhat (or even completely) different. Obviously, I am presenting *an* analysis—not *the* analysis—of the debate.

One of the central points of contention in the debate has to do with what is lost and what is gained by using Western concepts, such as fundamentalism, when one is talking about places other than the West. Defenders of global fundamentalism assert that concepts rooted in the West are used to analyze the rest of the world with great frequency. That assertion is undeniably true: we do not think twice about using concepts such as nationalism and capitalism when we are talking about Asia or Africa. But the defenders also argue that the prevalence of that practice guarantees the legitimacy of using the concept of fundamentalism to understand non-Christians. That is an odd argument. It is perfectly reasonable for us to rely on some Western terms and concepts—ritual, for example—when we are describing non-Western cultures and to avoid using other concepts—heresy, heathenism, and primitive religion, for example—that now seem inappropriate. And in fact there are some important similarities between fundamentalism and primitive religion. Both categories are deprecatory and both end up contrasting backward religious practices with ones that are thought to be more sophisticated. And from time to time both concepts have been said to be less than perfect but also irreplaceable. In 1965, the noted anthropologist E. E. Evans-Pritchard described the use of "primitive religion" in precisely those terms.[24] But these days we seem to get by just fine without using it; "primitive religion," it turned out, was not as indispensable as Evans-Pritchard thought. Claiming that the widespread use of "ritual" to analyze non-Western cultures somehow proves that "primitive religion" is legitimate and useful makes no sense whatsoever. But champions of global fundamentalism repeatedly defend that concept on very similar grounds. They suggest that if you say that it is helpful to use *some* concepts rooted in the West to analyze other parts of the world, you are therefore obliged to say that *all* Western concepts can be usefully applied to other parts of the world. I just don't think that's true.

I do think that the champions of global fundamentalism are right to say that the legitimacy of the concept does not stand or fall on the question of whether the people who are called fundamentalists think of themselves in those terms. In many contexts it is entirely legitimate to assign labels to people that they would not affix to themselves. Sometimes it makes perfect sense for us to say that someone who makes a half-million dollars a year is "a rich man" even if he insists that he is not. There are occasions on which it is completely appropriate to describe a person as a biped even if that is not a term she would ever use to describe herself. And even if Carl McIntire and Jerry Falwell were to insist, for some strange reason, that they were not Protestant fundamentalists, it would still be appropriate, in some contexts, to say that Protestant fundamentalists is exactly what they were.

But there is something peculiar about the comparisons that defenders of global fundamentalism draw between crabs and fundamentalists. Champions of global fundamentalism argue that, although crabs do not like to be classified as crustaceans that is nevertheless exactly what they are. One of the problems with this comparison is that it assumes that calling a Haredi Jew a fundamentalist is analogous to calling a crab a crustacean. But that assumption seems unwarranted. Calling such a Jew a fundamentalist might be like calling a crab a lobster. Not all crustaceans are crabs, and it is not helpful to use the category "crab" to describe lobsters, shrimp, and krill.[25] Haredi Jews and fundamentalist Christians could be thought of as constituting two of the many classes that belong to the same phylum. If that is the case, then it is not at all clear why we ought to use the name of one of the classes in the phylum—fundamentalist—to label all of the other classes. That is not how Linnaean taxonomy works. To put this another way, we could say that pinot noirs, zinfandels, cabernet sauvignons, and merlots are all red wines but that not all red wines are merlots. Calling a pinot noir a merlot is not helpful. Nor is it helpful, one could argue, to call a Haredi a fundamentalist.

That brings us to another point. When we are trying to decide whether or not to classify a wine as a merlot, we never pause to ask ourselves if that wine classifies itself as a merlot or as something else. The question is too foolish even to entertain. And, of course, asking if a crab thinks of itself as a crustacean is nearly as nonsensical. Although the champions of global fundamentalism have suggested, in a jocular manner, that a crab that heard itself being called a crustacean "would be filled with a sense of personal outrage," there are in fact no known reports of any actual crabs becoming agitated by scientists' classification of them.[26] Except when we are making jokes, we accept that there are very strict limits on what we can say about the way crabs understand themselves or others. There is very little that crabs can communicate to us or we to them. As far as we can tell, they do not care one way or the other whether we label them as crustaceans. But we can communicate with the people who are called fundamentalists. We know that many of them say that they are not fundamentalists and regard the fundamentalist label as an insult. We are not obliged to think about the people we call fundamentalist precisely the way they think about themselves, but their apprehension of themselves is accessible to us—and salient for us—in a way that crabs' understanding of themselves is not. Repeatedly comparing the people we call fundamentalists to crabs obscures that fact. The comparison seems to suggest that those people might not be fully human; it raises the possibility that they are, at base, nothing more than objects of inquiry.

Comparing fundamentalists to crabs does not, in any case, move us toward a satisfactory definition of global fundamentalism, and unless we can formulate such a definition the concept is not going to be of much help. And formulating an acceptable definition of global fundamentalism is, I believe, far more difficult than the champions of that concept are willing to admit. When considered carefully, many of the definitions turn out to be distressingly imprecise. That lack of precision makes it hard for us to do good empirical research. Although we have been talking about global fundamentalism for more than three decades now, we still are not in a position to provide clear answers to questions such as "What percentage of the world's fundamentalists live in cities?" or "Are most fundamentalists married?" After all this time, we cannot even answer a question as basic as "How many fundamentalists are there in the world?"

Scholars have often argued that empirical research has shed a great deal of light on the nature of fundamentalism. They have said, for example, that empirical investigations have demonstrated that fundamentalists are beleaguered true believers who are trying to stave off modernity. But I do not think that research has shown that to be true. The claim that fundamentalists are embattled people who are resisting modernity is best understood as an assumption upon which a great deal of the research on global fundamentalism rests, not as a proposition that has been validated by social scientific inquiry. We do not need to rely on empirical research if what we are trying to do is demonstrate that fundamentalism is what we have already defined it as being.

And some of the definitions that have been suggested—Minoo Moallem's, for example—are extraordinarily expansive. If we accept Moallem's definition of fundamentalism—"a regime of truth based on discourses identified with or ordained by God ... which binds observers to it"—then it will be difficult for us to find any devout theists who are not fundamentalists. Binding a believer to "a regime of truth" that is understood to have been authorized by God would seem to be something that all monotheistic religions do. A definition that comes close to making fundamentalism coterminous with monotheism is not of much use.

Although none of the definitions created by the leaders of the Fundamentalism Project were as expansive as Moallem's, many of them were so lacking in specificity that they seem to verge on the metaphysical. One of the Fundamentalism Project's most astute critics, Juan Campo, seems to have taken great delight in emphasizing and satirizing the ethereal nature of the definitions that were associated with it. Campo argued that Islamic fundamentalism is not really an Islamic phenomenon at all, and he did so using words that mimicked the ones the leaders of the Fundamentalism Project used. Campo called Islamic fundamentalism "a tendency, a habit of mind, found within scholarly communities" in the West, which "manifests itself as a strategy, or a set of strategies, by which beleaguered believers"—that is, believers in the Western project—"attempt to preserve their distinctive identity as a people or group."[27] Campo's parody of Marty and Appleby's attempt to define fundamentalism was perhaps a little mean-spirited, but it highlighted one of the problems that people ran into over and over again when they tried to define global fundamentalism. Determined to construct a definition roomy enough to house all the people they wanted to cram into it, they found themselves piling abstraction upon reification upon abstraction. The champions of global fundamentalism sometimes ended up defining the concept in ways that were almost completely detached from any concrete social reality.

Power

Champions of global fundamentalism are sometimes offended by skeptics' analyses of the concept's political implications. It is not difficult to see why. From time to time, critics of global fundamentalism speak as though they have discovered that people such as Marty and Appleby are part of a secret, centrally organized, well-funded, and powerful worldwide conspiracy to delegitimize and suppress fundamentalism.[28] Of course, no such conspiracy exists. The Pentagon did not direct the MacArthur Foundation to fund the Fundamentalism Project, and the Fundamentalism Project was not told to produce material that writers such as Karen Armstrong could mine. No government slush fund paid Armstrong to write polemics against fundamentalism. That is not how the world works. The people who write about fundamentalism are interested in a wide range of topics. Politics is not, by any means, the only thing they care about.

But it seems clear that politics is *one* of the things in which they are interested. And it seems strange that champions of global fundamentalism are perturbed by the questions skeptics raise about the political implications of relying on that concept. After all, they themselves sometimes emphasize those implications. Champions of global fundamentalism claim that studying fundamentalism helps us better understand the means by which religious movements oppress women and men and thereby points the way toward ending that oppression.[29] They say that their interest in fundamentalism is not purely academic and that it is also rooted in their desire to produce knowledge that will be useful to policymakers. The production of that sort of knowledge was clearly one of the primary aims of the Fundamentalism Project. There was never any confusion about that: in 1988, the leaders of the American Academy of Arts and Sciences said that it had accepted the grant used to study fundamentalism "*chiefly* for what it might have to say for public policy."[30] The leaders of the Fundamentalism Project explicitly said that they hoped it would produce knowledge that could be put to use by people who worked in the Pentagon and the State Department and in the analogous institutions of other nations. The leaders of the project wanted to be of assistance to "warmakers and peacekeepers."[31]

Strictly speaking, the phrase "warmakers and peacekeepers" is broad enough to include people who work for the governments of Iran or Sudan.

But there is no evidence to suggest that the leaders of the Fundamentalism Project were particularly interested in helping Iranian or Sudanese policymakers. They were, rather, hoping to be of assistance to policy makers who worked in nations with capitalist economies and democratic polities. The project's findings were intended to help a diverse group of well-educated and moderately powerful men and women who had not experienced any particular difficulties "adjusting to modernity" better understand various religio-political movements made up, for the most part, of people who were less well educated and less powerful than they were. The members of those movements were said to be having trouble adjusting to the reality of modern life. Once the tendencies and habits of mind of those troubled men and women had been dispassionately analyzed, the movements they joined would appear less mysterious. And when those movements were better understood, the threats they posed to the rest of the world could be minimized. The power of the troublemakers could be diminished. The world could be made a safer place.

Making the world safer is surely a worthwhile goal. But when you announce such a goal, you are likely to be asked, "Safer for whom?" For reasons I do not completely understand, the champions of global fundamentalism have a great deal of difficulty coming up with a straightforward answer to that question. The difficulty they experience when they try to respond casts doubt on the validity of global fundamentalism. As a general rule, champions of global fundamentalism also have trouble answering questions about the relationship between looking for knowledge and exercising power, about the relationship between modernity and the West, and about the wisdom of Western academics treating people who live in other parts of the world as objects of inquiry. Only a few of the champions of global fundamentalism—Ernest Gellner, for example—are willing to call themselves adherents of "Enlightenment Rationalist Fundamentalism."[32] But many of them are people who might be said to have something akin to Enlightenment rationalist fundamentalist *tendencies*, and few of them are equipped to give thoughtful responses to the questions postcolonial and poststructuralist texts ask. A good many of the champions of global fundamentalism behave as though they hope those sorts of questions will simply go away.

Behaving that way is not unreasonable. The influence of postcolonial and poststructuralist thinkers on how Americans view the world can be overstated, and it is certainly too early to make any final judgments about the durability of the questions those writers have posed. In the long run, they may prove to be quite ephemeral. But, in the short and medium terms, those questions seem very durable indeed and they have influenced—either directly or indirectly—the way a good many Americans view the world.[33] Americans who have been influenced by poststructuralism and postcolonialism are suspicious of Enlightenment rationalist fundamentalism. They do not assume that modernization theory provides the best starting point for analyzing the world we live in. They don't believe that the ideas of Max Weber ought to be treated with great deference. When given a choice between rereading a text written by Weber and one written by Edward Said, Michel Foucault, or Judith Butler, many of them will decide to lay Weber aside.

The questions poststructuralists and postcolonialists ask often make it difficult for conversations about global fundamentalism to proceed smoothly. People who want to talk about global fundamentalism are likely to discover that some of their conversation partners are convinced that the concept is patently bogus and that engaging in a conversation about it is a waste of their time. In the face of such skepticism, those who want to talk about global fundamentalism have to be prepared to explain why, in spite of everything, they think the concept is useful.

The scenario plays out over and over again. A speaker says something about global fundamentalism. A moment or two later another person confesses that she finds the concept extremely dubious and briefly explains why. The original speaker listens politely, presents a few counterarguments, and then tries to proceed with his argument. But then someone else interrupts and asserts that one of the speaker's counterarguments is based on an unwarranted assumption. A lively debate about the assumptions upon which global fundamentalism is based ensues. It lasts a long time. By the time the debate concludes, the conversation has gone off in so many directions that the point that the original speaker was trying to make now seems irrelevant.

It is clear that many of the champions of global fundamentalism have been part of conversations like the one just described. Quite understandably, those conversations have left them frustrated. Some of the most thoughtful champions of global fundamentalism respond to that sense of frustration by proposing that the range of phenomena to which the concept is applied ought to be dramatically narrowed. What they are trying to do, one might say, is to constrict global fundamentalism in order to save it. In *Strong Religion*—one of the most sophisticated of the texts the Fundamentalism Project generated—Gabriel A. Almond, R. Scott Appleby, and Emmanuel Sivan argued that many of the religious movements to which the fundamentalist label is frequently assigned are not really a part of fundamentalism proper. They drew a distinction between real fundamentalism—militant anti-secular movements that are rooted in one of the Western monotheistic religions—and the fundamentalist-like movements that are rooted in Eastern religions. After careful reflection, Almond, Appleby, and Sivan concluded that we should generally refrain from invoking global fundamentalism except when we are talking about Christians, Muslims, and Jews.[34]

And even when we talk about Muslims and Jews, the authors of *Strong Religion* said, there is usually no need to categorize them as fundamentalists. Generally, we should describe Muslims as Islamists rather than as fundamentalists. Likewise, most of the time we ought not to refer to the members of the Haredim or the Gush Emunim as fundamentalists; instead, we should use "specific Jewish designations" when we are talking about them. Almond, Appleby, and Sivan argued that we should speak of Jews and Muslims as fundamentalists only when we are presenting a comparative analysis of the monotheistic religions. At all other times, the only people we should describe as fundamentalists are Protestant Christians such as William Jennings Bryan and Jerry Falwell.[35]

This suggestion made a good deal of sense. Almond, Appleby, and Sivan's definition of global fundamentalism was more cohesive and less confusing than many of the other definitions of that term. But the analysis of global fundamentalism that they presented was open to the same sort of critiques, and they did not give their readers a convincing rationale for refusing to circumscribe the meaning of fundamentalism still further. Why not simply take another step or two and confine fundamentalism to Protestant Christians? Was all the fuss and bother and controversy and confusion connected to turning a specific historic concept into a universal comparative one really worthwhile? It seems like a very long way to go to gain a rather meager analytical advantage.

Conclusion

Earlier, I asked whether the term "fundamentalism" can be defended. The answer is clearly yes. Fundamentalism can be defended energetically. Fundamentalism can be defended ingenuously. But it is not at all clear that it can be defended successfully. On the whole, the arguments champions of global fundamentalism present are probably inferior to those the skeptics present. Showing that it is sometimes helpful to use Western concepts to explore non-Western societies does not demonstrate that doing so is always useful. Drawing comparisons between fundamentalists and crabs does not really work very well, and it tempts us to think of fundamentalists as something less than completely human. Champions of fundamentalism underestimate the difficulties connected to defining fundamentalism; many of their definitions are extremely vague. There is something odd about the way that scholars who study fundamentalism think about themselves: although they take umbrage when skeptics say that their work is deeply political, their work is as political as political could be. It is not a simple search for objective truth; it is an attempt to make the world safer. But safer for whom? It is an attempt to come up with results that could be useful to policy makers, and the kind of policy makers who are most likely to make use of it are those who work for the United States and its allies. In general, champions of global fundamentalism tend to be dismissive of the sorts of questions postcolonial and poststructuralist thinkers ask. That is not completely bizarre. But it does make it very difficult for champions of global fundamentalism to talk to people who have been influenced directly or indirectly by postcolonial and poststructuralist thinkers. Thus, a good many conversations about global fundamentalism have stalled rather quickly. People cannot argue about any specific questions connected to global fundamentalism without first arguing about whether the concept itself is useful. The most thoughtful champions of global fundamentalism are well aware of that fact. As a result, they end up dramatically circumscribing the meaning of global fundamentalism. Perhaps that is a smart thing to do. But it also gives skeptics an opening to ask a question for which there is no convincing rejoinder. Once one has gone that far, why not take a step further? Why not simply return to a stricter definition of fundamentalism?

3

The First Fundamentalists

The fundamentalist movement was created in the 1920s by Protestants who feared that America's churches had drifted away from the fundamental doctrines of the Christian faith. Those men and women were determined to stop that drift; they were committed to recalling America's churches to the doctrines that (in their view) were central to the Christian faith. In this chapter I look at the people who were a part of the fundamentalist movement—who they were, what they believed, and what set them apart from other Protestant Christians. Referring to that particular group of Protestants as fundamentalists is, everyone agrees, completely appropriate. They proudly called themselves fundamentalists, and their opponents called them that, too. Most people who have given any thought to the issue would say that a definition of global fundamentalism that is constructed in such a way as to exclude the people who belonged to the fundamentalist movements of the 1920s and 1930s is automatically suspect. If those people were not fundamentalists, then no one was—or is.

In the following pages I look at the fundamentalist movement of the 1920s and 1930s within the context of global fundamentalism. The defining characteristics of global fundamentalism have often been said to include a penchant for reading texts literally, a proclivity for mixing politics and religion, a determination to resist modernity, and a predilection for militancy. As it turns out, none of the supposed characteristics of global fundamentalism can be neatly applied to the fundamentalists of the 1920s and 1930s.

Origins

The fundamentalist movement took its name from a set of booklets called *The Fundamentals: A Testimony to the Truth*. Those pamphlets were based on the conviction that a sizable portion of Christendom had fallen into grievous error. *The Fundamentals*, which were published between 1910 and 1915, were edited by three evangelists: A.C. Dixon, Louis Meyer, and Reuben Torrey. The $200,000 required to produce and distribute the pamphlets came from a pious and influential oil tycoon named Lyman Stewart.[1] In keeping with Stewart's wishes, the essays in *The Fundamentals* admonished Christians to reject heretical ideas, cling to the truths that were set forth in the Bible, and dedicate themselves to disseminating those truths throughout the world.

The authors who contributed essays believed they were living in an age when many people within the church had an "uneasy and distrustful feeling" about the Bible. The authors assured their readers that there was no reason in the world why Protestant Christians should feel that way: God has revealed himself to his people, "the Bible is the record of that revelation, and that revelation shines in its light from the beginning to the end of it."[2] According to the conservative Protestants who wrote *The Fundamentals*, the Christian Bible is *absolutely* trustworthy; it contains no errors whatsoever. They viewed the Bible as God's definitive revelation of himself to man. To them, the claim that subsequent texts—such as *Science and Health*, the Book of Mormon, and the Qur'an—were somehow a continuation of the ongoing work of revelation was simply absurd.

In 1919, four years after the final volume of *The Fundamentals* was published, 6,000 people assembled in Philadelphia to take part in the creation of the World Christian Fundamentals Association (WCFA). Membership in the association was open to anyone who was willing to pay annual dues—associate members paid one dollar, full members paid five—and to sign the doctrinal statement upon which the WCFA was founded.[3] That statement affirmed the doctrine of the trinity, the inerrancy of the Christian scriptures, the virgin birth, Christ's substitutionary atonement for humanity's sins, the physical resurrection of Christ, and the imminent return of Christ to earth to inaugurate a thousand-year reign of peace.[4] These were the fundamentals whose importance the leaders of the WCFA wanted to reassert. The leaders believed that many of America's denominations included ministers and seminary professors who had rejected the fundamental doctrines of the Christian faith, and they hoped that the WCFA could protect Christians against the baneful influence of such people. The leaders of the WCFA believed that nominal Christians who had rejected the fundamental truths of biblical Christianity and yet continued to insist that they had the right to occupy positions of authority within the church were a terrible threat to the cause of Christ.[5]

Although the people who founded the WCFA were wholeheartedly committed to defending the fundamentals of the Christian faith, we can be certain that when those men and women gathered together in Philadelphia in 1919 they did not think of themselves as "fundamentalists" or as proponents of "fundamentalism." Neither of those words entered the English language until the 1920s. The word "fundamentalists" was invented the year after the WCFA was launched. Curtis Lee Laws, a pastor and journalist, coined the term while writing about the events that had taken place during that year's meeting of the Northern Baptist Convention. Laws used the word to refer to Protestants who were firmly committed to "the great fundamentals" of the Christian faith and who were willing to "do battle royal" on behalf of Christian orthodoxy.[6] The text in which Laws suggested that resolute defenders of orthodoxy call themselves fundamentalists was called "Convention Side Lights." It was not a long article, and most of it was concerned with matters other than what the opponents of theological liberalism ought to call themselves. Given how much influence it has had on the nomenclature we use to describe religious conservatives, "Convention Side Lights" said very little about what it was that the fundamentalists were trying to conserve. The article did not specify what Laws thought the fundamentals of the Christian faith actually were, and it did not describe the theological errors that fundamentalists ought to fight against. "Convention Side Lights" did not try to predict when and where the battles between the fundamentalists and their adversaries would take place. And the article said nothing about which social classes, which regions of the country, which denominations, and which institutions and publications could be counted on to support the fundamentalist cause. It also did not say who it was that the fundamentalists should turn to for leadership and guidance.

There is, however, nothing especially mysterious about those topics. From our present vantage point, they can be addressed with a fair degree of certitude. From the 1970s to the present day, an unusually astute group of historians has investigated the fundamentalist movement of the 1920s and 1930s. Their investigations have not, of course, produced a set of objective, universally agreed-upon generalizations about the true nature of fundamentalism. And there is good reason to suppose that historians' understanding of the nature of fundamentalism will be different in 2037 than it is right now.[7]

It also ought to be noted that the investigations of fundamentalism that historians have undertaken between 1970 and the present have not produced analyses of fundamentalism that are superior, in every single respect, to those produced in earlier decades. Older works such as Norman Furniss's *The Fundamentalist Controversy* and Richard Hofstadter's *Anti-Intellectualism in American Life* can still be read with profit.[8] But the analyses of fundamentalism that historians have produced in the past four decades are generally less tendentious, more fine-grained, and more sophisticated than the older interpretation of fundamentalism. They are also based on a greater familiarity with the primary sources that illuminate the history of the fundamentalist movements. These more recent analyses provide us with depictions of fundamentalists as imperfect human beings rather than as villainous monsters or saintly servants of God. Recent historical investigations have not told us everything we would like to know about fundamentalism, but they have shown us a fundamentalism with a human face.[9]

Of course, the various descriptions of fundamentalism that historians have given us in recent years differ from one another in a number of respects. In some settings, those differences are quite significant. But in the present context, the significance of those differences is easy to overstate.

For our purposes the important point is this: during the 1920s and 1930s fundamentalism was by no means coterminous with conservative Protestantism. All fundamentalists were conservative Protestants, but many conservative Protestants were not fundamentalists. In the 1920s and 1930s, fundamentalism was only one of the many tiles to be found in the conservative mosaic. And it was not necessarily the largest or most important tile. The fundamentalists certainly did not speak for all conservative Protestants. Most members of the Assemblies of God, the Church of the Nazarene, the National Baptist Convention, the Southern Baptist Convention, the Churches of Christ, and the Missouri Synod of the Lutheran Church never joined the fundamentalist coalition. And, as Joel Carpenter has pointed out, applying the fundamentalist label to conservative Protestants who did not choose to attach themselves to the fundamentalist movement makes it very difficult to understand those Protestants' beliefs and practices. Calling them fundamentalists makes it sound as if conservative Protestantism in America was far more homogeneous than it really was.[10]

Fundamentalism was a popular religious movement that won the allegiance of Protestant Christians from every region of the United States. It had its own distinctive institutions, publications, leaders, networks of influence, and doctrinal emphases that differentiated it from other forms of conservative Protestantism. Fundamentalists knew that they had much in common with other conservative Protestants, but their relations with conservative Protestants who were not a part of the fundamentalist movement were sometimes cool rather than warm.[11]

Fundamentalists never created an organization whose membership rolls included all the fundamentalists in the United States, and they never drew up a creedal statement that all of them recognized as authoritative.[12] But a fundamentalist, almost by definition, believed in the virgin birth, Christ's divinity, and the reality of the miracles recorded in the Bible. And a great many fundamentalists put tremendous emphasis on the doctrine of biblical inerrancy and on what they called the "blessed hope"—by which they meant "the personal, premillennial and imminent return" of Christ to earth.[13] Fundamentalists believed that they were living in an age when many powerful men and women disregarded the fundamentals of the Christian faith. They strove to live their lives in accord with the truths revealed in the Bible and endeavored to convince others that ignoring those truths was a dangerous thing to do. They wanted to give people throughout the world an opportunity to hear and accept the truths of the Bible. It seemed certain to them that God had graciously revealed a set of eternal truths, and they were sure that God had called them to teach those truths to others. So fundamentalism was, among other things, a sort of educational crusade.[14]

Fundamentalists believed that a great many of the colleges and universities in the United States were run by people who had rejected the fundamentals of the Christian faith. But they had confidence in schools such as the Bible Institute of Los Angeles, Bob Jones College,[15] Moody Bible Institute, Northwestern Bible and Missionary Training School, the Philadelphia School of the Bible, and Wheaton College. Fundamentalists were sure that if they sent their sons and daughters to schools such as these, they could be certain that their offspring would receive a godly education.

Fundamentalists listened devotedly to radio programs such as *Radio Bible Class*, *Bible Study Hour*, and *Old Fashioned Revival Hour*. They filled their bookshelves with texts that included *In His Image*, *The Conflict of the Ages*, *The Menace of Modernism*, and the *Scofield Reference Bible* and subscribed to magazines such as *The Fundamentalist*, *The King's Business*, *Moody Bible Institute Monthly*, *Our Hope*, *The Presbyterian*, *Revelation*, *Sunday School Times*, *Sword of the Lord*, and *Watchman-Examiner*.[16] Fundamentalists looked to men such as Bob Jones Sr., Charles E. Fuller, William Jennings Bryan, Arno C. Gaebelein, James M. Gray, G. Gresham Machen, Clarence E. Macartney, J. C. Massee, Carl McIntire, G. Campbell Morgan, J. Frank Norris, John R. Rice, William Bell Riley, Wilbur Smith, John Roach Straton, and Reuben Torrey for guidance and leadership.[17]

The movement that eventually came to be known as fundamentalism began to coalesce around the turn of the twentieth century. It gathered force during World War I and rose to national prominence in the 1920s. During that decade, fundamentalists threw themselves wholeheartedly into two distinct but related campaigns. The goal of the first was to make certain that America's most important denominations were controlled by conservative Protestants rather than by modernists. The goal of the second was to deter teachers in the nation's public schools from teaching their students the scientific theories developed by Charles Darwin.

Neither campaign was completely successful. Fundamentalists scored a few victories in the denominational battles of the 1920s, but they certainly did not succeed in driving their opponents out of the denominations. When the decade ended, a number of the nation's denominations were still what they were when the decade began: complex aggregations whose membership included modernists, moderates, and conservatives. And although fundamentalists and their allies did succeed in making it difficult for teachers in many of the nation's public schools to freely discuss Darwinian evolution, when the 1920s ended, many of the nation's public schools were continuing to expose their students to what the fundamentalists saw as the absurd scientific theories of a dangerous man.[18] The way that fundamentalists conducted themselves during the campaigns against teaching evolution made them appear foolish in the eyes of many well-educated Americans. When the 1920s ended, it was quite clear that fundamentalists were viewed as less than respectable in many circles. Many observers had come to believe that the fundamentalists had been exiled to the margins of American culture and that their years in exile would never come to an end.

But the defeats they suffered during the 1920s did not plunge the fundamentalists into inert despair. During the 1930s, fundamentalists exhibited great zeal and dedication. They flocked to summer conferences at which the fundamentals of the Christian faith were set forth with great conviction. Fundamentalists also poured a tremendous amount of energy into strengthening their congregations, Bible institutes, and colleges. And they expended a great deal of time and money on evangelistic campaigns in the United States and on missionary work in places such as China and Africa. By the time the United States entered World War II, there were a great many indications that the fundamentalist movement was flourishing rather than declining.

A disagreement over whether changed social and cultural conditions necessitated a rethinking of fundamentalists' traditional emphasis on opposition to theological error, however, caused the movement to falter in the early 1940s. Men such as Bob Jones Sr. and Carl McIntire thought that no change was necessary. People such as Billy Graham and Harold Ockenga came to believe that Bible-believing Christians should adopt a new set of tactics to advance the cause of Christ: they believed in a less confrontational approach to defending the fundamentals of the Christian faith. The debates over this issue were sometimes quite heated. Sometimes McIntire seemed to spend more time berating people such as Graham than he did condemning modernism. But the splintering of fundamentalism did not by any means put an end to fundamentalism's influence. Men who had grown up in the fundamentalist movement and who had been decisively shaped by their involvement in it played a large role in shaping the revival that occurred in the aftermath of World War II.[19]

Who They Were

It is sometimes assumed that the great majority of fundamentalists lived in the American South. That assumption is unfounded. A good many fundamentalists did live there, and a number of the leaders of the fundamentalist movement—Bob Jones Sr. and J. Frank Norris, for example—were southerners. However, fundamentalists could be found in every region of the United States, and many of the fundamentalist movement's most prominent leaders lived in cities in the North, the Midwest, or the West.[20] Clarence Macartney lived in Pittsburgh, J. Gresham Machen lived in Philadelphia, John Roach Straton lived in New York, and William Bell Riley lived in Minneapolis. Los Angeles, Boston, and Minneapolis were all places where fundamentalists were particularly active, and Chicago was arguably the most important fundamentalist stronghold in the nation.[21] To a much greater degree than is often realized, fundamentalism was a northern movement that appealed to men and women who lived in cities.

Although many fundamentalists lived in cities that had a great many African American residents, the vast majority of the people who were a part of the fundamentalist movement were native-born white Americans.[22] The leadership of the fundamentalist movement was lily white.[23] From time to time, an African American student would matriculate at a fundamentalist institution such as the Moody Bible Institute or Wheaton College, but such enrollments seem to have been quite uncommon.[24] And though many African Americans were deeply suspicious of Darwin's ideas, few African Americans threw themselves fully into fundamentalists' campaign to keep evolution from being taught in the nation's public schools. Indeed, some African Americans came to believe that the leaders of the crusade to keep Darwinism out of the schools were dangerous fools.[25]

The leaders of the fundamentalist movement who gained the most notoriety and the most fame were all men. But fundamentalism was not, by any means, a movement made up exclusively of men. Indeed, there is some reason to suppose that most of the rank-and-file members of the movement were women. Throughout all of American history, most congregations have had more women than men on their membership rolls, and there is little reason to believe that fundamentalist churches deviated from the general pattern. Indeed, we know for certain that most of the members of some of the most important fundamentalist congregations were women. During the 1920s, for example, women made up nearly 70 percent of the membership of Boston's Park Street Church.[26] We also know that even when fundamentalist leaders made a determined effort to convince men to come hear them preach, they still ended up addressing audiences in which women outnumbered men by a ratio of three to one.[27] It is also clear that many of the teachers in fundamentalist congregations and schools were women and that women made up a large proportion of the fundamentalist missionaries sent to foreign lands. Women also seem to have exercised a good deal of behind-the-scenes leadership in some fundamentalist organizations. It is difficult to gauge just how much covert influence women fundamentalists were actually able to exercise, but it is possible that it was considerable. It is certainly the case that male fundamentalists complained bitterly that Christian churches in the United States had been overly influenced by the values and outlooks of women.[28]

Relatively few of the women and men who actively participated in the fundamentalist movement possessed great fortunes. But the fundamentalist movement did win the allegiance of a few rich Christians and some wealthy fundamentalists—Robert G. Letourneau, Henry Parsons Crowell, John M. Studebaker, and Milton and Lyman Stewart, for example—who used their riches to advance the cause. Their generosity was one of the keys to the movement's strength. The fundamentalist movement was not, of course, a capitalist plot, but it certainly was a movement that enjoyed some support from wealthy capitalists. Fundamentalism also drew support from people who were poor and from people who were part of the working class. But the proportion of fundamentalists who made their living through manual labor and the proportion who were impoverished can easily be exaggerated. The fundamentalist movement seems to have appealed especially to people from the lower middle class, the middle class, and the upper middle class. A great many fundamentalists made their living working as semi-skilled craftsmen, tradesmen, teachers, or ministers. Some of them worked as lawyers or physicians. A good many fundamentalists were small businessmen. There is also some reason to believe that the fundamentalist movement included a large number of men and women who were upwardly mobile.[29] Indeed, in some instances, aligning oneself with the fundamentalist movement was, in and of itself, a form of upward mobility. Subscribing to a fundamentalist journal and reading it regularly could make you more learned. Mastering the intricacies of the dispensationalist scheme could sharpen your mind. Attending a fundamentalist Bible institute gave you a set of skills that could be used to live a life with wide horizons rather than narrow ones.

What They Believed

Most fundamentalists were obsessed with deepening their relationship with God and with living lives that glorified God. In order to do that, they engaged in a wide range of activities. Fundamentalists participated in prayer groups in which they asked God to meet the physical and spiritual needs of others and of themselves. They sang hymns that glorified God and gave personal testimonies designed to demonstrate God's power and might. Fundamentalists attended classes in which they learned about God and his ways. They read religious newspapers, magazines, and books that taught them how to live their lives in accord with God's will. They listened to sermons that exhorted and inspired them to do so.[30]

The sermons that fundamentalists heard were full of language and imagery drawn from the Bible. So were the testimonies they gave, the hymns that they sang, and the supplications they made. The newspapers, magazines, and books that fundamentalists read focused on the truths to be found in the Bible and on how Christians could apply those truths to their own lives. For fundamentalists, the Bible was quite literally a treasured gift from God. It was holy in the fullest sense of that word. It told them what God was like, and it taught them the true nature of the universe that God had created.

Fundamentalists believed that a very large proportion of the world's population had never embraced the truths to be found in the Bible. They believed that those men and women—both nominal Christians and those who were not Christians at all—were headed toward eternal torment.[31]

Fundamentalists were determined to save as many people as they could from that fate and to point them instead toward God. That determination pushed them to send missionary expeditions throughout the world and to launch evangelistic crusades throughout the United States. But a fundamentalist did not, of course, have to become a missionary or an evangelist in order to win souls for Christ. Fundamentalist preachers could—and did—make sure that their sermons ended with invitations for non-Christians to come to Christ. Fundamentalist laypeople could—and did—continually look for opportunities to ask their acquaintances, coworkers, neighbors, and friends to become Christians.[32] Once converted, new Christians were expected to live their lives in accord with the truths to be found in the Bible. Living this way would enable converts to look forward to spending eternity with God and it would also enable the Lord to make use of them in the here and now. As their understanding of biblical truths deepened, new Christians could encourage non-Christians to embrace those truths. Whatever else it was—and it was certainly many other things—the fundamentalist movement was also a zealous campaign to get people throughout the world to read the Bible, to interpret it properly, and to live out the truths it contained.

Fundamentalists often asserted that in order to understand the truths to be found in the scriptures, one had to interpret the Bible literally. They claimed that they relied on literal interpretation of the sacred text and that their modernist opponents relied instead on less trustworthy interpretations of the scriptures. Those claims had a good deal of validity. (Fundamentalists really did believe that many passages in the Bible that modernists tended to say were true spiritually rather than literally—those that said Mary was a virgin when Jesus was conceived, for instance—were in fact literal declarations about clear facts.) It is worth nothing, however, that fundamentalists did not always read the Bible "literally" in the fullest sense of that word. When fundamentalists read the fifteenth chapter of the Gospel of John—in which Jesus declares himself to be "the true vine"—they did not come away thinking that Jesus was a herbaceous plant. And though there are a great many passages in the Bible that refer to God's hand, fundamentalists did not believe that the Lord possessed a literal hand. Nor did they believe that Jesus's advice about what a Christian ought to do if he discovers that his right eye is leading him into sin—gouge out that eye—ought to be taken literally. If fundamentalists had interpreted that advice literally, then presumably the fundamentalist movement would have included a very large number of one-eyed Christians. Fundamentalists read the Bible in ways that suggest that they knew that it included a great many tropes. And though they seldom emphasized that point in their public pronouncements, fundamentalists did sometimes acknowledge that it was a mistake to interpret all the passages in the Bible in a literal fashion. Some fundamentalists said, for instance, that it was wrong to say that God had created the universe in six literal 24-hour days. It might well, they suggested, make more sense to assume that the days in the first chapter of Genesis were figurative days rather than literal ones.[33]

In general, fundamentalists seemed to have been far more interested in biblical hermeneutics than in politics. Most of them were more interested in making sense of the Book of Daniel than they were in trying to influence the outcome of elections. And even when fundamentalists did turn their attention to political events, they often seemed less interested in the social and economic effects of those events than in their implications for Christ's second advent: when they examined those events, fundamentalists focused their attention on how they dovetailed with the Bible's prophecies concerning the rapture, the tribulation, the rise of the Antichrist, and the battle of Armageddon.[34] Thus, interpretations of the fundamentalist movement that present it as a political phenomenon *rather than* a religious one simply cannot be brought into accord with the evidence to be found in the primary sources.[35] But to say that the fundamentalist movement was a religious phenomenon is not, of course, to say that it was not a political one. Politics is not just about who gets elected to office. It is also about how power is distributed, about how power can be used, and about the ends to which power ought to be used. Those sorts of questions were of great interest to the fundamentalists. Even fundamentalists who were least interested in politics in the narrowest sense of that term certainly were concerned with matters—whether women ought to work outside the home, for example—that are, when considered from certain points of view, as political as political can be.

One of the political issues in which fundamentalists took a special interest had to do with the Catholic Church. Fundamentalists tended to believe that Catholics had gained too much power in American society and that their political potency constituted a grave threat to American democracy. Fundamentalists were, therefore, frequently on the lookout for opportunities to reduce Catholics' influence on the U.S. government. As George Marsden has noted, a great many fundamentalists assumed that the "United States was a Protestant nation founded upon Biblical principles" and that fundamentalists had a duty to try to return the nation to its roots.[36] Fundamentalists wanted the American government to fully embrace Protestant norms and to take steps to cultivate virtue and to suppress sin. They often tried to get the government to prevent ungodly ideas from being taught in public schools. They also worked to get the government to do all it could do to limit the consumption of alcohol. Fundamentalists also attempted to convince the government to curb fornication, adultery, and divorce.

Although fundamentalists wanted the U.S. government to improve the nation's moral tenor, most of them seemed to think that it was unwise for the government to take direct action to try to solve economic problems such as poverty and homelessness. Such problems, they believed, were best addressed by spiritual revival and individual effort. Most fundamentalists had a good deal of sympathy for the tenets of laissez-faire liberalism. They tended to assume that, aside from encouraging its citizens to act morally, the government should play a relatively small role in shaping American society. They believed that in many respects the government that governed least was the one that governed best.[37] Although many fundamentalists who lived in the South routinely supported the Democratic Party, fundamentalists seldom displayed a great deal of enthusiasm for the New Deal. From time to time, they denounced it with great vigor. They often worried that the U.S. government had grown too large and too powerful. They also believed that the government placed too many restrictions on entrepreneurs: the contention that government has a duty to limit the power of businessmen and to support the rights of labor—a contention that a fair number of modernists were inclined to accept—was one that many fundamentalists rejected out of hand.[38]

Polemics

Fundamentalists were not categorically opposed to all the phenomena that we associate with the coming of modernity. They made skillful use of some modern inventions—the radio, for instance—to advance their cause.

And fundamentalists adopted some of the attitudes associated with modern commercial enterprise, such as tremendous confidence in the power of marketing and advertising, with great avidity. Indeed, some of the fundamentalists came to think of their evangelical endeavors as something very closely akin to a modern business venture. One fundamentalist leader, Mel Trotter, went so far as to calculate precisely how much money it took for his organization to save a soul. He concluded that each soul cost $1.60.[39]

Despite their great respect for the achievements of modern commerce, fundamentalists found some aspects of the modern age repellent. They tended to see the modern era as a time of darkness rather than light and as an epoch of wickedness rather than progress. In their eyes, the modern age was a time of lawlessness, sexual licentiousness, and cultural decline. Fundamentalists had little good to say about modern literature or modern art, and they enumerated the shortcomings of modern intellectuals such as Marx and Darwin with great zeal. Fundamentalists often believed that novel religious ideas were inferior to traditional ones; they were convinced that theological modernism was a collection of erroneous and dangerous hypotheses.

Protestant modernism was a complicated and multifaceted phenomenon. Some of the men associated with the fundamentalist movement—J. Gresham Machen, for example—had a very firm grasp of what the modernists wanted to do and what it was that they believed. Others did not. But even fundamentalists who knew relatively little about modernism were sure that they knew enough to understand that it was a terrible threat to true Christianity. Fundamentalists believed that modernists occupied positions of power within many of the large denominations and that they used that power to harass laymen and ministers who remained true to the fundamentals of Christianity.[40] Some fundamentalists, A. C. Gaebelein for example, believed that the modernists who were tormenting them were dangerous apostates.[41] Other fundamentalists, including Machen, adopted a more extreme position: they argued that modernists were adherents of a recently invented religion that was completely at odds with the Christian faith.

Machen was born in 1881 in Baltimore, Maryland. Both his mother and his father were well educated, accomplished, and well-to-do. His mother gave him a deep grounding in the fundamentals of the Christian faith as Presbyterians had traditionally understood them. Machen studied at Johns Hopkins University, Princeton Seminary, and Princeton University and then went to Germany to pursue more advanced work at the University of Marburg and the University of Göttingen. From 1906 to 1929, Machen taught New Testament at Princeton Seminary; he taught at Westminster Seminary from 1929 to 1937. During the course of his life Machen published several scholarly books—*The Origins of Paul's Religion* and *The Virgin Birth of Christ*, for example—and some popular ones, such as the *Christian Faith in the Modern World*, a book that was based on a series of talks Machen delivered on a radio station in Philadelphia. Machen's most famous book, *Christianity and Liberalism*, published in 1923, was enthusiastically received by many Christian theologians and by some secular intellectuals (both H.L. Mencken and Walter Lippmann admired it). Machen was reluctant to label himself as a fundamentalist; he thought of himself, rather, simply as a Christian. Nevertheless, during the 1920s and 1930s, Machen was generally thought of as one of fundamentalism's most important spokesmen. Machen is important to this discussion for two reasons. First, looking at him reminds us that fundamentalists such as Machen had a great deal in common with modernists such as Harry Emerson Fosdick. Second, focusing on Machen highlights the differences between the imaginary fundamentalists who fill the pages of antifundamentalist polemics and the actual fundamentalists who existed in the real world.

Machen argued that it was a mistake to view the religious controversies of the 1920s as a set of battles between Christians who adhered to fundamentalism and Christians who embraced modernism. The people who were commonly thought to be defending fundamentalism were, he said, actually trying to defend Christianity itself. He claimed that the opponents of fundamentalists did not subscribe to a sophisticated, forward-looking version of Christianity or even to a perverse form of Christianity.[42] They subscribed, rather, to an entirely different religion, a religion whose doctrines were on "almost every conceivable point" the opposite of Christianity. When both religions were carefully analyzed, it became obvious that one could not give one's loyalty simultaneously to both the religion of liberalism and the Christian religion. The two religions were "mutually exclusive."[43] Liberalism emphasized human goodness; Christianity focused on divine grace. Christianity was a supernatural faith; the religion of liberalism was rooted in a set of assumptions that were thoroughly naturalistic.[44]

Machen believed that modern liberals systematically downplayed the differences between liberalism and Christianity. Although liberals made use of reassuring traditional terms such as the atonement and the deity of Christ, they radically reinterpreted the meaning of those words.[45] Machen noted that those who had embraced liberalism generally refused to withdraw from the church and believed that they had a perfect right to exercise authority within the Christian church. To Machen, that belief was simply ludicrous. It seemed obvious to him that people who did not accept the fundamental doctrines of the Christian church should not try to serve as ministers in that church. Instead, they should make their way into voluntary associations that were explicitly devoted to the doctrines of the religion of liberalism. If liberals were to join such organizations, they could give them unfeigned loyalty. And after the liberals had emigrated, the church would be left firmly under the authority of those who were committed to core doctrines of the Christian faith.[46]

Machen had a knack for presenting his arguments in an irenic manner, and he sometimes leaned over backward to be respectful of persons with whom he disagreed.[47] He made a point of saying that he had no intention of questioning the sincerity of the liberals' beliefs, and he assured his readers that he did not believe that liberals' inability to embrace the doctrines of Christian faith demonstrated that they were bad people. Socrates, he noted, did not embrace those doctrines either, and he clearly towered "immeasurably above the common run of men."[48] Machen also said that he was not in a position to say whether any particular individual was or was not going to spend eternity in heaven. It was possible, Machen emphasized, that there were some liberals who were unable to accept the fundamental doctrines of the Christian religion but who nevertheless maintained an attitude toward Christ that constituted "a saving faith."[49]

In spite of the gentlemanly manner in which Machen presented his analysis of what was really at stake in the religious controversies of the 1920s, many modernists found his arguments exasperating.[50] That is entirely understandable. Machen made no real effort to give a sympathetic portrayal of modernists' understanding of Christianity; he had a great deal less to say about what liberals stood for than he did about what they were against. And although Machen said he did not mean to offend when he asserted that a good many people who thought of themselves as adherents of the Christian religion were in fact no such thing, it is not difficult to see how such a claim could be deeply offensive. That claim was, after all, somewhat analogous to arguing that a group of men and women who thought of themselves as loyal citizens of the United States of America were, in fact, subjects of the Empire of Japan. Moreover, the categories Machen used to analyze the controversies between people he called liberals and the ones he called Christians were remarkably brittle. Those categories consisted, in large part, of stark binaries that left little room for complexity or nuance. And, of course, there was nothing in Machen's analysis of the differences between liberals and Christians to indicate that the Christians might be mistaken. Machen wanted his readers to realize that on every single one of the issues about which liberals and Christians differed, the liberals were simply wrong. The liberals had misperceived the nature of the universe; Machen and his co-belligerents had gotten it right. Christians embraced the true religion; liberals had given their loyalty to a false one.

Even when it was presented as politely as Machen presented it, the message that "we're completely right and you're completely wrong" inevitably offended Machen's modernist opponents. And fundamentalist polemicists often spoke and wrote as though they had no intention of trying to be polite. They prided themselves on their militancy and on their willingness to ruthlessly critique modernists. J. Frank Norris, a prominent Texas fundamentalist, declared that modernists were "lepers" and "Judases."[51] A. C. Gaebelein said that modernists were leading the world toward atheism, communism, and ruin.[52] He also insisted that they lacked virility. W. B. Riley agreed: modernists, he said, were womanly.[53] Riley argued, too, that college professors who had embraced modernism posed a terrible threat to both democracy and Christianity.[54] The attacks fundamentalists launched on modernists were nothing short of militant. Not only were they not polite; they seemed to delight in launching savage verbal assaults against their enemies.

Fundamentalists' rhetoric was studded with metaphors drawn from warfare: they tended to speak of their encounters with modernists as skirmishes, battles, crusades, and battles royal. But the contests between fundamentalists and their opponents almost never involved actual physical violence.[55] The so-called theological battles of the 1920s were fought with sermons, books, and votes, not with knives, guns, and grenades. During the hard-fought contests for control of Princeton Seminary, for example, angry words were exchanged, but no shots. And when the men who were trying to protect the fundamentals of the faith lost control of Princeton, they accepted their defeat with a certain equanimity and then established a new institution, Westminster Seminary, that was firmly under their control and was located about forty miles to the south and west of Princeton. Fundamentalists' actions were far less violent than their words. The battles fundamentalists fought against the modernists were metaphorical ones.

Conclusion

The issue of militancy brings us back to the question of how we ought to define fundamentalism. A focus on topics such as literalism, politicization, modernity, and militancy does not illuminate the distinctive characteristics of the fundamentalist movement of the 1920s and 1930s. To be sure, fundamentalists did tend to interpret the Bible more literally than modernists did. Some fundamentalists did take an interest in partisan politics, and if we define politics broadly enough then it becomes clear that nearly all fundamentalists were interested in some of the political issues of their day. Fundamentalists viewed the modern world with deep suspicion, and their rhetoric was sometimes quite militant indeed.

But the militancy of the Protestant fundamentalists of the 1920s and 1930s can easily be overstated. They sometimes spoke and acted in ways that could be described as moderate. And their attacks on modernists were almost always metaphorical rather than literal. Fundamentalists' resistance to modernity was sometimes inconsistent and half-hearted. Their interest in politics, as it is conventionally understood, was sporadic rather than obsessive. They believed that most political problems were little more than symptoms of spiritual disorder. And fundamentalists did not interpret all of the passages of the Bible literally; they realized that a good deal of the language in the Bible is figurative rather than literal.

The scholarly literature on Protestant fundamentalism in the 1920s and 1930s indicates that fundamentalism was not simply a heterogeneous assortment of combative men and women who did not approve of the modern world. The fundamentalist movement was not tightly structured, but it was well organized, and it possessed its own institutions, leaders, concerns, and doctrinal emphases. The men and women who attached themselves to the fundamentalist movement had a good deal in common with other conservative Protestants. But they were also, in a number of respects, somewhat atypical.

Within the context of American religious history, fundamentalism is a concept that is most valuable when used with precision and specificity; in that context, at least, the more elastic fundamentalism becomes, the less useful it is. The next three chapters will look at the imaginary fundamentalists who were conjured into existence in the polemics written by antifundamentalists. Although those imaginary fundamentalists had some things in common with the real ones, the actual fundamentalists of the 1920s and 1930s do not conform precisely to the stereotypes of antifundamentalist discourse. By looking at the actual fundamentalists of the 1920s and 1930s, we can guard against our tendency to treat the assertions of antifundamentalist polemicists as objective, accurate, and unbiased analyses. We can prepare ourselves to consider the possibility that the antifundamentalist polemicists are unreliable narrators.

4

Invention

J. Gresham Machen died on January 1, 1937, in Bismarck, North Dakota. In the years since his death, many people have expressed admiration for the dexterity with which he explained the differences between conservative Christians and theological modernists. But almost no one has tried to use the rigid binary he created—real Christians versus phony ones—to analyze the fundamentalist controversies of the 1920s. That is, of course, a good thing: anyone relying on Machen's binary could not possibly do justice to the complexities of the struggles between the fundamentalists and their adversaries. For the same reasons that an adequate history of the American Revolution cannot assume that Loyalists' descriptions of Patriots are completely truthful, an accurate account of fundamentalist controversies must not take their descriptions of modernists at face value.

Similarly, relying on modernists' descriptions of fundamentalists will not lead to a fair history of the controversies of the 1920s. That might seem like an obvious point, but it is still worth making. Many people who have written about the fundamentalist controversies have relied heavily on the polemics penned by fundamentalism's opponents. As a result, many accounts of the fundamentalist controversies present the arguments of the modernists as though they were the gospel truth. Even worse is that those tendentious accounts have in turn provided a pattern for interpreting controversies that occurred at other times and places: Iran in 1979 and Afghanistan in 2001, for example. A set of stories fabricated during an intramural struggle between Protestants in a relatively small portion of Christendom have ended up being applied to a group of believers whose presence was supposedly detected in nearly all of the inhabited world. A local narrative became a global one; a Protestant story became an account of religion in general.

A Superseded Religion

In this chapter, we are going to look at three classic expressions of early antifundamentalism: Harry Emerson Fosdick's "Shall the Fundamentalists Win?" (a 1922 sermon), Kirsopp Lake's *The Religion of Yesterday and To-morrow* (1925), and Frederick Lewis Allen's *Only Yesterday* (1931). Fosdick, Lake, and Allen were all Protestants who held progressive views on the religious controversies of their day. All three men had strong ties to prestigious educational institutions: Allen was a member of the board that oversaw Harvard University, Lake was a professor there, and Fosdick was a professor at Union Theological Seminary. Although they sometimes professed a certain amount of respect for fundamentalists, Fosdick, Lake, and Allen were not completely sure that fundamentalists were their intellectual equals; they tended to view them with a certain degree of condescension. Fosdick, Lake, and Allen were certain that the doctrines to which the fundamentalists subscribed were outdated and in the process of being replaced by more sophisticated ideas that better accorded with the modern world. All three men associated fundamentalism with the past; they believed that fundamentalists were on the wrong side of history.

In addition to being the bête noire of the fundamentalists, the man who preached "Shall the Fundamentalists Win?" was one of the most prominent modernist theologians of his day. Harry Emerson Fosdick was born in Buffalo, New York, in 1878. Religion was taken quite seriously in his childhood home, and Fosdick made a public confession of faith and was baptized before he reached his eighth birthday. As a child, Fosdick had to listen to some preachers who had fallen prey to what he would later come to regard as "bibliolatry."[1] He received bachelor's degrees from Colgate University and Union Theological Seminary in New York City and an MA from Columbia, but he never earned a PhD. Fosdick was asked to join the faculty of Chicago and Harvard but decided instead to make Union Theological Seminary his academic home. He was a gifted teacher, an energetic reader, and a prolific author, and his preaching won him national renown. For years he occupied the pulpit of one of the most famous churches in the United States, and for nearly two decades his radio sermons were broadcast nationally by the National Broadcasting Company. His voice was thus familiar to millions of Americans. He was also a personal friend of John D. Rockefeller Jr., and at several crucial junctures in Fosdick's career Rockefeller went out of his way to offer him moral support and financial assistance.[2]

Fosdick was a Baptist minister, but many people who were not Baptists admired his sermons. In 1919 he was installed as a minister of one of New York City's most historic churches, First Presbyterian, a gorgeous structure on Fifth Avenue between Eleventh and Twelfth Streets. Although installing a Baptist minister in a prominent Presbyterian congregation was an unusual course of action, it was a reflection of the fact that many Presbyterians were deeply committed to pan-Protestant ecumenism. Fosdick's own outlook was profoundly ecumenical; he often said that he was "at heart a Quaker." Installing Fosdick in a Presbyterian pulpit was also a reflection of his great skills as an orator. The lay leaders of the congregation included some of New York's most powerful and wealthy men. During his time at First Presbyterian, Fosdick attracted huge crowds. The lines to hear him preach routinely extended for several blocks, and visitors to New York City often made a point of coming to hear him.[3]

Fosdick delivered "Shall the Fundamentalists Win?" on May 21, 1922. (At the time, the term "fundamentalists" had been in use for less than two years.) The importance of the sermon was recognized immediately and fundamentalists were quick to denounce it. It quickly appeared in print in liberal Protestant journals, including *The Christian Century* and *Christian Work*, and John D. Rockefeller had a slightly revised version printed as a pamphlet that, according to some reports, was sent to every Protestant clergyman in the United States. If someone was looking for a date to mark precisely when the fundamentalist controversies of the 1920s began, May 21, 1922, would be as good as any.[4]

"Shall the Fundamentalist Win?' includes several passages in which Fosdick expressed respect for conservative Christians. He acknowledged that their devotion to the doctrines that they held dear—the virgin birth of Christ, for example—was sincere. Many conservatives were, Fosdick said, openhearted and charitable; the best religious conservatives could often give lessons to religious liberals about "true liberality of spirit."[5] Much of the sermon sounds friendly, generous, and conciliatory. However, its general tone is condescending. It also has a combative side. The provocative title implied that a battle was taking place and raises the possibility that a fundamentalist victory would be a disaster. Moreover, Fosdick repeatedly asserted that the questions fundamentalists viewed as issues of great importance—the nature of the atonement, for example—were not really all that significant. This assertion implied that the fundamentalists had completely failed to see which aspects of the Christian faith were primary and which were secondary. There are real problems facing the world today, Fosdick said; atrocities—such as the Turks burning Armenian Christians alive—are reported regularly. Christians needed to focus on real problems like that. Fosdick seemed to be saying that getting caught up in doctrinal debates with fundamentalists was a waste of time.[6]

Committed fundamentalists surely could not find Fosdick's arguments compelling. Although Curtis Lee Laws's condemnation of the sermon—"a remarkable illustration of the intolerance of liberalism"—was probably overly harsh, it is not difficult to see why a fundamentalist might find the sermon deeply offensive, for part of what Fosdick did in "Shall the Fundamentalists Win?" was to argue that there were important similarities between fundamentalists and the Jews who persecuted the first Christians.[7] In Fosdick's sermon, the people who rejected Christ were pictured as the forerunners of the fundamentalists; the people who accepted Christ were seen as the forerunners of people like Fosdick.

"Shall the Fundamentalists Win?" opens with an evocation of a famous episode in church history that is recorded in the fifth chapter of the Book of Acts. The story concerns the relationship between the apostles of Jesus and the religious leaders of the Jewish people. The high priest and his associates became jealous—so the story goes—of the apostles and had them thrown into jail. Miraculously, the apostles escaped from jail and, following instructions given by an angel, entered the temple to proclaim the gospel. They were seized once again and brought before the Sanhedrin for further questioning. The apostles refused to be cowed. "The God of our fathers," the apostles said, "raised up Jesus, whom ye slew and hanged on a tree." God has exalted Jesus, they continued, and made him "a Prince and a Savior." The people who killed Jesus should repent of their sins and ask God for forgiveness. The Sanhedrin were enraged and decided to kill the apostles. But Rabbi Gamaliel suggested a superior course of action. He told the members of the Sanhedrin that they ought to allow the followers of Jesus to go in peace. If their teachings were of merely human origin, then they would die of their own accord. If they were divine in origin, then nothing could be done to keep them from prospering.

Tragically, Fosdick says, "the Jewish leaders" failed to follow the "wise" program of "tolerance" Gamaliel had sketched for them. Instead, they clung to their "bitter antagonism" and ended up excising Christianity—"the finest flowering out that Judaism ever had"—from their synagogues.[8] Much of the rest of the sermon spells out the modern-day application of the Bible story. There are, Fosdick asserted, new ideas afoot in Christendom. These new ideas have made the fundamentalists jealous. The fundamentalists, who have failed to see that they had been superseded, have been seized by a spirit of persecution. Fosdick insisted that their plans to persecute the modernists must not grow to fruition. Instead, conservative Christians must be persuaded to follow Gamaliel's advice. Twentieth-century conservative Christians must not be allowed to persecute liberals. They must not be allowed to treat their opponents the way the Jews who did not accept Jesus as the Messiah treated those who accepted him as the Christ.

This line of argument is at the heart of Fosdick's antifundamentalist polemic. Persecution is unwise and un-Christian, and the fundamentalists of the twentieth century seem to have been possessed by a persecuting spirit similar to the one that prevailed among the Sanhedrin. But that is not all that the Sanhedrin and the fundamentalists have in common, Fosdick said. Both groups failed to understand how to think about sacred texts and about revelation. Fosdick warned his readers against granting the Bible too much authority. He encouraged them to conclude that they should never assume that something is true simply because the Bible asserts that it is. He warned that Christian fundamentalists—like Jews—have a tendency to cling to offensive and outdated religious ideas and that they have failed to appreciate the importance of progressive revelation. Fosdick urged them to understand that biblical assertions, like all assertions, ought to be interpreted in an enlightened and progressive way.

There are people in the church, Fosdick noted, who believe that the scriptures were "dictated by God to men." Such people believe that everything in the Bible—"scientific opinions, medical theories, historical judgments, as well as spiritual insight"—is absolutely infallible. When modern Christians hear Muslims claim that the Qur'an was dictated by God to humankind and is absolute truth, they know that such a claim is suspicious, for when they read the Qur'an, they find God conceived of "as an Oriental monarch" and learn that fatalistic submission to his will is humanity's chief duty and that the use of force on unbelievers, polygamy, and slavery, is acceptable. Such notions and practices are clearly outdated, Fosdick said. No modern person can accept them.[9]

When Christians turn to their Bible, they find much the same. God is "thought of as an oriental monarch; there, too, are patriarchal polygamy, and slave systems, and the use of force on unbelievers." What makes the Bible preferable to the Qur'an, Fosdick argued, is just this: in the Bible, revelation is progressive—God as king gives way to God as father; polygamy is replaced by monogamy; "slavery, never explicitly condemned before the New Testament closes," is nevertheless brought into question; and harsh treatment of unbelievers is replaced by "appeals to love." This is why the Bible, correctly understood, is so beautiful. In the Bible, "revelation is progressive" and the lower elements of religiosity are "always being superseded." Thus, for modernists such as Fosdick, even the New Testament would be superseded where necessary. Revelation did not end when the New Testament was completed. It continues right up to the present day.[10]

Jesus, Fosdick claimed, clearly understood this fact. Jesus was by no means an enemy of the Jews. He deeply appreciated the prophets. His ideas about God, about the proper way to live one's life, and about the future were all deeply rooted in the Old Testament. Jesus wanted to fulfill, not destroy, the beliefs and practices that were his "racial heritage." But Jesus knew that God was not dead and that God's "words and works" did not come to an end in the final chapter of the book of Malachi.[11] The God Jesus taught about was not confined to ancient history. His God was, rather, "a contemporary God—a God who was still speaking and still working. He was a God who wanted to lead his people from a 'partial truth' to a 'fuller truth.'" Thus, Jesus believed in progressive revelation. The Jewish leaders to whom Gamaliel spoke did not believe in progressive revelation; they clung to old truths and were afraid of new ones.[12]

Fosdick thus set before his readers two paths. The first was associated with progressive revelation, with the New Testament, Jesus, true Christianity, reason, toleration, and openness. The other was associated with fundamentalism, the Old Testament, the Qur'an, the traditions of the Jews, persecution, and the forces of reaction. Fosdick was sure that the great preponderance of Christians would eventually choose the right road. The church was faced with some real challenges and liberals had a positive program to address them. The fundamentalists did not. All they could do was persecute forward-looking Christians. Their atavistic banner was not one that could attract the allegiance of many Christians. There was no chance, Fosdick said, that the fundamentalists were going to succeed.[13]

A Hostility to Experimentation

Kirsopp Lake's *The Religion of Yesterday and To-morrow* was published in 1925, a year when the battles between the fundamentalists and their adversaries were being fought with great passion. Lake presented fundamentalism as a large, well-organized movement that was determined to prevent thoughtful Christian leaders from revising the doctrines of the Christian church to align with modern thought. Although he had been living in the United States for more than a decade when he wrote the book, Lake's roots were in Europe.[14] He was an Englishman by birth and was educated at St. Paul's, London, and at Oxford. Early in his career, Lake served as a curate in an Anglican church. In 1904, he moved to Holland to teach at the University of Leyden. Lake, whose theological views were quite progressive, flourished in the climate of intellectual freedom he found in Leyden. His years teaching there were perhaps the happiest of his life. In 1913, Lake crossed the Atlantic to teach at the Episcopal Theological School in Cambridge, Massachusetts. A year later, he joined the faculty of the Harvard Divinity School, where eventually he would occupy an endowed chair. Although his chair was in ecclesiastical history, Lake's scholarly interests also included theology, New Testament, archeology, and Greek paleography. Both his research and his private life—Lake divorced in 1931 and remarried in 1932—were reported with some avidity in U.S. newspapers. After his divorce, Lake resigned his position at the divinity school but did not leave Harvard. Instead, he joined the faculty of Harvard College.

Lake was a man of enormous erudition, and scholars greatly admired many of his articles and books. *The Beginnings of Christianity,* for example, a five-volume text that Lake (in collaboration with F. J. Foakes-Jackson and Henry Cadbury) produced in the 1920s and 1930s, deeply influenced historians' understanding of the early church.[15] But Lake was no pedant. The courses he taught for the college, in which he talked about history, literature, and his own philosophy of life, won him a loyal following among Harvard undergraduates. He also had a knack for writing accessible prose. He wrote for popular magazines such as *The Atlantic Monthly* and a number of lucid scholarly monographs. The prose to be found on the pages of *The Religion of Yesterday and To-morrow* is personal and informal, in some instances almost chatty. Read aloud, the book sounds like one well-educated gentleman talking to another. In spite of its casual style, the book's message carried substantial weight. According to Lake, the church's future greatly relied on the demise of fundamentalism. In Lake's view, three distinct ecclesiastical parties were involved in the fundamentalist controversies: the institutionalists, the fundamentalists, and the experimentalists. Although he tried to present accurate analyses of all three of those parties, Lake made it clear that he was not a neutral observer of the struggles among the three. He was himself an avid experimentalist; he hoped the experimentalists would win and the fundamentalists would lose.[16]

Lake applied the "experimentalist" label to Christians who had been deeply influenced by theological modernism and did not want to rely primarily on revealed religion to make sense of the universe. Instead, they wanted to rely on the truths human beings learned from their own experiences. Experimentalists were eager to embrace the findings of modern science and modern scholarship; they were wary of ancient creeds. They tended to be well educated, and they realized that some of the teachings found in the Bible, including "Love your enemies" and "Resist not evil," were too simplistic and too utopian to provide sure guidance to sophisticated modern beings.[17]

Lake used the term "institutionalist" to refer to churchmen who were trying to find a middle way between the bold embrace of the new ideas for which the experimentalists stood and the unbending defense of biblical doctrine upon which the fundamentalists insisted. In his view, the institutionalists were men who were especially committed to preserving the church from division and schism. They were always looking for a compromise that would keep the church from being torn apart. At several points in *The Religion of Yesterday and To-morrow*, Lake made it clear that the institutionalists often said and did things that he found distasteful. They were not candid enough and they were far too timid. But Lake had no intention of antagonizing them. He wanted the institutionalists and the experimentalists to find ways to work together to limit the power of the fundamentalists.[18]

Such working coalitions were necessary, Lake suggested, because the fundamentalists had considerable resources at their disposal. Some of their arguments—such as their claim that they were defending ancient Christian ideas and their insistence that the experimentalists embraced ideas that previous generations of Christians would have rejected—were completely convincing. A number of the fundamentalists were very effective public speakers; most of them were full of energy and determination. Their economic and political views tended to be "antirevolutionary"; thus it was not impossible that the fundamentalist movement might end up receiving a great deal of financial assistance from wealthy industrialists, leaving them with deeper pockets than either the experimentalists or the institutionalists. Already it was clear that the fundamentalists had a good deal of political power. And it was also clear that fundamentalists had won the allegiance of a huge number of U.S. Protestants. Additionally, it was quite likely that fundamentalists outnumbered both experimentalists and institutionalists in the Protestant churches of the United States.[19]

But the fundamentalists also had some quite obvious weaknesses, Lake said. One of these was rooted in money. In the United States, Lake observed, men who want to become ministers could follow two different routes. The first, which was more expensive, involved attending a university and a seminary. The second, which was far cheaper, was to simply attend a Bible school. Understandably, many poor men chose the second option. The Bible schools were staffed by men who had spent a good deal of time reading the Bible and who could sometimes give persuasive sermons and talks. But the education they could offer young men who were studying for the ministry was distinctly second rate. The men who graduated from these schools were full of zeal but were only "half-educated." They did not really know much about reason or logic, they knew little about history or philosophy, and they knew even less about science. It was from this class of men that the fundamentalist party drew its recruits.[20]

Fundamentalists subscribed, Lake wrote, to a "quadrilateral of belief": the divinity of Christ, the reality of his second coming, the efficacy of his blood atonement, and the infallible inspiration of the New and Old Testaments. This last point was, Lake thought, especially important. Fundamentalists believed that the Bible was "God's word written." They believed that Christians had a duty to embrace and defend the teaching set forth in the Bible and that the faith delivered to the early church had to be kept pure and inviolate. Fundamentalists were therefore unwilling to learn from experience if the truths that experience revealed could not be harmonized with the propositions set forth in the Bible. They believed that all the truths a person needed to know were to be found in the ancient scriptures. Fundamentalists were therefore often quite content to remain "willfully ignorant" of modern science and modern scholarship.[21]

Given how cut off they were from the main currents of modern intellectual life, it was little wonder that fundamentalists failed to see the necessity of allowing the traditions of Christianity to evolve so that they better accorded with modern discoveries and outlooks. Rather than accept that fact, fundamentalists sought to drive the people who had grasped it out of the church. There was a deeply intolerant side to fundamentalism, and its adherents did not really debate the religious issues of the day fairly. They caricatured their opponents' careful arguments and responded to them with crude appeals to biblical authority.[22]

Lake believed that fundamentalists were too poorly educated to grasp the traditional teachings of the Christian church at their most capacious. They did not really understand, for example, what the church had traditionally taught about the nature of the Trinity. So it would be a mistake to conclude that fundamentalists were simply fighting for traditional Christianity. What they were fighting for was, rather, some desiccated fragments of the old faith. The theology of the fundamentalists was only "a partial and uneducated survival" of the theological formulations that had prevailed in previous centuries. Fundamentalists were not really defending Christian orthodoxy in the fullest sense of that term. They were, instead, asserting what one might call orthodoxy for dummies.[23]

An Unseemly Spectacle

Frederick Lewis Allen was the son of a clergyman who served on the staff of one of Boston's most famous congregations, Trinity Episcopal Church. Allen, who could trace his family's New England roots back to 1620, grew up among Boston's cultural elite. He studied at Groton and Harvard and maintained his ties to Harvard throughout his life. During the late 1910s and early 1920s, Allen served as Harvard's publicity director, and during the 1940s and 1950s he served on its Board of Overseers. Allen was a talented writer and a fine amateur historian. His work as an editor for magazines such as *The Atlantic* and *Harper's* won him national fame, and the history books he wrote were highly intelligent and beautifully written. They were also quite influential. The analysis of the 1920s that Allen presented in *Only Yesterday: An Informal History of the Nineteen-Twenties* was one that many readers—including many professional historians—found compelling. *Only Yesterday*, which was published in 1931, set the terms for a good many historiographical debates that have continued up to the present day.[24]

Allen presented the era his book described, beginning with the Armistice and ending with the coming of the Depression, as one that was clearly delineated from the rest of history. Although Allen began writing the book in the spring of 1930, his account of the previous decade portrayed a time that seemed far off and difficult to understand.[25] Parts of the book have the tone of a man reviewing, in the cold light of a sober morning, the strange things he had done the night before while under the influence of a great quantity of alcohol. The book must have led more than one reader to wonder what in the world the American people had been thinking. Why did they do so little to protest the hysteria of the Red Scare? Why did they invest their money so recklessly? Why did they fall for so many fads? Why did they get so emotionally involved in the Scopes trial? The book's overall tone suggests that the 1920s were a time when the American people, still suffering from the aftereffects of the world war, did a great number of odd things. Chief among their odd behaviors was their willingness to support the fundamentalists' campaigns to drive liberals out of leadership positions in Protestant churches and to prevent evolution from being taught in the nation's public schools.

Allen's account of the religious history of America in the 1920s begins by noting the degree to which the American people were committed to Protestantism. Five out of every eight church members in the United States belonged to a Protestant denomination of one sort or another. According to Allen, America's Protestant churches were not in very good shape at the time. Church membership was steady, but church attendance seemed to be declining. And many of the people who did attend church could not give particularly compelling reasons for doing so. The pews in Protestant churches had a good number of unfilled seats, and the people who were sitting in the pews were not quite sure why they were there.[26] During the 1920s, Allen suggested, the American people had suffered from spiritual starvation.[27]

The loss of vitality was partly the result, he suggested, of the decision of many Americans to focus their attention on making money or on having a good time instead of on spiritual matters. But the loss of vitality was also the result of Americans' growing tendency to turn to science rather than religion for knowledge about the nature of the universe and for guidance on how to solve social problems. Allen suggested, echoing his contemporaries Fosdick and Allen, that some Protestants, people who called themselves modernists or liberals, had responded to science's growing prestige by self-consciously adapting the traditions of the Christian church to better accord with the findings of science and the spirit of the age. However, another group of Protestants, the fundamentalists, went another way. They believed in "the letter of the Bible" and refused to accept any ideas, even those backed by the prestige of modern science, that conflicted with Christian scripture.[28]

In Allen's view, the conflict between the modernists and the liberals reached its climax in the famous Scopes trial of the summer of 1925. The fundamentalists' claim that evolution should not be taught in the public schools of Tennessee was, Allen said, not a ridiculous one. If the taxpayers of that state did not want evolution to be taught in the schools they funded, then a case could be made that evolution should not be taught in those schools.[29] In Allen's telling of the story, the fundamentalists failed to make that case during the Scopes trial. Instead, they, with the help of many others, created a spectacle that made everyone associated with it seem foolish.

During the trial, the town of Dayton was festooned with signs that displayed the odd brand of piety that dominated rural Tennessee. Evangelists of every stripe came to Dayton, and revival meetings were held throughout the trial. Prayers were said in the courtroom, and the trial itself gave William Jennings Bryan ample opportunity to try to explain his peculiar religious beliefs. The spectacle at Dayton was also a commercial enterprise. Debates about the nature of the universe were mingled with displays of fashion and the selling of lemonade and hot dogs. The whole trial was in some respects simply an attempt to bring crowds and reporters to Dayton in order to "put Dayton on the map."[30] The Scopes trial was a piece of theater that revealed the nature of both modern hucksterism and old-time religion.

As Allen saw it, the spectacle ended disastrously for the fundamentalists. Scopes was convicted, of course, and the Supreme Court of Tennessee found a way to avoid having to rule the anti-evolution statute unconstitutional. But Bryan, under Darrow's merciless questioning, had confessed that he believed that the world had been created in 4004 B.C. and that Noah's flood had occurred in 2348 B.C. Bryan also said that he believed that Jonah had literally been swallowed by a giant fish and that human linguistic diversity was the result of human beings' attempt to build a tower whose top would reach into heaven. These were beliefs educated modern men could not take seriously. Bryan had been personally humiliated and had given the world a painful glimpse of fundamentalism's intellectual bankruptcy. Fundamentalism, as the Scopes trial revealed, was simply unable to defend itself against the questions modern skeptics posed. In the aftermath of the trial, fundamentalism became a laughingstock. People in the hinterlands might still find ways to keep their religious beliefs "locked in a science-proof compartment," but "civilized opinion everywhere had regarded the Dayton trial with amazement and amusement." The high point of the fundamentalist-modernist controversies had done nothing to stop the nation's drift away from the religious beliefs the fundamentalists championed. Instead, it had brought those beliefs into dispute. "Fundamentalism had lost."[31]

Muslim Fundamentalists?

Of course, Allen was wrong to think that fundamentalists had suffered a crushing defeat at the Scopes trial. The trial did not leave teachers in all of America's public schools free to teach the theory of evolution, and there is a good deal of evidence to suggest that during the 1920s fundamentalists actually managed to make it more difficult for evolution to be discussed in classrooms. Allen was certainly wrong to imply that the outcome of the trial had turned fundamentalists into a universal laughingstock. In the late 1920s and early 1930s, many Americans still had enormous respect for fundamentalists. And, as things turned out, the fundamentalists and their descendants have played a crucial role in shaping U.S. Protestantism from 1931 to the present. However, Allen's analysis of the fundamentalist controversies contained a grain of truth. In the aftermath of these years, fundamentalists were not as secure as they had been before and modernists were still welcome in many of the nation's most prominent denominations. Additionally, many Americans disapproved of the fundamentalist movement's goals and tactics. By the time the controversies were over, fundamentalists had been subjected to fierce criticism. Widely circulated and skillfully written polemical attacks had deeply influenced the way many Americans thought about them. By the time Allen wrote *Only Yesterday*, the set of overlapping conversations, beliefs, assumptions, prejudices, and feelings I am calling antifundamentalism had begun to coalesce.

If the comparison is not pushed too hard or too far, it is useful to think of antifundamentalism as a communications network. We could say that the creation of the network began nearly a century ago and that the network as it stands today is complex, formidable, and vast. We could also observe that the network continues to grow and transform even today. When compared to the network that exists today, the one that existed when Allen's *Only Yesterday* was published was fairly modest. It's a bit like comparing the telephone system that existed in 1931 to today's Internet. In 1931 the antifundamentalist network was largely a North American affair: nearly all of the people who had created it lived in North America and nearly all of the people who were called fundamentalists lived in either the United States or Canada. The network was also overwhelmingly Protestant. The people who had created it and nearly everyone to whom the fundamentalist label was assigned were Protestant Christians. Thus, the people who wrote the first antifundamentalist polemics were attacking Protestant Christians; their polemics did not focus on Catholics, Buddhists, Hindus, Sikhs, or Jews.

However, in 1931 the outlines of antifundamentalism as it presently exists were already clearly visible. The people who created the network had already suggested that fundamentalism had won the allegiance of a great many believers and that fundamentalists were particularly prevalent in backward regions. Fundamentalists had been linked to ignorance and intolerance. They were accused of clinging to religious beliefs that had been superseded by more modern and sophisticated ideas. Fundamentalists' approach to scripture had been labeled naïve and defective. Fundamentalists had been described as people who were bound to fail; they were said to be on the wrong side of history.

It is also worth pointing out that by 1931 a miniscule number of thinkers had begun to suggest that Muslims who were fanatically devoted to tradition could be thought of as fundamentalists. One of these people was the writer Edwin W. Hullinger. In the summer of 1926 he published a story in the *New York Times*, "Islam's Ties of Unity Are Loosening," that examined how the Muslims of North Africa were responding to Mustafa Kemal Atatürk's attempts to reform Turkish society. Hullinger referred to Muslims who were hostile to the reforms as "fundamentalist Arabs." (Atatürk wanted to make sure that the Republic of Turkey, which had been founded in 1923, was more secular and more fully modern than the Ottoman Empire had been.)[32]

The fundamentalists were particularly appalled, Hullinger said, by Atatürk's insistence that Turkish men start wearing modern hats. He said that a surprisingly large proportion of the men who lived in North Africa were deeply attached to turbans and fezzes and that they had no intention of wearing anything on their heads that resembled the hats Europeans wore. Hullinger assured his readers that they should not be unduly alarmed by the large number of fundamentalists to be found in the Muslim world. He said that the disagreements between fundamentalists and progressives were an indication that Muslim unity was disintegrating and that disintegration was, on the whole, a very good thing. The divisions that had appeared among the Muslims of North Africa indicated that the prospects for "Christian dominion" in that region were far brighter in the mid-1920s than they had been just a few years earlier. The Christian nations of the world seemed to be realizing that pursuing a policy of "divide and rule" would enable them to strengthen their control of North Africa. The tensions between progressive and fundamentalist Muslims should be interpreted as a hopeful sign, Hullinger said.

Hullinger clearly had more sympathy for progressives than he did for fundamentalists. He thought that the kind of religion fundamentalist Arabs practiced did not have all that much to do with either the mind or the soul; it focused on matters of form rather than substance. Fundamentalists' religious beliefs led them to pour an unreasonable amount of energy into fighting battles over issues—such as the way men dressed—that were of no real importance. Fundamentalists were a little ridiculous, Hullinger's article suggested. William Jourdan Rapp, the author of another story that appeared in the *Times* in the mid-1920s, had even less sympathy for Muslim fundamentalists than Hullinger did. In "Islam Fundamentalists Fight Modernist Trend," Rapp told readers that Muslim fundamentalists were absolutely sure that Islam was the only true religion and that they viewed all non-Muslims with contempt. They stubbornly clung to the notion that God had commanded them to bring all the nations in the world "under the sway of Islam." Fundamentalists were determined to create a world in which all social, political, and economic matters had been transformed into religious questions.[33]

Rapp told his readers that Muslim fundamentalists had much in common with Christian fundamentalists; they too sought to "jealously guard the old religious ideas and beliefs in all their details." But he also emphasized the differences between Muslim and Christian extremists. Rapp asserted that modern scientific inquiry had conclusively demonstrated that Muhammad, the prophet to whom Muslim fundamentalists had given their allegiance, was a deeply flawed human being. He was "opportunistic," "voluptuous," and "cruel." In contrast, Christian fundamentalists—in spite of their many weaknesses—were still the religious descendants of Jesus. Modern scholarship had shown that Jesus was "a religious leader of unique purity, courage and understanding." The implication was clear. Muslim fundamentalists were even worse than Christian fundamentalists. Christian fundamentalism was an aberrant form of a great religion. Islamic fundamentalism was a debased form of an inferior sect.

Rapp said that some forward-looking Muslims were attempting to fashion a sophisticated form of Islam that was somewhat comparable to

Christian theological modernism. But Rapp told his readers that attempts to create a more progressive form of Islam were likely to end in failure. The underlying assumptions that Islam rested upon were remarkably narrow and incredibly naïve. That meant that it was nearly impossible to embrace the truths of modernism while holding onto the doctrines of Islam. There was a sense, Rapp implied, in which all *true* Muslims were, by definition, fundamentalists. Rapp came close to saying that when it came to Islam, fundamentalism was really the only game in town.

These writings by Rapp and Hullinger; in spite of their relevance to the subject at hand, were not particularly influential. Throughout my research on antifundamentalism, I have never run into a reference to either piece, and it is possible that neither article exerted a direct influence on the subsequent history of antifundamentalism. Moreover, I cannot be absolutely sure that Hullinger really believed that such a thing as Islamic fundamentalism actually existed. When he talked about "Arab fundamentalists," he made a point of putting scare quotes around the phase. That might indicate that he was not completely convinced that it was possible for Muslims to be fundamentalists in the fullest sense of the word. It is possible that when Hullinger labeled Muslims as fundamentalists, he was simply using a figure of speech.

In any case, it is absolutely clear that the concept of Islamic fundamentalism did not come into general use in the 1920s. In that decade, the number of publications in which Muslims were called fundamentalists was infinitesimally small in comparison to the number of texts that assigned the label to Christians. However, there is good reason to suppose that in the 1920s hundreds of thousands of texts were published in which Protestants were called fundamentalists.[34]

In the years when the fundamentalist controversies in the United States were at their height, writers such as Rapp and Hullinger toyed with the idea of describing Muslims as fundamentalists. In the next few decades, only a handful of writers followed their example. Imagine a line on a graph that showed the number of English-language texts about Muslim fundamentalists that were published in any given year from 1920 to 1980. The line would have one tiny bump in the mid-1920s and another small bump in the mid-1940s. But otherwise it would be almost completely flat from 1920 to 1950. It would begin to inch up slightly in the 1950s and 1960s, but the rate of increase would be very modest. Writers did not begin to refer to Muslims as fundamentalists with any frequency until the 1970s.[35]

But the stories Rapp and Hullinger wrote illustrate a significant point. Even in the mid-1920s, it was clear that the concepts of fundamentalist, fundamentalists, and fundamentalism could be used to demean as well as to describe Muslims. Hullinger and Rapp had shown that it was possible to take the polemics against Christian fundamentalists, adjust them slightly, and turn them into diatribes against Muslims who were thought to be obstructing the march of progress.

5

Ratification

This chapter focuses on three texts of the 1930s and 1940s that built upon and went beyond the polemics of the 1920s. The first, H. Richard Niebuhr's "Fundamentalism," appeared in a highly respected reference work published in 1931, the *Encyclopedia of the Social Sciences*. The second, an informal memo by Talcott Parsons called "Memorandum: The Development of Groups and Organizations Amenable to Use against American Institutions and Foreign Policy," was written in 1940. The third text is Carl F. H. Henry's 1947 book *The Uneasy Conscience of Modern Fundamentalism*.

During the 1930s and 1940s, people who were not fundamentalists paid less attention to fundamentalists than they had in the 1920s. There were no real analogues to the drama of the Scopes trial or the fundamentalists' much-publicized efforts to expel modernists from the ranks of Northern Baptists and Northern Presbyterians. The words "fundamentalist," "fundamentalists," and "fundamentalism" appeared in print somewhat less frequently than they had in the 1920s. And of course they occurred far less frequently than did terms such as "Depression," "New Deal," "Nazism," and "world war."

However, during the 1930s and 1940s, the nature of antifundamentalism underwent several important changes. During these decades, antifundamentalism embedded itself in standard reference works in a way that suggested that it was a simple truth, not one side of a controversy. Social theorists used ideas rooted in antifundamentalism to create a general theory of fundamentalism. According to this theory, fundamentalism was rooted in the failure of human beings to cope successfully with the coming of modernity. And in the 1930s and 1940s antifundamentalism also began to embed itself in the minds of the Protestant Christians who eventually came to be known as "evangelicals." Criticizing fundamentalism became a way for evangelicals to say who they were and what they stood for.

Objectivity

H. Richard Niebuhr, the author of one of the first encyclopedia articles on fundamentalism, was one of the most highly respected Christian theologians of his day. He was born in Wright City, Missouri, in 1894; earned his PhD at Yale in 1924; and then returned to the Midwest, where he worked as a seminary professor and college administrator. In 1931, Niebuhr was asked to join the faculty of the Yale Divinity School. He accepted the invitation and remained at Yale until his death in 1962.[1] In addition to his work at Yale, Niebuhr pursued graduate work at Washington University, the University of Michigan, the University of Chicago, Columbia University, and Union Theological Seminary. At Union, Niebuhr studied with Harry Emerson Fosdick.[2]

Niebuhr never reached the level of national prominence Fosdick achieved, and he was never quite as famous as his older brother, Reinhold Niebuhr. But H. Richard Niebuhr was arguably a more gifted scholar than his brother. For decades, Niebuhr was one of the intellectual leaders of the Yale Divinity School. Between the late 1920s and the early 1960s, Niebuhr published a set of brilliant explorations of the relationship between the church and the world. A number of his books—*The Social Sources of Denominationalism*, *The Kingdom of God in America*, *Christ and Culture*, and *Radical Monotheism and Western Culture*—are still read today.

In many of his scholarly works, Niebuhr analyzed the dangers of parochial attachments. He believed that such attachments could prevent Christians from living faithful lives. Loyalty to one's own race, class, region, nation, or religion, Niebuhr warned, might easily become idolatrous.[3] In Niebuhr's view, much of what passed for religion in the United States in the twentieth century was terribly deficient. He suspected that the religious practices of most twentieth-century Americans centered on the adoration of tribal gods rather than on the worship of the one true God.[4] Americans' strong local allegiances—to their own class or nation, for example—left them with a faith that was both shallow and narrow. Niebuhr came by his fear of parochialism honestly, for he himself was a man of the provinces. If his life had worked out slightly differently, he might well have ended up editing a newspaper or pastoring a church in a small town in Missouri or Illinois. Niebuhr's father was a clergyman in a tiny denomination whose members lived mostly in the environs of St. Louis, Missouri. The members of the denomination—the German Evangelical Synod of North America—were mostly emigrants from Germany. Niebuhr's first language was German, and German was the language of instruction in both the small college and the insular seminary Niebuhr attended as he was preparing to become a minister in the Evangelical Synod.

The ethos that prevailed in his childhood synod was not an especially progressive one. According to one of his most perceptive biographers, Niebuhr viewed it as "embarrassingly out of step with the march of life in America."[5] Some members of the synod thought that Niebuhr's views were so advanced that he was unfit to teach in its schools.[6] And one of the professors at the synod's seminary, Manfred Manrodt, charged that Niebuhr had sought to have him fired simply because the ideas he expressed in his courses conflicted with Niebuhr's "modernist predilections."

Manrodt's charge was never proved. And given Niebuhr's deep regard for traditional Christian beliefs and practices, it is not accurate to call him a modernist. But as a young man, Niebuhr had to make his way in a world in which conservative men—men whom opponents might have thought of as fundamentalists—wielded considerable power.[7] Those men sometimes made his life rather difficult, and those difficulties, in turn, affected how Niebuhr thought about fundamentalism.

In "Fundamentalism," the highly influential article he published in 1931, Niebuhr asserted that fundamentalists had several distinct aims. They wanted to prohibit instructors in public schools from teaching evolution, they wanted to prevent liberal Christians from influencing Protestant seminaries and colleges, and they hoped to expel liberal Christians from their denominations.

Accordingly, Niebuhr defined fundamentalism as "an aggressive conservative movement in the Protestant churches of the United States in the decade after the [First] World War." Fundamentalists gave allegiance, Niebuhr said, to "the five points of fundamentalism": the inerrancy of the scriptures, the supernatural atonement, the virgin birth of Jesus, his physical resurrection, and the authenticity of the Gospel miracles. Fundamentalists were Protestants who wanted to "impose" their creed on the nation's public schools and its denominational colleges and seminaries. It was not accurate, Niebuhr said, to think of fundamentalists simply as religious "conservatives"; they were *aggressive* conservatives. A good many conservative Protestants viewed this aggressiveness with great suspicion. The fact that fundamentalists never succeeded in creating a coalition that included all conservative Christians was one of the reasons why they were not able to fully achieve their goals.[8]

Niebuhr emphasized that the fundamentalists had won a number of partial victories. In some cases, teachers at denominational schools had been forced to either subscribe to the fundamentalist creed or face dismissal. In other instances, fundamentalists had created new denominational schools whose faculty were compelled to subscribe to a creed. And the fundamentalists' attacks on academic freedom had also significantly affected the nation's public schools. Fundamentalists had succeeded in creating outright bans on the teaching of evolution in Tennessee, Oklahoma, and (for a time) Mississippi. And in many other states—California, West Virginia, Kentucky, Missouri, Arkansas, Texas, Florida, Georgia, and Alabama, for example—fundamentalists had convinced large segments of the electorate that it was entirely inappropriate for evolution to be taught in the public schools. In this new climate of opinion, teachers, administrators, and school boards felt pressured to exclude evolution from their curriculums.

Niebuhr left his readers with the clear impression that fundamentalists had created an atmosphere of intolerance throughout great swaths of the nation. He led them to believe that the spirit that animated the fundamentalist movement was similar to the one that animated movements to suppress racial minorities; "in some localities," he claimed, the fundamentalist movement was "related" to the Ku Klux Klan.[9]

Niebuhr was well aware, of course, that there were a great many fundamentalists in the U.S. South, and he was willing to grant that fundamentalism was, in part, a vehicle for southerners to express their differences with the North. But Niebuhr did not place much emphasis on the role the divisions between North and South played in the history of fundamentalism. Instead, he consistently linked fundamentalism with the agrarian values of rural America. Fundamentalism's most well-known spokesman, Niebuhr noted, was William Jennings Bryan, a politician who had made his reputation championing the interests of farmers. Niebuhr asserted that fundamentalism's strongholds were in "isolated communities in which the traditions of pioneer society had been most effectively preserved and which were least subject to the influence of modern science and industrial civilization." In such communities, the educational institutions were inadequately developed. The laypeople and clergymen who lived in such regions tended to "distrust reason" and put a great deal of emphasis on emotion. Obsessed with finding ways to acquire God's help in securing bountiful harvests, rural people practiced an unsophisticated form of religion that had much in common with simple magic.[10]

People living in rural America tended to live lives that were dominated by the timeless rhythms of agriculture; their culture tended to be "static." They, unlike people who lived in cities, were reluctant to see "change as a primary law of life."[11] But change was, of course, inevitable, and some of the changes the United States was experiencing were bound, Niebuhr implied, to undercut the strength of fundamentalism. Rural areas were increasingly tied to the rest of the country by new forms of communication that were disseminating new ideas. The educational institutions of the countryside were improving. Clergymen were increasingly attending schools where the life of the mind was taken quite seriously. The sermons they preached were more erudite. The worship services over which they presided were less emotional. Those services were becoming more and more liturgical.[12]

Fundamentalism and Modernity

Few readers of Niebuhr's analysis of fundamentalism are likely to have concluded that the battles between fundamentalism and modernism would be long and drawn out; fewer still would have come to think that the future belonged to the fundamentalists. Niebuhr's article suggested that the progress of history would eventually make fundamentalism irrelevant. This way of thinking about fundamentalists—as people whom history was passing by—also figured prominently in Talcott Parsons's "Memorandum: The Development of Groups and Organizations Amenable to Use against American Institutions and Foreign Policy." For Parsons, fundamentalism was at base simply resistance to the rationalizing of society that inevitably accompanied the coming of modernity. One could make the case that Parsons's ideas about fundamentalism were deeply flawed. They certainly do not seem to have rested on a deep familiarity with the fundamentalist movement that I described in chapter 3. But they were nevertheless influential.

Parsons's social theories have often been subjected to withering critiques.[13] Functionalism, the type of social analysis with which he is associated, is now widely regarded as having led the sociologists who practiced it into a dead end. Parsons has often been dismissed as being insufficiently sensitive to the injustices created by the social structures he analyzed. Indeed, sometimes he has been thought of as little more than an apologist for capitalism. Parsons's tendency to see social development in evolutionary terms has often been dismissed as naïve.[14] And the abstract prose with which Parsons communicated his ideas has been ridiculed mercilessly.

It is also true, however, that Parsons's ideas have influenced many great intellectuals. Jeffrey Alexander, Harold Garfinkel, Uta Gerhardt, Jürgen Habermas, Niklas Luhmann, David Schneider, and Bryan Turner, for example, have all drawn inspiration from Parsons's work. And there can be no doubt that for several decades, Parsons was widely regarded as one of the most important social theorists in the United States.[15] That might have been a stretch, but certainly no one could deny that Parsons played an important role in shaping the study of religion in the United States.[16] Parsons played a key role in disseminating the analysis of religion Émile Durkheim and Max Weber developed, and two of Parsons's protégés, Robert Bellah and Clifford Geertz, decisively influenced how educated Americans think about religion.

Parsons's interest in religion was probably rooted at least in part in his family history. On his mother's side, Parsons was a direct descendant of one of America's most influential Christian intellectuals, Jonathan Edwards.[17] Parsons's father, Edward Parsons, was a Congregationalist minister who had been educated at Amherst College and Yale Divinity School. Edward Parsons's theological views were liberal rather than conservative, and he had been influenced by the ideas of the social gospel movement. After his ordination, Edward Parsons moved to Colorado to pastor a church. It was there that Talcott Parsons was born. He spent portions of his childhood in Colorado, Ohio (where his father worked as the president of a college that had been founded by Congregationalists), and New York (where his father worked for the Young Men's Christian Association). Parsons was educated at Amherst and Heidelberg and began teaching in Harvard's economics department in 1927. Although some of the members of Harvard's faculty were unsympathetic to his work,[18] Parsons was eventually offered tenure, and he remained at Harvard until his retirement in 1973. Throughout the middle decades of the twentieth century, he exerted great influence on the way that Harvard's faculty approached the study of sociology, anthropology, and psychology. He received numerous academic awards and honors, and near the end of his life he was asked to serve as president of the American Academy of Arts and Sciences, the organization that eventually sponsored the Fundamentalism Project.[19]

In the summer of 1940, a time when he suspected that world civilization might well have arrived at one of its most important turning points,[20] he wrote his memorandum on groups that could be used against American institutions. The memo was written for a group, the Council of Democracy, that was attempting to limit the power of fascism.[21] In the essay, Parsons tried to explain the features of U.S. society that had produced groups that might sympathize with the Nazis. He sought to name those groups and suggest ways that thoughtful Americans could limit the power of those potential subversives. He wanted to determine which sort of Americans would be most susceptible to Nazi propaganda so that steps could be taken to prevent them from sabotaging (through either action or inaction) the struggle against the fascists. One of the most dangerous groups, Parsons said, was the fundamentalists.[22]

The memorandum is a creative work that includes many passages that bear witness to Parsons's scholarly habits of mind. But it also appears to have been written in some haste. It was partly typed and partly written by hand. It is not well organized, and its prose is unnecessarily opaque. It is also poorly documented; it lacks a bibliography and contains only a single footnote. Thus, a reader cannot always tell where Parsons's ideas are coming from. Are they rooted in the results of scientific research? Do they reflect what Parsons, an inveterate reader of newspapers, had learned from journalists?[23] Nevertheless, it is not difficult to identify some of the groups Parsons believed had the potential to become subversive. Those groups include fundamentalists, non-Protestants, non-Anglo-Saxons, and people who are not successful.

Parsons believed that class resentment had played a crucial role in the rise of Nazism. The Nazis had been able to create a socialist program that appealed to Germans who did not have much money. Such a program might also have considerable appeal, Parsons feared, to some segments of the American people. American society is arranged, Parsons wrote, in a pyramidal structure. The bottom of the pyramid is quite broad and the top is quite narrow. Inevitably, only a small proportion of the people who start at the bottom can reach the top. Widespread frustration results that leads unsuccessful people to create scapegoats whom they blame for their failure. Parsons suggested that this might well be exploited by the Nazis. Unsuccessful Americans—not all, but some—were thus potential subversives.[24]

People who had not fully embraced the Anglo-Saxon values upon which the American political system is founded might also have the potential to be subversive. It was quite probable, Parsons asserted, that some segments of America's polyglot population contained a good many people who appeared to be "good Americans" but who might well be susceptible to Nazi propaganda.[25] Who were these people? Well, one could begin by specifying who they were not: they were not Anglo-Saxons. The traditions of the Anglo-Saxons formed a powerful bulwark against Nazi subversion. The potential for trouble came from immigrants—especially immigrants whose roots were in societies that are backward.[26] Some immigrants to America had assimilated quite fully to Anglo-Saxon values, but some of them had not. They might well end up aiding the Nazi cause.[27]

Some Catholics might also be susceptible to Nazi propaganda, Parsons suggested. To some Catholics, the Nazis might appear to be nothing more than sound conservatives who provided a fine alternative to the anticlericalism that was sometimes found among liberals and leftists. And some Catholics might find the collectivist and antidemocratic aspects of Nazism to be highly attractive. The Catholic Church's "basic structure" tended toward authoritarianism. For that reason, many Catholics lacked self-reliance and an adequate attachment to freedom.[28]

In a way, Parsons's fears about Catholics are not at all surprising. Worries about whether Catholics fully embrace American values have surfaced time and time again.[29] For centuries Catholics were used as a dangerous other against which Protestants could define themselves. What is somewhat more surprising is Parsons's repeated insistence that fundamentalists might well end up aiding the Nazi cause. The fundamentalists of the 1920s and 1930s were no less worried than Parsons about the tension between Catholicism and American values. And fundamentalists sometimes expressed their love of the United States and what it stood for in the most extravagant of terms. What was it about the fundamentalists that made Parsons worry about their loyalty to America?

Parsons suspected that fundamentalism was hostile to the core values of America. He believed that America's "great national tradition" stemmed from the Enlightenment of the eighteenth century and was built around values such as individual rights, democracy, and freedom.[30] There was a sense in which the United States of America had always tended to be a forward-looking nation—a nation that was especially open to the coming of modernity and to the rationalization (in the Weberian sense of the term) of society. And rational technology, science, and critical thought now played absolutely central roles in American culture. Parsons believed that what fundamentalism was, at its core, was a backlash against rationalization. Fundamentalism was a refusal to accept what modern American society had become and a rejection of the Enlightenment ideals on which America was founded. It was difficult to see, therefore, how a person could be fully loyal to both fundamentalism and America.[31]

The case Parsons made for seeing fundamentalists as people who might be susceptible to Nazi propaganda was in some sense a philosophical one. He stipulated what America stood for and then asserted that fundamentalists stood for something else. But it is also possible that Parsons's fears about the possibility of alliance between fundamentalists and Nazis was also based on what he had been reading in newspapers. During the Depression, a number of groups emerged on both the far right and the far left of the political spectrum. Parsons believed that fundamentalists were disproportionately represented in the groups on the extreme right. Of course, the number of fundamentalists (in the strictest sense of that word) who were actively involved in extreme right-wing political organizations during the Depression was tiny. But when Parsons spoke about fundamentalism, he was using the word in a very loose way.

When he spoke of fundamentalism, he did not have in mind a group of men and women who were tied together by loyalty to certain doctrines and by a desire to keep Christian churches from drifting away from those doctrines. Nor did he have in mind a group of people who wanted to prohibit the teaching of evolution. For Parsons, fundamentalism was something more diffuse than that. He sometimes used the term to refer to all social groups that did not enthusiastically accept the rationalization that Max Weber believed was the hallmark of modern societies. Thus defined, the word "fundamentalist" could be stretched to cover a huge number of American Protestants. It might be used, for example, to describe Protestants who sympathized with the ideas of William Jennings Bryan or who supported Charles Lindbergh's efforts to prevent the United States from becoming involved in World War II or who voted for politicians such as Huey Long.

But I cannot be completely sure about that. In his writing, Parsons made very few empirical claims about who the fundamentalists were or which specific movements and institutions attracted their support. For him, specificity was not the point. He did not see fundamentalism as a specifically Protestant—or even as a specifically religious—phenomenon. Nor was it a specific movement or set of movements. It was, instead, an attempt to resist the inevitable rationalization of modern society. In fact, Parsons was willing to use the term "fundamentalism" to analyze the Nazis themselves and to talk about Americans he suspected of being susceptible to Nazi propaganda. Since he believed that one of the defining characteristics of Nazism was its hostility to social rationalization, he was quite willing to say that Nazism and fundamentalism had a great deal in common.[32] Some passages in the memorandum seem to suggest that fundamentalism is simply a New World version of Nazism and that Nazism is simply a European variant of fundamentalism. For Parsons, fundamentalism and Nazism were both examples of social pathology rooted in the inability of some human beings to accept the changes that rationalization brings.[33] In emphasizing the links between fundamentalism and Nazism, Parsons presented an interpretation of fundamentalism that was a good deal more derogatory than those advanced by the writers I have already described. For him, fundamentalism was an example of one of humanity's most dangerous flaws: its tendency to react to the coming of modernity with fear and resentment.

An Evangelical Critique of Fundamentalism

Parsons's fears about the possibility that American fundamentalists might make common cause with the Nazis proved, of course, to be completely unfounded. During World War II, fundamentalists were no less loyal to the United States than other Americans were. If anything, fundamentalists might have been especially patriotic: during the war years, fundamentalists sponsored huge rallies in which young men and women were encouraged to publicly demonstrate their passionate devotion to both God and country. Those campaigns made it clear that fundamentalists were not the subversives Parsons suspected they might be.[34]

During the 1940s, fundamentalists took steps to challenge the authority of religious organizations they saw as insufficiently committed to the fundamentals of the Christian faith. One of the groups whose authority they especially wanted to challenge was the Federal Council of Churches. The organization, which had been founded in 1908, advised the radio networks about which Protestant ministers should or should not be given free radio time to talk about religion. It also helped supervise the selection and training of Protestant chaplains in the armed forces. The Federal Council enjoyed the support of many of the nation's most prominent Protestant denominations and sometimes acted in ways that implied that it had a right to speak on behalf of American Protestantism as a whole. Fundamentalists were certain, however, that the Federal Council had no right whatsoever to speak for them. It gave its support to religious and political causes they opposed, and it made pronouncements that fundamentalists found deeply offensive.[35]

In the early 1940s, fundamentalists such as Carl McIntire, J. Elwin Wright, and Harold John Ockenga set out to create an organization that could provide an alternative to the Federal Council of Churches. Eventually two new organizations were founded: the American Council of Christian Churches in 1941 and the National Association of Evangelicals in 1942. McIntire was aligned with the former, Ockenga and Wright with the latter. The creation of two distinct organizations was symptomatic of an important process: in the 1940s, the heirs of the original fundamentalists were beginning to separate themselves into two camps. The camp associated with the American Council of Christian Churches consisted of Christians who continued to call themselves fundamentalists. The other camp, which was more sympathetic to the National Association of Evangelicals, included both people who thought of themselves as evangelicals *and* people who thought of themselves as fundamentalists.

The differences between the groups can easily be exaggerated. Both were deeply committed to the fundamentals of the Christian faith as the fundamentalists of the 1920s and 1930s had understood them. They were both highly suspicious of the social gospel, and both believed that modernist versions of Christianity were heretical. Both groups were intensely patriotic, and both hoped that God could use them to call America back to Christ. Both groups sometimes used militant rhetoric when outlining their goals: they routinely spoke about launching crusades and joining in campaigns.

But there were some important differences between them. McIntire and the other leaders of the American Council of Churches were reluctant to build coalitions with conservative Protestants who were not fundamentalists. They believed that all orthodox Christians ought to separate themselves fully from all the denominations in America that were willing to tolerate modernism. They were unwilling to make any compromises with modernists and were determined to denounce the evils of modernism in the strongest possible terms. They believed that the National Association of Evangelicals had failed to take a strong enough stand against the Federal Council of Churches. The leaders of the American Council of Churches associated the National Association of Evangelicals with "confusion," "compromise," and "appeasement."[36]

The fundamentalists who associated themselves with the National Association of Evangelicals did not, of course, think of themselves as appeasers. But some of them were quite willing to maintain their membership in denominations that were clearly apostate in the eyes of fundamentalists such as McIntire. The fundamentalists who joined the National Association of Evangelicals were eager to establish working coalitions with conservative Protestants—Pentecostals, for example—who were not fundamentalists. From the very outset, the leadership of the National

Association of Evangelicals included many men who were not fundamentalists in the strict sense of the word. They were not as interested as McIntire was in simply preserving the fundamentalist heritage. They hoped to build broad coalitions that could evangelize and transform America and wanted God to use them to spark a national revival of authentic Christianity. Wright, Ockenga, and other men aligned with the National Association of Evangelicals thought that it was easy to exaggerate the efficacy of denouncing modernism over and over again. A purely negative approach, they believed, simply would not do. They believed that Christians should present the world with a positive message of hope and sought to chart a middle course that avoided the perils of both modernist laxity and extreme fundamentalist rigor.[37]

In retrospect, the founding of the National Association of Evangelicals appears to have been a clear harbinger of the creation of what eventually became known as American evangelicalism. As time went on, the Christians associated with this group generally came to refer to themselves as evangelicals *rather* than fundamentalists. Saying that someone was a fundamentalist implied that he stood for more or less the same things that McIntire stood for; saying that someone was an evangelical implied that his sympathies lay with the program outlined by people such as Wright and Ockenga. The people who created evangelicalism—leaders such as Wright, Ockenga, and Billy Graham—were sometimes willing to criticize certain aspects of fundamentalist Christianity. Their criticisms of fundamentalism enabled evangelicals to say what it was that made them different from the fundamentalists of the 1920s and 1930s and from fundamentalists such as McIntire and to state who they were by stating who they were *not*.

One of the most famous critiques of fundamentalism to be produced by an evangelical Christian was Carl F. H. Henry's *The Uneasy Conscience of Modern Fundamentalism*, published in 1947. In that book and in a series of articles Henry published in 1948, he presented a sympathetic critique of fundamentalism. Henry enthusiastically endorsed all of the fundamentalist doctrines and ideas. However, he also said that fundamentalists had made a number of crucial mistakes that had harmed the Christian church and that trying to ignore those mistakes was counterproductive. Christians who were committed to the fundamentals of the Christian faith needed to acknowledge where the fundamentalists had gone wrong and develop a positive program that would demonstrate the redemptive power of the gospel to modern Americans.

Henry, who grew up on Long Island, pursued his undergraduate studies at Wheaton College and earned doctorates from both Northern Baptist Theological Seminary and Boston University. Henry was studying at Boston University, only a couple of miles away from the school where Parsons taught, while he was writing *The Uneasy Conscience*.

Of course, Henry was more religious than Parsons; he was, in fact, an ordained Baptist minister. Henry was also a gifted journalist; at the urging of Billy Graham, he became the first editor of *Christianity Today*. That journal eventually became one of the most important Protestant magazines in the United States. Henry was also a skilled organizer; he played an important role in the creation of the National Association of Evangelicals and participated in the founding of Fuller Theological Seminary, a school that instantiated evangelicals' commitment to the life of the mind.[38] Henry's theological writings earned him a reputation as one of the finest evangelical theologians in the United States. When he died, the *New York Times* ran an obituary whose headline described him as the "brain" of the "evangelical movement."[39] That was an overstatement, of course. But in many evangelical circles in postwar America, Henry's prestige was immense.

Henry's critique of fundamentalism was based on the assumption that theological modernism was in trouble. He asserted that modernists were passionately committed to two cardinal ideas: "man's essential goodness" and "inevitable world progress." Those ideas could never be squared with the truths of the Bible. And now it was also clear, he said, that those ideas could not be squared with human history: the events of the previous three decades had revealed that it is absurd to believe in ineluctable human progress or in the essential goodness of humanity.[40] Modernism was intellectually bankrupt. That bankruptcy, he wrote, provided an opening for the fundamentalists, but it did not make a fundamentalist triumph inevitable. It was possible that fundamentalists were not equal to the task that God had set before them. If they failed, secular ideas—ideas that in many respects were even more pernicious than those of the modernists—might well carry the day.[41] It was imperative that fundamentalists take a clear-eyed look at their strengths and weaknesses so they could minimize their weaknesses and accentuate their strengths.

Henry defined fundamentalism largely in terms of the doctrines and ideas it stood for. He said that fundamentalists believed in a personal God and a purposeful universe that was created by God's supernatural power. Fundamentalists rejected the theory of "naturalist evolution" and insisted that a Christianity shorn of its supernatural elements was no Christianity at all. Fundamentalists believed that human beings' predicament was the result of their revolt against God and that the solution to that predicament was Jesus Christ. They insisted that the Christian scriptures were different in kind from all other texts and that those scriptures alone light the way to redemption through Christ. Fundamentalists rejected the claim that history is completely open-ended; they maintained that history is moving toward a conclusion in which the entire human race will be judged by God.[42]

He believed that the fundamentalists were right and that the modernists and secularists were wrong. The fundamentalists remained loyal to the essentials of "the Hebrew Christian outlook" in a way that the modernists had not.[43] Moreover, he believed that many of the liberal attacks on fundamentalism were terribly unfair. When liberals said that Christians should not make the mistake "of taking the whole Bible literally, or of thinking God dictated it without respecting the personalities of the writers, or of contending that God stopped working in human history 1900 years ago," they were attacking a straw man. No "representative" fundamentalist, Henry said, believes any of those things. Liberals' attacks on fundamentalists were lacking in charity. Indeed, they were determined to nail fundamentalists to a cross, Henry said. From his perspective, it seemed people like Fosdick had got it backward: the fundamentalists were not the persecutors; the liberals were.[44]

But, Henry argued, fundamentalists had made a number of important mistakes. They spent too much time discussing the inessential matters upon which they could not reach complete unity and too little time proclaiming the central truths of the Christian gospel upon which they all agreed. For example, fundamentalists devoted far too much time to internal debates about the fine points of eschatology. They spent a great deal of time trying to figure out how biblical prophecies applied to present world events, and they criticized each other too fiercely whenever they did not see eye to eye on those matters.[45] Of course, Henry believed, there was nothing wrong per se with fundamentalists focusing their attention on the coming of the kingdom of God. He believed that the kingdom of God really was at the heart of the biblical message. But fundamentalists tended to think about the kingdom of God in ways that were overly pessimistic. Sometimes it seemed that they spent more time discussing who the Antichrist was than they did talking about God's redemptive power.

Indeed, Henry said, a tendency to underestimate the hopeful side of the Christian message was one of the fundamentalists' most debilitating shortcomings. Fundamentalists were right to stress that human beings were powerless to save themselves, but they were wrong not to emphasize God's power to redeem the people he had created.[46] Fundamentalists tended to focus their energies on trying to preserve "a faithful remnant" that was still loyal to the gospel and on saving individual sinners from damnation. That was a grievous mistake, Henry said. They should instead be trying to turn the world upside down. Fundamentalists had too much to say about individual sins (such as playing cards and smoking) and too little about the great social evils of the day, such as aggressive warfare, racial intolerance, and economic injustice. Fundamentalists had done far too little to ameliorate the social problems of the twentieth century and had given people the impression that they cared about social injustice less than secularists and modernists did. Henry argued that the fundamentalists had gotten a great deal right. But they had gotten some things wrong, too. Christians who were committed to the fundamentals of the faith needed to learn from the fundamentalists' mistakes.

Conclusion

I do not want to exaggerate the difference between the antifundamentalist texts I have looked at in this chapter and the ones I examined in the previous one. Niebuhr's analysis of fundamentalism, for example, clearly had a good deal in common with those Harry Emerson Fosdick and Kirsopp Lake presented. But there is also an important difference between Niebuhr's analysis of fundamentalism and those of his predecessors. Fosdick and Lake wrote in ways that made it abundantly clear that they regarded fundamentalists as their adversaries. Niebuhr did not. Unlike Lake and Fosdick, Niebuhr avoided saying anything that was overtly polemical. He did not make any explicit value judgments about fundamentalism; he presented his analysis of fundamentalism as a straightforward exposition of objective social scientific truth. During the 1930s and 1940s, antifundamentalism moved away from being a set of arguments toward becoming a set of propositions whose truthfulness was beyond question in the minds of many. The article Niebuhr wrote for the *Encyclopedia of Social Sciences* is an important example of that process.

Although Parsons's analysis of fundamentalism certainly had a good deal in common with the analyses Niebuhr, Lake, and Fosdick presented, it was more abstract and less specific than theirs. It was also more ambitious. Parsons began to develop what might be called, for lack of a better term, a general theory of fundamentalism. For Parsons, fundamentalism was a quasi-philosophical category that could be used to identify a set of extraordinarily dangerous tendencies. For him, fundamentalism was a nebulous social force that might be lurking anyplace where modernity's effects had been felt and resented.[47]

When fundamentalism is thought of in that way, it is entirely possible to argue that fundamentalists do not necessarily have to be Christians. One can say that there is no reason why Jews, Muslims, and Hindus cannot become fundamentalists. In his memorandum on groups that might not be loyal to the United States, Parsons did not claim that fundamentalists could be found outside Christendom. But that is of course precisely the claim that subsequent writers have made time and time again. Many of them did so, at least in part, because they had been influenced by the work of Martin Marty, a man who was deeply impressed by Parsons's work.

It is clear that in the late 1970s and early 1980s, Marty turned to Parsons's work to help him understand the "sociopsychological underpinnings" of fundamentalism. And there can be no doubt that Marty's claim that fundamentalism has to be understood as a problematic response to the strains created by the coming of modernity echoes some of the central themes in Parsons's analysis of fundamentalism. Since Marty has done as much as anyone else in the world to establish and elaborate a theory of global fundamentalism, Parsons's direct influence on Marty's thinking suggests the possibility that Parsons has had an indirect but important influence on how millions of people think about fundamentalism. In principle, at least, one can imagine a world in which Marty, forced to grapple with fundamentalism without reference to Parsons's ideas, could have come up with a different—and less problematic—approach to understanding it.[48]

Although the ideas Henry expressed in *The Uneasy Conscience* do not seem to have had much influence on how Marty thought about fundamentalism, they nevertheless played an important role in the history of antifundamentalism in America. As men such as Henry, Ockenga, Wright, and Graham were creating the coalitions that eventually came to define American evangelicalism, they consciously distanced themselves from fundamentalists such as McIntire. As they did that, they sometimes talked about fundamentalism in ways that were similar to how Fosdick and Lake talked about it. Of course, evangelicals such as Henry found far more to admire in fundamentalism than people such as Fosdick and Lake did. The doctrinal positions evangelicals such as Henry adopted were not that different from those fundamentalists such as McIntire adopted. But in the 1940s evangelicals such as Henry began to define themselves as conservative Protestants who were *not* fundamentalists. They sometimes made it clear that they believed extreme fundamentalism—or even fundamentalism itself—was a trap that Christians ought to avoid. As the 1940s drew to a close, then, antifundamentalist sentiment was not confined to the world of secularists and religious liberals. It was also present in the movement that became evangelicalism. In subsequent decades, millions of Americans who thought of themselves as evangelicals believed that fundamentalism was a danger to be warded off or a problem to be solved.

6

THE DUSTBIN OF HISTORY

Flannery O'Connor's 1952 novel *Wise Blood* follows the religious quest of a troubled young zealot named Hazel Motes. After fighting in World War II, Motes returns to the South and suffers a series of failures and disappointments. Near the end of the novel, Mrs. Flood, who owns the house in which Motes is staying, tries to convince him to abandon one of the extreme forms of self-mortification that has become a part of his daily regime. She tells him: "It's not normal. It's like one of them gory stories, it's something that people have quit doing—like boiling in oil or being a saint or walling up cats. . . . There's no reason for it. People have quit doing it." Mrs. Flood's observation does not describe the situation with complete accuracy. If everyone in the world had stopped engaging in extreme forms of self-mortification, there would have been no need for her to tell Motes to change his regime. Her observation does, however, express common modern sentiments: a longing to place "religious extremism" firmly in the past and a desire to demonstrate that it has no place in the modern world.[1]

Fundamentalism has, of course, often been described as a noxious form of religious extremism that has been consigned to the dustbin of history. Almost as soon as the fundamentalist coalition was created, its opponents began arguing that the fundamentalists had been soundly defeated and firmly placed on a path to certain extinction. Since the 1920s they have claimed with great passion and apparent conviction that fundamentalists are ridiculous fanatics whom no one can take seriously. They have also asserted that fundamentalism is not an option that any person living in the modern world could take seriously. Its critics began writing obituaries for it in the 1920s. They are still doing so today.

In this chapter I examine three different attempts to write a fitting obituary for Protestant fundamentalism. The first, Stanley Kramer's 1960 film *Inherit the Wind*, portrays fundamentalism as a reactionary movement whose intellectual bankruptcy was dramatically revealed in a famous trial about the teaching of evolution. The other two obituaries—Norman F. Furniss's *The Fundamentalist Controversy, 1918–1931* (1954) and Richard Hofstadter's *Anti-Intellectualism in American Life* (1963)—were both written by professional historians. Both books present fundamentalism as a form of Christianity that *in the past* blocked Americans' search for knowledge; both assert that religious fundamentalism's influence peaked in the 1920s and then went into steep decline.

We also look at another book written by a professional historian: Ernest R. Sandeen's *The Roots of Fundamentalism: British and American Millenarianism, 1800–1930* (1970). In sharp contrast to *The Fundamentalism Controversy* and *Anti-Intellectualism in American Life*, Sandeen's book does not read at all like an obituary for an antiquated form of Christianity. He believes that fundamentalism is a thoroughly modern movement that rests on an innovative reinterpretation of traditional Christianity. He also believes that there is no good reason that fundamentalism is doomed to extinction; to him it seems clear that fundamentalism displayed many signs of resilience and vitality in the 1930s, 1940s, 1950s, and 1960s.

Although *Roots of Fundamentalism* has won the admiration of many scholars who specialize in the study of fundamentalism, it has not received very much attention from nonspecialists. Sandeen's interpretation of fundamentalism never became as well known as that described in *The Fundamentalist Controversy*, *Anti-Intellectualism in American Life*, or *Inherit the Wind*. Sandeen's analysis of fundamentalism is almost as obscure as it is brilliant.[2]

A Threat to Freedom

Norman Furniss's *The Fundamentalist Controversy*, one of the first serious monographs on the history of fundamentalism, appeared in 1954.[3] Subsequent students of fundamentalism have had some harsh things to say, but when it first appeared Furniss's book was seen as a compelling account of an important episode in American history. Positive reviews of the book appeared in journals such as Church History, the *Journal of Southern History*, and the *Mississippi Valley Historical Review*. One reviewer concluded that the book was "a model of objectivity of appraisal and clarity of statement." The book reveals a great deal about how historians thought about fundamentalism in the 1950s.[4]

Furniss, who was born in New Haven in 1922, received his education at the Hotchkiss School and at Yale University, where he earned his bachelor's, master's, and doctoral degrees. The home in which Furniss was raised was not an especially devout one, and he never became a regular churchgoer. But he thought that religion was interesting, and, when it came time to choose a dissertation topic, Furniss decided (perhaps with some prodding from his dissertation adviser, Ralph Henry Gabriel) to investigate fundamentalism. Furniss received his PhD in 1950 and accepted a position teaching history at a school that was then called Colorado A&M and that is now known as Colorado State. While teaching in Colorado, Furniss transformed the dissertation into a book.

Furniss did not try to provide his readers with a precise definition of fundamentalism, and he did not provide them with a simple explanation for why fundamentalism arose when it did. He observed, however, that, in the years between 1865 and 1918, a great deal of "progress" had been made in theology and science and posited that perhaps many "humble Americans" were unable to accept the new ideas. Instead, they clung to "nineteenth-century orthodoxy."[5] These Americans were, moreover, inclined to believe that these new ideas were weakening the nation's moral standards. During World War I, some humble Americans came to believe that "new forms of knowledge" posed a threat to the nation analogous to that posed by the armies of the German Kaiser. And some Americans concluded that the events of the war demonstrated that optimistic assessments of human history were less accurate than the more pessimistic views of history inculcated by preachers who insisted that human history was spiraling toward disaster.[6] The result of this concatenation of trends and events was the rise of fundamentalists. They reached the peak of their power in the 1920s, and by 1931 their power had already begun to wane.

The reasons for fundamentalism's decline, Furniss admitted, were not entirely clear. The death of William Jennings Bryan, he thought, had dealt a terrible blow to the fundamentalist movement.[7] Additionally, some fundamentalists decided to direct their energies elsewhere, including the enforcement of Prohibition and efforts to raise money to repair the damage the Depression had wrought on church finances.[8] The demise of fundamentalism was also the result, Furniss asserted, of "the spread of knowledge." By 1931, the American people were less ignorant than they had been about evolution and modernism. As their ignorance waned, so too did their fear.[9]

Furniss devoted one chapter of *The Fundamentalist Controversy* to describing and analyzing fundamentalists' efforts to prevent the teaching of evolution in schools and colleges. Most of the remainder of his book consisted of discrete essays in which he narrated the battles between liberals and conservatives in the various Protestant denominations in the United States. Furniss focused special attention on the battles that took place among Northern Baptists and Northern Presbyterians, but he also surveyed controversies among the Disciples of Christ, Methodists, Episcopalians, Southern Baptists, and Southern Presbyterians. Furniss had no special interest or expertise in theological matters, and he did not attempt to provide his readers with a detailed analysis of the theological issues that divided fundamentalists from other sorts of Protestants. Nor did he have much to say about religious practice. Rather, he kept his focus on the political maneuvers in which the fundamentalists and their opponents engaged. Although he found these maneuvers interesting—somewhat like one might find the moves made during a game of chess interesting—Furniss also found them somewhat distasteful.

Furniss—in sharp contrast to Harry Emerson Fosdick, Kirsopp Lake, Frederick Lewis Allen, H. Richard Niebuhr, and Talcott Parsons—systematically examined a range of published primary sources that shed light on the history of fundamentalism. His book included an appendix in which he gave his readers a careful overview of the vast literature fundamentalists and their opponents had created. And Furniss's book, unlike the texts produced by Fosdick, Lake, Allen, Niebuhr, and Parsons, was packed with footnotes. *The Fundamentalist Controversy* was written by a man who wanted to provide as much empirical evidence as possible to back up his ideas about what fundamentalism was and the sources of its appeal.

His analysis of the primary sources led Furniss to believe that some of the claims writers such as Fosdick, Lake, Allen, Niebuhr, and Parsons made were probably false. He concluded, for instance, that there was little to support the claim that fundamentalists had received a great deal of support from the leaders of the Ku Klux Klan. He also expressed a good deal of skepticism about the idea that fundamentalism was, in large part, an agrarian protest movement aimed at protecting the values of rural America. (Furniss noted that the books, articles, and pamphlets fundamentalists published did not evince any special interest in agrarian issues and that many of the leaders of the fundamentalist movement lived in large cities.) He also concluded that there was a dearth of evidence to back the claim that the fundamentalist movement derived much of its power from the willingness of wealthy businessmen to secretly fund its operations.

The differences between *The Fundamentalist Controversy* and earlier interpretations of fundamentalism can, however, be easily overstated. Furniss, like the authors of many earlier texts on the subject, had little sympathy for fundamentalists. He viewed them, in fact, as forerunners of McCarthyites. He consistently portrayed fundamentalists as bullies who were intent on taking away the freedoms of other Americans. Those bullies, in his telling of the story, had two chief aims. First, they wanted to take away the freedom of those who wanted to teach evolution—in other words, to curtail academic freedom. Second, the fundamentalists wanted to compel church members to accept church dogma wholeheartedly—in other words, to limit the freedom of Christian believers who wanted to think for themselves even if that meant moving away from old ideas.

Furniss expressed a grudging admiration for the tremendous stores of energy upon which the leaders of the fundamentalist movement seemed to draw as they carried out their attacks. And he was willing to admit that a handful of them seemed to be intelligent and well educated. Furniss also made it clear, however, that he believed that the leaders of the movement were, on the whole, a remarkably unimpressive collection of human beings. His analysis of the leaders stressed four characteristics: sentimentality, egotism, ignorance, and anti-intellectualism. The leaders of the fundamentalist movement, as Furniss tells the story, included a good many men who were in need of psychiatric assistance and more than a few who should have been imprisoned.[10]

A Metaphor for McCarthyism

Inherit the Wind, a black-and-white film that was released in 1960, may well be the most influential cinematic exploration of fundamentalism ever created. It was based on a popular Broadway show with the same name. The play was adapted for the screen by Harold Jacob Smith and Nedrick Young, both Academy Award winners. Young was also famous in Hollywood circles for having refused to cooperate with the House Un-American Activities Committee.[11] The film starred Spencer Tracy, Fredric March, and Gene Kelly. It was directed by Stanley Kramer, one of the men in Hollywood who was most strongly committed to making "message" films. (Kramer also directed *The Defiant Ones*, *On the Beach*, *Judgment at Nuremberg*, and *Guess Who's Coming to Dinner*.)

Inherit the Wind was nominated for four Oscars and influenced the way that millions of Americans think about fundamentalism. Many Americans have a harder time bringing to mind images from the actual events of the Scopes trial than they do conjuring up images from the trial portrayed in *Inherit the Wind*; it is easier for them to picture Matthew Harrison Brady (March), Henry Drummond (Tracy), and E.K. Hornbeck (Kelly) than it is for them to remember the faces of William Jennings Bryan, Clarence Darrow, and H.L. Mencken.

The film's first public showing was in June 1960 at the Berlin International Film Festival. The next month, *Inherit the Wind* was screened in Dayton, Tennessee, the site of the actual trial. John Scopes, whom Kramer had asked to help publicize the film, was present at the screening and later said that he enjoyed the movie and that he thought it did a good job of capturing "the emotions in the battle of words between Bryan and Darrow." But he also noted that the movie departed in a number of respects from the historical events that inspired it.[12] He was right, of course.

Kramer, Smith, and Young were determined to make a film that demonstrated how detestable McCarthyism really was. They were unwilling to let the facts of the Scopes trial get in the way of telling a story whose moral was crystal clear. In the movie, the fundamentalists are misguided fools; the foes of fundamentalism are men who are willing to take chances in order to protect the right of human beings to search for the truth.[13]

In the film, Dayton has been transformed into the fictional town of Hillsboro. A few of the people who live in Hillsboro are reasonable people. There is a banker—a man who assures the townspeople that he is committed to the fundamentals of the faith—who believes that it is unwise to outlaw the teaching of evolution in the public schools. And some of the boys in the town's high school seem to be decent and kind. And, of course, there is also a young teacher—whose name in the movie is Burt Cates—who is determined to teach the theory of evolution to his students. But Cates, whom one of the characters in the film calls the only intelligent man in Hillsboro, is locked up in jail.

Hillsboro is full of religious fanatics. They march through the streets, legs and arms swinging in perfect rhythm, carrying torches, waving placards denouncing evolution, and singing Christian tunes that includes lyrics such as "we'll hang Burt Cates from a sour apple tree." The spiritual leader of the town is Rev. Jeremiah Brown. In his spare time, he sits at home alone and plays hymns on his organ. During an emotional nighttime service in Hillsboro, Brown prays for God to condemn Cates to an eternal punishment. When Brown's own daughter, Rachel, expresses sympathy for Cates, Brown loses his temper and asks God to damn her to hell.

As it happens, Rachel Brown is also Cates's fiancée. The film seems to suggest at several points that what the entire trial is really about is a struggle for Rachel Brown's love and loyalty. Brown's father is an angry patriarch; Cates is a kind, somewhat mild man who loves to dream. He is passionately devoted to Rachel Brown, but he also knows that she can have no life with him unless she breaks from her father. Throughout much of the movie, it is not clear whom she will choose. Rachel does not seem fond of her father, but she clearly fears him. It is not at all obvious that she will have the courage to defy him and the small-town conformism with which he is allied. In the end, she casts her lot with Cates.

The other major female character in the movie is Sara Brady. She has a great fondness for her husband, a famous Midwestern fundamentalist who has made three unsuccessful attempts to become president of the United States. But Sara Brady is also on good terms with Henry Drummond, the well-known Chicago lawyer who is defending Cates. Drummond treats her with an almost courtly respect and compliments her profusely. He asks her to dine with him and invites her to join him in laughing at her husband's peculiarities. Throughout the film, Mrs. Brady strives to maintain cordial relations with Drummond without doing or saying anything that would be disloyal to her husband. She, like Rachel, is torn between two men.

The men who made *Inherit the Wind* gave Matthew Harrison Brady several different peculiarities. He is fat; his doctor has asked him to watch what he eats, but Brady has a huge appetite that he indulges at every turn. He is in the habit of telling jokes that are not especially clever and then laughing at them heartily. He has a stentorian voice and a great deal of self-confidence. He is the sort of man who might be accused by his enemies of thinking of himself as God's mouthpiece. All in all, the film leaves the audience wondering how in the world such an odd man could have developed such a huge popular following. Drummond, on the other hand, is wise and heroic. When the townspeople of Hillsboro—many of whom seem to believe that Drummond is literally in a league with the devil—seek to confront him, Drummond generally responds with a tolerant gallantry. He is not looking for trouble. He has come to Hillsboro simply to defend a human being's right to think for himself.

About 90 minutes into the 128-minute film, Drummond calls Brady to the stand to talk about the Bible. Drummond begins his questioning by asking Brady whether it is safe to assume that Brady is an authority on the Bible. Brady tells Drummond that it is. But within a few moments, Brady has been forced to admit time and time again that there are things about the Bible that he simply does not understand. He has also declared that he has never read Darwin and never will. He thereby makes it clear that he has no way of knowing whether Darwin's theory and the Bible can be reconciled. He has said that all acts of sexual intercourse—including those that take place within holy matrimony—are sinful. Brady has also asserted that he knows for a fact that God created the world at 9 A.M. on October 23, 4004 B.C. As Brady's testimony proceeds, it becomes more and more apparent that he is overmatched. The sympathies of the men and women in the courtroom begin to shift from him to Drummond. At the end of the testimony, some of the people in the courtroom seem to view him with pity.

The next day, the jury finds Cates guilty. But the judge fines him only $100. Brady, who wanted to make an example out of Cates, is outraged; he wants to see a "drastic" punishment imposed. He demands that the judge allow him to make a statement that he hopes will help him regain his dominance over the courtroom. Instead, the judge tells him that such a statement would be out of order but that he is perfectly free to make his statement after the trial is adjourned. The judge then gavels the trial to its conclusion. Brady tries to make his speech, but no one in the courtroom seems much interested. They have better things to do with their time than listen to him. Brady tries to press on, but he cannot finish his remarks. Stricken by an apparent heart attack, he falls to the floor, dead.

The filmmakers seem to have gone out of their way to encourage viewers to enjoy a few laughs at Brady's expense, and in a number of scenes in the movie the journalist E. J. Hornbeck, a character modeled on H. L. Mencken, repeatedly points out Brady's absurdities. Hornbeck views Brady with more contempt than does Drummond, who sees in Brady a man who has a history of caring about justice. Brady is also, Drummond knows, a man who is deeply flawed, someone who is unable to accept progress and a man with a terrible lack of intellectual curiosity. Brady's limitations are also apparent to his wife. He is, she believes, a man with many gifts but one who is sometimes prone to making serious mistakes. Some of his actions strike her as wrongheaded, even immoral. During the last hours of Brady's life, his wife does not think of him as a defender of the faith. Instead, she views him almost as a little boy who needs her maternal support in order to avoid making himself into a laughingstock.

I am not at all certain that Kramer, Smith, and Young intended to make the Brady character into an embodiment of fundamentalism. Perhaps all they were trying to do was to produce an embodiment of McCarthyism. But whatever their intentions, the men who made *Inherit the Wind* ended up creating a film that alerted tens of thousands of Americans—including me—to the supposed dangers of fundamentalism. Until I first saw the movie—probably in 1968 or so—I had never really thought of fundamentalists as a threat. I spent most of my childhood in rural towns in the West and the South. Many of the people who lived in those towns were conservative Protestants. I knew from experience that some of them were not especially well educated or especially open to new ideas. But I did not see them as fanatics, extremists, or fundamentalists. I did not think of them as particularly sinister.

Watching *Inherit the Wind* prompted me to see the conservative Protestants who surrounded me in a new light. It enabled me to consider the possibility that they constituted a threat. Seeing that possibility encouraged me to want to fight for people such as Drummond and against people such as Brady. For me, as for lots of other Americans, *Inherit the Wind* served as a catechism for the set of feelings, assumptions, and beliefs I am calling antifundamentalism.

An Illustration of the Dangers of Anti-Intellectualism

In 1964 Richard Hofstadter, one of the most well-known historians in the nation, received his second Pulitzer Prize, this one in recognition of a beautifully written book called *Anti-Intellectualism in American Life*. In *Anti-Intellectualism* Hofstadter tried to show, with limited success, that fundamentalists had played a formative role in creating a national culture that was hostile to the life of the mind. Hofstadter, who was born in Buffalo in 1916, was the son of a Jewish father and a Protestant mother. He was baptized in the Lutheran Church and sang in a church choir, but he was never especially devout. For most of his life he seems to have been far less interested in religion than in politics. Hofstadter attended a high school named after Harry Emerson Fosdick's father; he performed brilliantly there and was awarded a scholarship to attend the University of Buffalo. After graduating from college, Hofstadter moved to New York City and began studying for a legal career. However, law school bored him and he eventually dropped out and began studying history instead. In 1942, Hofstadter received a PhD in history from Columbia University. After a brief stint teaching at the University of Maryland, he moved back to New York to join the faculty of Columbia's history department.[14]

Hofstadter stayed at Columbia for the rest of his life. There he found a circle of friends—men such as Daniel Bell, David Herbert Donald, Peter Gay, Lionel Trilling, and C. Wright Mills—who shared his passionate commitment to the life of the mind. Hofstadter was deeply loyal to the school he made his home; he loved being a Columbia professor. He certainly did not, however, love everything about teaching at Columbia. His salary was a good deal lower than he wished. He did not take much pleasure in teaching Columbia undergraduates and sometimes seems to have regarded undergraduates as an annoying distraction from his real work: writing his books and training his graduate students. And Hofstadter found the behavior of Columbia's student radicals in the 1960s to be reprehensible.[15]

As a young man, Hofstadter moved in leftist political circles. He was even briefly a member of the Communist Party, but his experiences in the party left him deeply disillusioned. The party was not the kind of organization, Hofstadter concluded, for a man who liked to think for himself. As he grew older, Hofstadter's political views moved somewhat to the right. During the 1950s and 1960s, many of the people who had known him during his youth were puzzled by how far he had moved from his earlier leftist sentiments. In their eyes, he had become a complacent liberal—or even, perhaps, a centrist.[16]

Hofstadter's later political positions clearly grew out of his sense that the intelligence and trustworthiness of the American people ought not to be overstated. He believed that mass political movements that attracted support from people on the left could do a great deal of damage to American society. The same was true, he was convinced, of movements that drew their support from the right. He distrusted Communists, but he also believed that anti-Communists such as Joseph McCarthy posed a terrible threat to American society. Hofstadter's concerns about the power of McCarthyism helped shape his approach to the history of American intellectualism, as too did his indignation over the American people's tendency to choose leaders such as Dwight Eisenhower over "eggheads" such as Adlai Stevenson. Indeed, *Anti-Intellectualism* begins with a meditation on the 1952 election and on the fact that Americans preferred to be governed by a man whose mind was (in Hofstadter's opinion) clearly second rate than by a highly intelligent man who had received his education at Choate, Princeton, and Northwestern.[17]

Hofstadter believed that throughout their history, Americans had displayed an unseemly suspicion of men who valued reflection, comprehension, and the pursuit of knowledge for its own sake. Americans tended to be overly pragmatic and overly utilitarian, he argued.[18] They were insensible to the need to support the work of intellectuals and inclined to think the worst of what intellectuals do and what they stand for. A great many Americans, he wrote, tended to see intellectuals as "pretentious, conceited, effeminate, and snobbish."[19] Hofstadter was quite willing to admit that intellectuals are far from perfect, but he also believed deeply in their worth. And he was impressed by their selflessness and generosity of spirit. Hofstadter believed that the history of Western civilization demonstrated that "of all the classes which could be called in any sense privileged," it was "the intellectual class" that was most concerned about "the well-being of the classes which lie below it."[20]

There is little evidence to suggest that Hofstadter spent much time studying the primary sources that have a bearing on the history of fundamentalism, but his interpretation of fundamentalism was provocative, forcefully argued, and beautifully written. It was inspired, at least in part, by the sociological theories about right-wing movements that men such as Daniel Bell and Theodor Adorno had developed and drew on books such as Ralph L. Roy's *Apostles of Discord*, William G. McLoughlin's *Billy Sunday Was His Real Name*, and Norman Furniss's *The Fundamentalist Controversy*.

Hofstadter believed that fundamentalism grew out of Americans' rebellion against religious establishments and their love of evangelicalism. He noted that the religious establishments that had dominated religious life in the colonies of New England were not without their flaws, but he emphasized their great virtues and their tremendous respect for learning. As soon as they possibly could, Hofstadter noted, the men who founded the Massachusetts Bay Colony created a college in Cambridge that demonstrated their determination to give pious, erudite men a large say in the colony's affairs. The authority of the religious establishment was challenged almost as soon as those new institutions were created. Almost immediately after the Massachusetts Bay Colony was created in 1630, its peace was disturbed by Anne Hutchison's heated attacks on "learned ministers" and "university education."[21] As Hofstadter saw it, the history of religion in the United States was marred by regular outbreaks of popular hostility to the idea of allowing the life of the mind to affect religious beliefs and practices. Evangelical Protestants, he believed, had developed a form of Christianity that systematically denigrated learning. Indeed, there are passages in Hofstadter's book that assert that Americans' hostility to religious establishments and their enthusiasm for evangelical religion are the wellsprings out of which American anti-intellectualism flows.

Hofstadter believed that there were two kinds of fundamentalism: serene and militant. He confessed that he was not especially interested in serene fundamentalism; he had little to say about it in *Anti-Intellectualism*. What Hofstadter was concerned with was militant fundamentalism. When Hofstadter used the term "fundamentalism" in the pages of that book, it was militant fundamentalism that he had in mind.[22] Hofstadter believed that fundamentalism was a particularly obscurantist and dangerous variant of evangelicalism that had come into existence in the second half of the nineteenth century. He saw it as a "revolt against modernity" and argued that fundamentalists often demonstrated a deep-seated need "to strike back against everything modern—the higher criticism, evolutionism, the social gospel, rational criticism of any kind."[23] Fundamentalists were suspicious of education, learning, and the life of the mind and were against libraries.[24] They were quite willing to condemn their children to living lives of ignorance in order to prevent them from coming into contact with any ideas that might disturb their dogmatic certitude.[25]

Hofstadter was unwilling to say that fundamentalism could be reduced to a psychological malady, but he was convinced that there was such a thing as "a generically prejudiced mind" and that the minds of many fundamentalists suffered from this affliction.[26] Fundamentalists' pronouncements tended to be shrill and petulant.[27] They could not see the world in all in its complexity; instead, they saw the world as set of crude binaries.[28] They were an intolerant lot, obsessed with demonstrating their "toughness and masculinity" and "terrified of their own sexuality."[29]

The fundamentalists, Hofstadter believed, had lost more battles than they had won. By the end of the nineteenth century—two decades before they had even been given the name "fundamentalists"—these reactionary Protestants had lost much of their influence and their respectability.[30] Decisively defeated in the battles of the 1920s, they "retired sullenly" from the fields on which they had battled their enemies, looking for some other ground on which to "smite" them.[31] Eventually, the fundamentalist movement became more secular and was transformed—through a set of processes that Hofstadter left quite vague—into a political movement. Indeed, the irrational crusades the radical right launched in the 1950s and

1960s were, in part, simply more secular versions of the campaigns the fundamentalists had waged—and lost—in the 1920s.

Anti-Intellectualism was not Hofstadter's best book. He himself seems to have believed that it should not have been awarded a Pulitzer Prize. A number of scholars found the book's argument to be either opaque or wrongheaded. David Herbert Donald confessed to Hofstadter that he was not sure that the real target of the book was anti-intellectualism; perhaps, Donald suggested, the book was really an attempt to explore some of the weaknesses of democratic societies.[32] The reviews of *Anti-Intellectualism* that appeared in the *Journal of American History*, the *Journal of Southern History*, and the *American Historical Review* were unenthusiastic. So were the reviews written by Philip Gleason and Daniel J. Boorstin. In a dyspeptic essay called "Elitism on the Left," Kenneth Lynn dismissed *Anti-Intellectualism* as a set of parables and myths that bore only the slightest relationship to the actual history of the United States. Lynn found Hofstadter's analysis of the history of evangelicalism amazingly wrongheaded. In a private letter, Hofstadter's close friend C. Vann Woodward told him that his analysis of fundamentalism was seriously flawed.[33]

> You . . . refer to "the one-hundred percent mentality"—and here I am not clear whether you are talking about the fundamentalist, the far right, or both, or whether you have shifted categories. Anyway, you say that it is not only anti-intellectual but then you let go with both barrels: millennial, apocalyptic, puritanical, cynical, nationalistic, quasi-fascist, anti-foreign, anti-Semitic, anti-statist, anti-Communist, anti-liberal. Now I think that you can make a case that the present-day fundamentalists, or some of them, are guilty of those charges, though I think you have been more circumspect and cautious in charging this and other classes with anti-intellectualism. . . . Dick you just can't do this.[34]

The passage of time has not burnished the book's reputation. In 2006, David S. Brown argued in *Richard Hofstadter: An Intellectual Biography*, his much-acclaimed analysis of Hofstadter's life and work, that *Anti-Intellectualism* ought to be read in part as "a study in self-interest" in which an American intellectual argued that American intellectuals were not being treated deferentially enough.[35] Brown noted that the book was marred by Hofstadter's elitist assumptions and his tendency to write about people who were not intellectuals with condescension or even mockery.[36] One could argue that *Anti-Intellectualism* sheds more light on the anxieties experienced by American intellectuals than it does on the nature of Protestant fundamentalism. From many points of view, Hofstadter's ambitious attempt to understand American fundamentalism ended in confusion and failure. It might be said to represent the nadir of the historical profession's understanding of fundamentalism.

An Innovative Theological Movement

By 1970, the year when Ernest Sandeen's *Roots of Fundamentalism* was published, things had begun to get better. Sandeen was acutely aware of the weaknesses of Hofstadter's *Anti-Intellectualism*. He eventually came to believe that its arguments about fundamentalism were both superficial and "perverse." Sandeen also thought that Furniss's *The Fundamentalist Controversy* was an unreliable account of fundamentalism; he regarded it as a shoddy book that contained a great many errors and little rigorous analysis. In *Roots of Fundamentalism* and in a set of articles that appeared in the late 1960s and early 1970s, Sandeen tried to present an interpretation of Protestant fundamentalism that sidestepped the traps that had snared other scholars. Sandeen's work on fundamentalism has some weaknesses and many strengths, but it has never been wildly popular. Today, when readers want to learn about fundamentalism, they are more likely to read a book written by Joel Carpenter or George Marsden than they are to read Sandeen's *Roots of Fundamentalism*. But Sandeen's approach to fundamentalism clearly influenced Carpenter and Marsden. Indeed, Sandeen's influence can be discerned in a great many of the best accounts of the history of fundamentalism. When *Roots of Fundamentalism* was published, it was almost immediately recognized as a major contribution to the field. Reviewers sometimes took issue with Sandeen's arguments, but they also asserted that no better account of the history of fundamentalism had ever been written.[37]

Sandeen was a Midwesterner. He was born in 1931 in one of Chicago's western suburbs and earned his BA from Wheaton College, located just twenty miles or so from the place where he was born. Sandeen earned both his MA and his PhD from the University of Chicago. After completing his doctorate, he taught for several years at North Park College, a Chicago school with strong ties to the Evangelical Covenant Church, and then moved to Macalester College, a small liberal arts college in St. Paul, Minnesota. He remained on the faculty of Macalester until his death in 1982. Although he also wrote a book about the history of St. Paul, Sandeen's scholarly reputation was built very largely on *Roots of Fundamentalism.*

Roots of Fundamentalism is a work of great erudition. It is also a passionate work that clearly expresses both Sandeen's admiration for the accomplishments of the fundamentalists and his conviction that the fundamentalists' approach to understanding scripture was, in the final analysis, deeply flawed. In *Roots of Fundamentalism* and in the articles he published around the time the book appeared, Sandeen insisted that it was a mistake to see fundamentalism exclusively in terms of the psychological makeup of the fundamentalists or the social conditions in which fundamentalists lived. He also argued that in order to describe fundamentalism clearly, one had to get clear of a "semantic muddle" that stretched all the way back to the 1920s. The problem was that the "fundamentalist" label was applied to too large a set of people; using it to describe everyone who supported Prohibition or every American who thought that Earl Warren ought to be impeached was simply absurd. Nor were fundamentalists simply a collection of people who wanted to battle modernity.[38]

There was an appealing modesty to Sandeen's approach to studying fundamentalism. He admitted that his definition of fundamentalism did not work perfectly and that it would not be universally accepted. That was fine with him, he said. What he objected to was the practice of writing about fundamentalism without trying to accurately define what fundamentalism actually was. Fundamentalism was a movement, not "an amorphous entity" or "an abstract category." If one wanted to draw an accurate portrait of fundamentalism, one had to pay attention to what fundamentalists "believed and taught." One also had to pay attention to who fundamentalists regarded as their friends and who they trusted.[39]

Sandeen had a good deal of firsthand experience of fundamentalism. When he began his graduate work at Chicago, he still thought of himself as a fundamentalist.[40] He later left the fundamentalist fold, and he was sometimes fiercely critical of some of the distinctive doctrines to which fundamentalists were committed.[41] But he never abandoned his belief that whatever else fundamentalism was, it was also an "authentic and distinctive" religious movement. If one saw fundamentalism primarily as a set of political maneuvers aimed at expelling liberals from certain denominations and getting the teaching of evolution banned from the nation's public schools, one could never make sense of what it was that fundamentalism offered its adherents. Fundamentalism was not simply a set of denunciations. It was also a positive movement that gave its adherents powerful tools to understand the world in which they were living and specific guidelines for how to live a meaningful life.

Sandeen asserted that fundamentalism was, at base, a religious movement and that it had to be understood, at least in part, in religious terms. Beginning around 1875, he noted, fundamentalists had succeeded in building a set of institutions that helped them propagate a distinctive theological vision. The fundamentalist movement was an alliance between Protestants who had been influenced by dispensationalism and those who were drawn to the so-called Princeton Theology, which had been developed in the nineteenth century by a group of scholars who taught at Princeton Seminary, including Archibald Alexander, Charles Hodge, Archibald Alexander Hodge, and Benjamin B. Warfield.[42] Those men, who were deeply committed to intellectual rigor and to Christian orthodoxy, placed great emphasis on the authority of scriptures. They were unalterably opposed to any approach to the scriptures that left open the possibility that the Bible should be read as a text that reflected the foibles and imperfections of the people who wrote it. Accordingly, Princeton theologians argued that every affirmation in the Bible had to be understood as an infallible "utterance of God."[43] They asserted that the Bible was free from all errors and that each word in it was the word of God. This unshakable belief that each word of scripture was a direct expression of God's will became one of the two defining characteristics of fundamentalism, Sandeen argued.

The other was dispensationalism—an approach to interpreting the Bible that was developed in the nineteenth century by men such as John Nelson Darby, James Brookes, and William Gladstone. Dispensationalists believed that human history was divided into distinct epochs and that human beings' relationship to God varied from one epoch—or dispensation—to another. Dispensationalists were convinced that the present age was a time when most human beings and most human institutions had turned their backs on God. The present age, they maintained, was characterized by increasing wickedness, not (as some liberals declared) by progress toward the millennial kingdom. That kingdom would not be established by human effort. Rather, it would come only as the direct result of the personal bodily return of Jesus Christ. The three and a half years before Christ's return to earth would be years of terrible "tribulation"; the awful human suffering that would be inflicted during that time of trial would be brought to an end when Christ's army triumphed in the Battle of Armageddon. None of these events could, dispensationalists believed, be consigned to the distant future. Human beings were living on the verge of a precipice: the tribulation was about to break out, and Christ was preparing to return to earth to establish his kingdom.

Sandeen knew that dispensationalism and the Princeton Theology were not perfectly compatible, but he also believed that beginning in the 1870s, the proponents of the two theological systems had managed to create an alliance that worked fairly smoothly up until 1918. The coalition frayed in the 1920s, but the fundamentalist movement was certainly not crushed during that decade. When examined carefully, the theological views of the fundamentalists were not traditional in the strictest sense of the word. The fundamentalists were creative theologians who developed a new approach to understanding the Bible. They then used books, magazines, courses in Bible institutes, conferences, public lectures, and sermons to spread these new ideas throughout the nation.[44] The fundamentalists were, as Sandeen saw them, far from anti-intellectual. They were, rather, people who were obsessed with learning and teaching.

Conclusion

Sandeen's interpretation of fundamentalism was pathbreaking. Unlike many other writers, Sandeen did not believe that fundamentalists were fanatics who had taken leave of their senses. He did not assume that the outcome of the controversies of the 1920s had put them on a path to extinction. He presented fundamentalists as adherents of an innovative religious movement, not as participants in a simpleminded backlash against changing social conditions. Sandeen showed that many fundamentalists were deeply interested in reading and thinking: he made a point of carefully exploring fundamentalists' ideas about eschatology and hermeneutics seriously and did not dismiss those ideas as absurd or irrelevant.

Sandeen's *Roots of Fundamentalism* included many brilliant analyses of fundamentalists' ideas about how the Bible should be interpreted and what it said about the end of days; they have often been praised by scholars who specialize in the history of American fundamentalism. But readers who lack a strong interest in hermeneutics or eschatology have sometimes found reading *Roots of Fundamentalism* to be a tough slog. For readers like that, Sandeen's attempts to explain the nature of fundamentalism often seemed less than compelling. It is easy to exaggerate the number of admirers *Roots of Fundamentalism* has won in the years since its publication. The number of people who have actually read it in its entirety is not very large.

Few traces of Sandeen's ideas are evident in the conversations about fundamentalism that took place in the 1970s and early 1980s. Traces of the interpretations of fundamentalism men such as Hofstadter, Kramer, Furniss, Parsons, Niebuhr, Allen, Lake, and Fosdick created are, in sharp contrast, everywhere to be seen. In the 1970s and early 1980s, when Americans talked about "fundamentalists" they were often using the word as a sort of shorthand for "poorly educated religious zealots who have failed to successfully adapt to the coming of modernity." The fundamentalists they were talking about bore very little resemblance to fundamentalists whose ideas were explored in the pages of Sandeen's book.

7

Reinvention

In the autumn of 1985, scholars from throughout the United States gathered at Harvard University to explore the relationship between religion and politics in nations such as Iran, Egypt, Saudi Arabia, Iraq, Afghanistan, and Pakistan. The conference, which attracted national attention, was organized by Nadav Safran, the scholar who directed the university's Center for Middle Eastern Studies. Newspapers referred to it as "a conference on Islamic fundamentalism."[1]

A few weeks before the conference, a rumor began to circulate that the funding for it had come from the Central Intelligence Agency. The rumor turned out to be true, and it created controversy. Safran had not told the invitees who would be paying for the meeting. He had also kept the conference's links to the CIA hidden from his colleagues at Harvard, which infuriated some members of the university's faculty. They argued that the funding for the conference lent credence to the widespread belief that American scholars who worked on the Middle East were in the pocket of the CIA and that the CIA's sponsorship might well give outsiders the impression that Harvard was acting in concert with the U.S. military-industrial complex.

For a few days it looked as though Harvard administrators might cancel the conference. In the end, however, they allowed it to proceed. The administrators noted that Safran's contract with the CIA did not *require* him to keep his relationship to the agency secret and that if Safran had wanted to, he could have told his colleagues about the CIA's involvement. The decision to keep the CIA's identity concealed was Safran's and Safran's alone. The administrators argued that the fact that the CIA did not demand that its connection to the conference be kept confidential demonstrated that the conference did not have to be canceled because it showed that the CIA's motives were not nefarious. To many scholars, this argument seemed entirely bogus.

Although the conference on fundamentalism was allowed to proceed, it was not a great success. Many of the people who had been scheduled to give presentations decided not to attend, and there was a fair amount of unhappiness among the scholars who did show up. Some of the participants believed that they should have been told about the CIA's sponsorship when they were invited to participate, and some of them objected to the fact that a good deal of the conference was closed to the public. In their view, that created a bad impression.

Shortly after the conference concluded, Safran stepped down as director of the Center for Middle Eastern Studies. Although the university's formal report on the conference and the controversies that surrounded it did not constitute a formal censure of Safran, it made clear that he had made a number of significant mistakes in managing his relationship to the CIA and in organizing the conference. If he had not made those mistakes, the report noted, the conference would not have created so much controversy.

From some points of view, the controversies that the conference did *not* create are as important as the ones it did. As far as I can determine, no one involved in the debates about the conference claimed that there was no such thing as Islamic fundamentalism. No one suggested that Islamic fundamentalism did not deserve scholarly investigation. No one said that U.S. policy makers ought not to reflect on who Islamic fundamentalists were and on what they were trying to do.[2]

Of course, the newspaper stories on the Harvard conference were not the first instances of journalists linking fundamentalism to Islam. As I have already noted, a few journalists attached that label to Muslims in the 1920s. A few other journalists did the same thing in the 1930s, 1940s, 1950s, and 1960s, and in those decades a handful of scholars referred to Muslims as fundamentalists. In the early 1930s, A.J. Toynbee, the famous student of the rise and fall of the world's great civilizations, noted the persistence of "old-fashioned Islamic Fundamentalists" in Syria, Iraq, and Turkey. In books published in the late 1940s, H. A. R. Gibb, one of most highly respected orientalists of his generation, used fundamentalism to analyze a wide range of Islamic movements. In the early 1960s, one of Gibb's protégés, a political scientist named Leonard Binder, discussed the influence of Muslim fundamentalists on Pakistani politics.[3]

But it would be a mistake to make too much of that. The routine use of the terms "fundamentalist," "fundamentalists," and "fundamentalism" in connection with any religion other than Christianity is a very recent phenomenon. From the 1920s through the 1960s, almost no one had anything to say about forms of fundamentalism other than Christian ones. Dictionaries and encyclopedias published in those decades made it clear that fundamentalism was strictly a Christian phenomenon. Very few—if any—of the published books that focused on fundamentalism in those years had a word to say about any religion other than Christianity. In those decades, a book about fundamentalism that focused on Islam would have seemed idiosyncratic, bizarre, and absurd.

Between the mid-1960s (when Ernest Sandeen was conducting the research for *Roots of Fundamentalism*) and the mid-1980s (when Safran organized the Harvard conference), the role fundamentalism played in American culture was radically transformed. First, the range of phenomena to which the concept was applied expanded quite dramatically. In the mid-1960s, when Americans talked about fundamentalism, they were almost always saying something about Protestant Christianity. In the mid-1980s, when Americans talked about fundamentalism, they were frequently discussing Hinduism, Sikhism, Buddhism, or Islam. Second, fundamentalism attracted far more attention in the mid-1980s than it had in the mid-1960s. Exactly how much more is, of course, hard to say. But it is entirely possible that fundamentalism was attracting ten times more attention in the mid-1980s than it had in the 1960s.[4] Third, in the mid-1980s, far more Americans were willing to say that fundamentalism posed a significant threat to the nation than were willing to say that two decades earlier. Indeed, by the mid-1980s, some Americans were beginning to suspect that fundamentalism was as menacing as Nazism or communism.

This chapter analyzes the developments that set the stage for the reinvention of fundamentalism. It also examines three texts that illustrate the uses to which fundamentalism was put during that time. The first is a brief article, Martin Marty's "Fundamentalism Reborn," that appeared in the *Saturday Review* in the spring of 1980. It used the ideas of Talcott Parsons to comment on the dangers inherent in the rise of global fundamentalism. The second text, *Holy Terror* (1982), was written by two journalists, Flo Conway and Jim Siegelman. The book attempted to demonstrate that fundamentalists all over the globe are engaged in systematic campaigns against freedom, justice, progress, and democracy. The third text, "Islamic Fundamentalism and Islamic Radicalism," is a transcript of congressional hearings that took place in the summer of 1985.[5] It illustrates some of the ways governmental officials—and the experts who advised them—thought about fundamentalism in the mid-1980s.

A World Transformed

In the 1960s and 1970s, some observers came to question the notion that as societies become more modern, religious institutions inevitably become less connected to government organizations, less influential, and less robust. As early as 1965, British scholar David Martin expressed doubts about the validity of some aspects of so-called secularization theory. Three years later, one of Talcott Parsons's most highly regarded protégés, Robert Bellah, argued that college students in the United States seemed to be far more interested in religion (and far more likely to practice it) than the secularization theory suggested. Bellah reported that many of his students at Berkeley did not believe that well-educated moderns were obliged to reject religion. "Enlightenment fundamentalism" held no allure for them. In the early 1970s, Andrew Greeley, a scholarly cleric with a particular interest in sociology, said that there was very little reason to believe that the world was becoming less religious. He claimed that the salient empirical data simply did not confirm the predictions that theorists of secularization had advanced. Greeley argued that the data clearly demonstrated that the world's people were still remarkably "unsecular."[6]

Greeley's claims certainly did not go unchallenged. But in the 1970s his contentions did not seem to be at all implausible. Even the champions of secularization theory had to admit that religion was—by at least some measures and in at least some regions—still surprisingly robust. And in a good many countries, religion and politics seemed to be intertwined in ways that were hard to reconcile with the predictions of some theorists. In some nations, politics and religion were still deeply enmeshed. The political cultures of Latin American nations such as Brazil and Nicaragua were transformed by the rise of liberation theology. Christian critiques and defenses of apartheid shaped political debates in South Africa. Hindu nationalism—and hostility toward it—played a significant role in shaping Indian politics. Religious controversies affected politics in Egypt, Pakistan, and a number of other Muslim nations.

In the very late 1970s, some of the most vivid indications of the connections between religion and politics came from Iran. In January 1979, the shah of Iran, Mohammad Reza Pahlavi, who had ruled the nation since 1941, was forced to leave the country. On February 1, Ayatollah Ruhollah Khomeini, an Islamic philosopher and jurist whose opposition to the shah's regime had forced him to live in exile for fourteen years, returned to Iran. Millions of Iranians filled the streets of Tehran to celebrate. Ten days later, the secular regime that the shah had created completely collapsed. In June, the draft of a new constitution was made public; it included provisions to ensure that the government did not adopt any laws that were un-Islamic. In November, Iranian students stormed the embassy of the United States; one month later, Khomeini was named the supreme leader of Iran.

The overthrow of the shah, the establishment of an Islamic Republic, and the capture of the American embassy took America by surprise. Anyone who was living in the United States at the time will remember how these events became part of Americans' everyday lives. I was working as a janitor during the hostage crisis. The crew to which I belonged worked from four in the afternoon until one in the morning. Each night we took our break at 11:30 and gathered around a tiny black-and-white television set to watch a show called *America Held Hostage*. Members of the crew, as I recall, routinely referred to the students who had taken the embassy personnel hostage as assholes, bastards, and sons of bitches. To my coworkers, the national humiliation the American people had suffered at the hands of those students was comparable to the wounds they had suffered at the hands of the Communists in Vietnam. What was happening in Iran left us disoriented and bewildered.

As Americans searched for a way to make sense of the Iranian Revolution, some were struck by the apparent similarities between the religious revolutionaries in Iran and the revolutionaries in Latin America who had been influenced by liberation theology. They noted that Khomeini was in contact with Nicaraguan Catholic leftists such as Ernesto Cardenal. (Cardenal was both a Jesuit priest and the minister of culture in the leftist Nicaraguan regime.) Those connections made American observers nervous. A few writers warned that Khomeini might be trying to propagate an Islamic analogue to liberation theology.[7] The Iranian clerics who guided the Iranian Revolution and the Roman Catholic priests who developed liberation theology did have some things in common. Both groups included brilliant intellectuals. Both were struck by how much damage had been done to poor people throughout the world in the name of modernization. Both had a certain degree of contempt for governmental officials who cooperated closely with the U.S. government and U.S. corporations.

But whatever its intrinsic merits, the inclination to understand the Iranian Revolution as a Middle Eastern analogue to radical Catholicism in Latin America never gained much traction. Another analogy—one that stressed the similarities between people such as Khomeini and Protestant fundamentalists—turned out to be far more compelling. By the time the shah's regime began to totter, a great many Americans had begun to suspect that Protestant fundamentalism was not destined for extinction, as they had previously believed. Indeed, by the late 1970s, some thoughtful observers had begun to hypothesize that more conservative forms of Protestantism were more robust than liberal ones in the United States.[8] That hypothesis was probably quite sound. By the late 1970s, a good deal of evidence had accumulated that membership of many denominations that had made a conscious commitment to reconcile Christianity with modern thought was in decline. The statistics also suggested that membership in many denominations that refused to make such a commitment was on the upswing.[9] (Membership in Congregationalist and Unitarian churches was shrinking, for example, while membership in Southern Baptist churches was growing.) In the late 1970s, a good many Americans thought they were living in a world that was the mirror image of the one that progressives such as Kirsopp Lake had envisioned in the 1920s. Liberal Protestantism looked as if it was in trouble. Conservative forms of Protestantism such as fundamentalism seemed to be flourishing.

The groups people pointed to as embodiments of the continuing vitality of fundamentalism were extraordinarily heterogeneous. The practice of referring to the members of those groups as fundamentalists failed to recognize the diversity of the adherents. To be sure, some of the conservative Protestants whom outsiders labeled fundamentalists—Carl McIntire, Bob Jones Jr., and John R. Rice, for example—really were fundamentalists in the strict sense of the term. Those men called themselves fundamentalists and they were the direct spiritual descendants of the fundamentalists of the 1920s and 1930s. McIntire, Jones, and Rice admired the zeal with which the first generation of fundamentalists had battled theological modernism and they believed that those battles still needed to be fought. They did not shy away from conflict; they relished it. The numerical strength of the type of fundamentalism associated with men such as McIntire, Jones, and Rice should not be exaggerated, but it did win the allegiance of millions of Americans.

Another variety of conservative Protestants often associated with fundamentalism—the form associated with so-called evangelicals such as Carl Henry and Billy Graham—was, in some respects, a reaction *against* the perceived excesses of the fundamentalists of the 1920s and 1930s. For that reason and for others, evangelicals such as Graham and Henry made a point of *not* labeling themselves fundamentalists. They preferred to call themselves neo-evangelicals or evangelicals. Of course, evangelicals such as Henry and Graham embraced all the doctrines that they saw as fundamental to the Christian faith, and many of them had strong links to the fundamentalists of the 1920s and 1930s. But evangelicals such as Graham and Henry believed that the fundamentalists of those earlier years had made a number of strategic mistakes. Those mistakes were enumerated in books such as Henry's *The Uneasy Conscience of Modern Fundamentalism.*

Evangelicals tended to think of men such as McIntire, Jones, and Rice as rigid, extreme, and cantankerous. They liked to think of themselves as flexible, moderate, and irenic. Evangelicals insisted, with good reason, that on some issues there was a world of difference between fundamentalists such as McIntire, Jones, and Rice and themselves. But many of the distinctions between the two groups were lost on observers. Outsiders often labeled both groups fundamentalists.[10] Thus, the successes of evangelicals such as Graham and Henry were often interpreted as signs of fundamentalism's continuing strength. And of course, those successes were considerable. In the late 1970s, very few, if any, religious leaders in the United States could match Graham's popularity or influence, and it was obvious why he had come to be known as "America's pastor."[11]

Evangelicals and fundamentalists were not, of course, the only two groups of conservative Protestants in the United States. Members of many other groups—the Assemblies of God, the Church of the Nazarene, the National Baptist Convention, the Church of Christ, and the Missouri Synod of the Lutheran Church, for example—had relatively few direct links to the fundamentalist movement of the 1920s and 1930s. These conservative Protestants, unlike evangelicals, did not have to make a conscious effort to distance themselves from fundamentalism; they had never been strongly attached to it in the first place. While the members of these other groups of conservative Protestants seldom called themselves fundamentalists, outsiders often labeled them that way. Indeed, during the 1960s and 1970s, many outsiders frequently used the fundamentalist label to refer to almost any group within American Protestantism that was not firmly committed to the tenets of liberal Christianity. If one adhered to this practice, then fundamentalism was alive and well in America in the 1970s. It seemed that fundamentalists were everywhere you looked.

In the 1970s, the role fundamentalists played in the political realm was particularly conspicuous: they helped create a movement—the so-called New Christian Right—that transformed American politics. The leaders of the New Christian Right, people such as James Dobson, Pat Robertson, and Jerry Falwell, emphasized the importance of limiting secular humanism's influence on the government and of putting Godly men in positions of power. The leaders of the New Christian Right worked to ease restrictions on prayer in public schools and to ban homosexuals from teaching in those schools. They tried to prevent the Internal Revenue Service from revoking the tax-exempt status of Christian schools and colleges (Bob Jones University, for example) that practiced forms of segregation outlawed by the civil rights laws of the 1960s. They worked to defeat the Equal Rights Amendment and to overturn *Roe v. Wade*. To many moderates, liberals, and leftists, it seemed as if the leaders of the

New Christian Right were convinced that everything that had happened in America since about 1956 or so was bad. They seemed determined to put an end to progress. It almost seemed as though they wanted to find a way to go backward in time.

The leaders of the New Christian Right have sometimes exaggerated the movement's power. So have its critics. But its significance should not be minimized. The New Christian Right helped create a large bloc of poor and middle-class whites who were suspicious of the policies and candidates of the Democratic Party and who helped make the South a bastion of Republican strength. Without the backing of the New Christian Right, Republicans would have not had as much influence as they have had in the U.S. Congress in recent decades. Had they not enjoyed the support of the New Christian Right, Ronald Reagan, George H. W. Bush, and George W. Bush might not have been elevated to the White House.[12]

Many of the leaders of the New Christian Right were closely identified with some form of conservative Protestantism. And many of them—including Jerry Falwell—wore the fundamentalist label as a badge of honor. Beginning around 1976, Falwell began to receive a fair amount of press attention. By 1979, journalists were far more interested in him than they were in McIntire, Jones, or Rice. By then Falwell was, for many Americans, the embodiment of fundamentalism and its political power.

There is good reason to suppose that if Americans had not been so deeply interested in the political power of fundamentalists such as Falwell or so concerned about it, they might not have relied on the concept of fundamentalism to try to make sense of the Iranian Revolution. But Falwell and his co-religionists were very much on Americans' minds in the late 1970s and early 1980s. When Americans tried to understand the Iranian Revolution, noting how much Khomeini and Falwell had in common seemed like the obvious place to start.[13]

Going Back to Parsons

The similarities between Falwell and Khomeini were central to Martin Marty's "Fundamentalism Reborn: Faith and Fanaticism." The article, which was intended for a broad audience, was illustrated with photographs of Khomeini's face and an image of Falwell standing at a microphone clutching a Bible. At the very beginning of "Fundamentalism Reborn," Marty noted that before the outbreak of the Iranian Revolution, many Americans believed that religion was of no importance in shaping the modern world. That belief was hard to reconcile with television reports about what was happening in Iran. On their TV screens, Americans had seen millions of Muslims, linked by a "fanatic loyalty to fierce Shi'ite Islam" and by a deep allegiance to a "scowling Ayatollah," take to the streets to overthrow the government of one of America's most important allies in the Middle East. Less than a year later, Americans watched militants storm the American embassy and take scores of Americans hostage. "Embarrassment," Marty said, "turned to terror."[14]

Marty argued that Khomeini's followers had a great deal in common with the militant Christian fundamentalists who lived in the United States. He said that "meanness" was the distinguishing characteristic of Protestant fundamentalists in the United States: they were people who took satisfaction in scowling. Marty associated fundamentalists with fanaticism and self-righteousness. He believed that they were engaged in a crusade against humanism and liberal religion and against evangelical Christians—such as Billy Graham—who were unwilling to excoriate liberals and humanists. American fundamentalists were to be found in organizations such as the Religious Round Table and the Moral Majority, Marty said. They controlled a large proportion of the nation's Christian radio and television stations. With the help of direct-mail consultants such as Richard Viguerie, fundamentalists had created mammoth fund-raising networks; they were better funded, Marty said, than either the Democratic or the Republican Party. Under the leadership of men such as Jerry Falwell and Pat Robertson, fundamentalists had achieved great political power. They had already unseated two U.S. senators, and they had the means to consign other legislators to "political oblivion." When he listened to the harangues of Protestant fundamentalists in America, Marty wrote, he could hear "echoes" of the pronouncements the militants in Iran had made.[15]

Marty tried to use the terms "fundamentalist," "fundamentalists," and "fundamentalism" with a certain amount of precision. He noted that many scholars with special expertise in Islam argued that it made no sense to call Muslims fundamentalists. He admitted that their argument could not be dismissed out of hand. He also asserted that it was important to remember that not everyone who was called a fundamentalist really was one in the strict sense of the term.[16] He said, for instance, that although John Paul II was sometimes classified as a fundamentalist and although the pontiff really did have something in common with men such as Khomeini and Falwell, it was not helpful to apply the fundamentalist label to him.[17] But the range of movements that Marty saw as expressions of fundamentalism—or at least of phenomena that were very similar to fundamentalism—was quite remarkable. Conservative Roman Catholics who insisted on "clinging to the Latin Mass" were fundamentalists. Some Russian Pentecostals were fundamentalists. So were people such as Alexander Solzhenitsyn who were devoted to a "rigid Eastern Orthodox outlook." Some of the "Hindu fanatics" in India were fundamentalists, as were some of the orthodox Jews who lived in Israel and in settlements on the West Bank. Some of the Muslims in Saudi Arabia—those, for example, who wanted to overthrow the Saudi regime and replace it with one that better accorded with traditional Muslim ideals—were fundamentalists. So were the members of some of Japan's "Buddhist sects."[18]

Marty observed that in recent years, strong religious movements had sprouted up throughout the world, most of them "militantly antimodern," "fanatical," and contemptuous of the principle of "separation of church and state." Under the leadership of men such as Falwell and Khomeini, these fundamentalist movements had gained numerous adherents. They seemed to be reshaping the world. All over the globe, "religious recalcitrants" were on the march.[19] Marty argued that these movements were in large part a "sociopsychological" reaction to modernity.[20] People who wanted to understand them would do well to consult the insights of Talcott Parsons.

Drawing on Parsons's work, Marty argued that fundamentalism ought to be understood as an irrational backlash against modernity. In the 1960s, he said, it seemed clear that the world was headed toward modernity. Secularization was on the advance. The most prominent forms of religion had been deeply influenced by liberalism and rationality. In that decade, it seemed as if religion would have to accommodate itself to modernity or watch itself be confined to the margins of society. But in the early 1980s, Marty said, the forms of religiosity associated with liberalism and rationality seemed to be losing power. In many parts of the world, fundamentalists were gaining ground. In the United States, they were making a determined effort to alter America's political system. In Iran, they had toppled one government and created another one.

Marty said that in order to understand fundamentalism's power, people needed to think about modernization and the people who found that process troubling. He explained that the process of modernization, especially under regimes such as that associated with the shah of Iran, is often experienced as disruptive. It creates a world in which facts and values have been torn asunder and life feels "all chopped up" and "too full of choices." In its wake, people experience a "hunger for wholeness." The coming of modernity makes many men and women feel uneasy, and fundamentalism builds on that unease. At base, it is a militant attack on modernity and on the people associated with it.[21]

Although many of the developments Marty discussed in "Fundamentalism Reborn" left him feeling apprehensive, the overall tone of the article was not especially pessimistic. Marty assured his readers that while it was clear that fundamentalists were on the march, it was also quite possible that a defensive alliance could thwart their attacks. The alliance Marty envisioned had two chief components: "humanists" and "open-minded theists" committed to the same ideals as Pope John XXIII, Mohandas Gandhi, Abraham Joshua Heschel, and Martin Luther King Jr. If such an alliance could be created, Marty argued, it was possible that the future would not have to be ceded to religious fanatics such as Falwell and Khomeini. Modernity and the forms of religiosity amenable to it might still carry the day.

When read as a polemic, "Fundamentalism Reborn" is not a difficult text to understand. Marty was warning the readers of the *Saturday Review* about the dangers of religious fanaticism and he was asking them to consider the possibility that people who were religious in reasonable ways and people who were not religious at all could form working alliances that would defend the world from the crusades religious fanatics were mounting. But when read as an attempt to make sense of contemporary religious movements, "Fundamentalism Reborn" is a puzzling text. Marty was surely aware of the carefully modulated interpretation of fundamentalism Sandeen had presented in *Roots of Fundamentalism*. The book had been widely reviewed and it had quickly become the standard scholarly interpretation of Protestant fundamentalism. But Marty's article advanced an interpretation of fundamentalism that was very far removed from Sandeen's. Marty's interpretation of religion in the United States and of religion throughout the world seemed to grow out of an uncritical acceptance of the ideas of Parsons, whose reputation had taken a beating by 1980. Parsons's belief that he knew exactly what modernity and progress were had begun to seem overconfident, hubristic even. By 1980, it was a commonplace in some scholarly circles that what was sometimes called "modernization" could also be labeled "imperialism." This point was so obvious that a good many college undergraduates could, by 1980, make it at the drop of a hat.

So "Fundamentalism Reborn" was, in some respects, extremely old-fashioned. But it was also pathbreaking. The arguments sketched out in the piece would be fleshed out over and over again in the next thirty-five years. Marty might well have gotten fundamentalism wrong in 1980, and indeed, one of my conversations with him made me suspect that he is not especially proud of "Fundamentalism Reborn." But if Marty got fundamentalism wrong, he did so in an extremely influential way. Thirty-five years later, his ideas about fundamentalism are still echoing in both popular and scholarly conversations.

A Global Syndrome

Holy Terror: The Fundamentalist War on America's Freedoms in Religion, Politics, and Our Private Lives, one of the first books that presented a set of ideas similar to Marty's, reads like a muckraking exposé. As journalists Flo Conway and Jim Siegelman presented fundamentalism, it was not simply a primitive form of religion; it was a noxious "syndrome." People who had been influenced by that syndrome embraced all sorts of ridiculous beliefs. They also subscribed to preposterous conspiracy theories. Many fundamentalists had concluded, for example, that secular humanists had begun a ruthless campaign to take over the United States. That was simply false. A campaign to take over the country really had been launched, but the people who were directing it, Conway and Siegelman argued, were not secular humanists. They were the fundamentalists themselves.[22]

As they went about trying to conquer the United States, fundamentalists used a set of techniques they had borrowed from the world of advertising. Fundamentalists turned out to be hucksters for Jesus. But the range of techniques that fundamentalists were willing to employ went far beyond the bounds of hucksterism. They had developed sophisticated forms of "mind control," and they used those strategies with merciless efficiency.[23] Fundamentalist leaders insisted that their followers submit themselves unreservedly to the will of Jesus. That insistence enabled the leaders to turn rank-and-file fundamentalists into obedient pawns. Becoming a fundamentalist was, in many respects, just like joining a combative religious cult.[24]

Conway and Siegelman told their readers that it was almost impossible to exaggerate the scope of the changes fundamentalists wanted to bring about: "master plots" such as the one fundamentalists had developed were simply outside "the American experience."[25] In order to understand what fundamentalists were up to, one had to look for analogues in other nations: to Russia and the Bolsheviks and to Germany and the Nazis.[26] And the fundamentalists' goals were, when fully understood, even more sweeping than those of the Nazis. Fundamentalists wanted to control the heart and mind of every single human being over whom they held sway. They were determined to control every aspect of American culture and every aspect of American society. Churches, governments, the media, personal relationships would all, the religious fanatics hoped, be controlled by fundamentalists.[27]

There were a great many indications, Conway and Siegel asserted, that fundamentalists had already made great strides toward reaching their ultimate goal. Men such as Jerry Falwell, Bunker Hunt, Bill Bright, and Pat Robertson had attracted millions of followers who were willing to do their bidding. Propaganda was being disseminated, funds were being raised, and adversaries were being bullied into submission. Politicians who dared to resist the fundamentalists were run out of office; those who were eager to cooperate with fundamentalists were being put in control of the U.S. government. Ronald Reagan's victory over Jimmy Carter was a case in point. Under Reagan's leadership, the U.S. government had begun to construct a polity based on a set of blueprints that fundamentalists had drawn up.[28]

Conway and Siegelman told their readers that it was a mistake to think of fundamentalism as an exclusively Christian phenomenon. They said that their research had convinced them that fundamentalism was a far more expansive phenomenon than people had previously believed: it was a *worldwide* syndrome that grew out of human beings' resistance to "modernization and social change." Although Conway and Siegelman admitted that there were some differences among the various expressions of fundamentalism, they insisted that Christian, Muslim, Jewish, Hindu, and Sikh fundamentalists were all hostile to freedom and democracy. All fundamentalists were devoted to the "subjugation" of other religious traditions. They all wanted to impose their religious "beliefs and social values" on anyone who disagreed with them. Wherever it reared its ugly head, fundamentalism created terrible problems.

Conway and Siegelman were convinced that both Hindu and Sikh fundamentalists were involved in dangerous plots to take control of the government of India. They believed that Jewish fundamentalists had come to exercise an extraordinary amount of power in Israel, using their political clout to win special privileges for themselves and to dictate the rules that governed what all Israelis could and could not do on the Sabbath. They also asserted that many Muslims had embraced fundamentalism. According to them, fundamentalists had overthrown the shah of Iran and put Ayatollah Khomeini in charge of the Iranian government and within months of the fundamentalist takeover of Iran, fundamentalist influence had spread throughout much of the rest of the Middle East. Fundamentalists were on the march in Saudi Arabia and in several other Gulf States. In Egypt, fundamentalists had succeeded in killing the head of state. Conway and Siegelman warned their readers that the things that Islamic fundamentalism had done in Iran, Israel, and India were indicative of what Christian fundamentalists wanted to do in America. In nations such as Iran, Americans could "see a forecast" of what the United States was in danger of becoming.[29]

A Foreign Policy Challenge

It would be hard to argue that *Holy Terror* was anything like an attempt to present an evenhanded analysis of global fundamentalism. In fact, attempts to present evenhanded analyses of global fundamentalism were relatively rare in the mid-1980s. But there were some: from time to time, fundamentalism was used as something akin to a neutral category of analysis. Consider, for example, the congressional hearings on Islamic fundamentalism that were held in the summer of 1985. They were sponsored by a subcommittee of the House Committee on Foreign Affairs and chaired by a Democratic member of Congress from Indiana, Lee Hamilton. The transcripts of the hearings do not indicate that the people who participated in them were simply using them to create a bogeyman. They suggest rather that members of the U.S. Congress were troubled by developments in the Islamic nations of the world and that they were quite willing to turn to experts for help in trying to understand what was going on.

Islamic fundamentalism, as the term was used in the course of the hearings, was a rather elastic concept. Indeed, the people who participated in the hearings sometimes confessed that they were having difficulty figuring out what fundamentalism meant. During the course of the hearings, the term "fundamentalism" sometimes seemed to be used as shorthand for "religious movements that are hard to understand and that might transform the Middle East." Most of the questions that the representatives who took an active role in shaping the hearings (Harry Reid, Tom Lantos, Stephen Solarz, Benjamin Gilman, and Lawrence Smith, for example) asked seemed to be real questions, not rhetorical ones. The questions sounded like honest attempts to learn about the relationship between religion and politics in the Muslim world. What would an organizational chart of Islamic fundamentalism look like? Are there any important differences, one member asked, between Sunni fundamentalists and Shiite fundamentalists? What are the chances that fundamentalists will get control of the Egyptian State? Might the fundamentalists lose control of Iran when Khomeini dies? Are fundamentalists opposed to the West per se or only to certain policies Western nations had adopted? Are some forms of fundamentalism somewhat compatible with democratic values?[30]

To get answers to those sorts of questions, the subcommittee turned to seven expert witnesses. One of the experts, Hermann Eilts, had served as an ambassador to Egypt; another, Gary Sick, had worked as a White House aide. Two of the experts, Augustus Norton and William Olson, were scholars who worked for the U.S. Army. Another of the expert witnesses was John Esposito, a religious studies professor who had done some consulting work for the State Department. The other two experts, Fouad Ajami and Shahrough Akhavi, were political scientists.[31]

Fundamentalism, as one of the scholars who testified before the committee defined it, was simply "a renewal of Islam in personal and public life." Its manifestations were said to include an increased interest in religious observance, "calls for the implementation of Islamic law," and the "proliferation of religious publications and media programming." Fundamentalists, the scholar asserted, believed that Islam was a "total way of life." They were convinced that Islamic beliefs and practices ought to suffuse political life as well as the private sphere. In order to understand Islamic fundamentalism, another scholar asserted, we have to accept the fact that many Muslims believe that there ought not to be any wall of separation between politics and religion.[32]

Fundamentalism was not, the witnesses emphasized, a "monolithic entity." Rather, it was "a multifaceted admixture of parties, societies and movements with a correspondingly diverse collection of goals, programs, and motives." The witnesses told the subcommittee that it was extraordinarily difficult to make meaningful generalizations about who fundamentalists were and what they wanted to do. In order to make sense of fundamentalism, one often had to avoid advancing theories about fundamentalism in general and instead embrace specificity and particularity.[33]

The men who testified at the hearing said there was no reason to conclude that *all* Islamic fundamentalists were hostile to the West. Some fundamentalists had an essentially anti-Western outlook, but others did not. Some fundamentalists were simply opposed to some of the policies Western nations had adopted. Under some circumstances, they suggested, the United States ought to consider the possibility of abandoning the policies to which the fundamentalists objected. The United States might, for example, consider distancing itself from Israel's ongoing efforts to place Jewish settlers in the occupied territories. And the United States might also want to consider cutting back on the support it offered to secular regimes in the Middle East that were clearly corrupt, authoritarian, and incapable of meeting even the most basic needs of the people over whom they ruled. Doing that might decrease fundamentalists' hostility to the United States.[34]

Some fundamentalists—Iran's Akbar Hashemi Rafsanjani, for example—seemed to be fairly open minded and relatively pragmatic. On some issues, fundamentalists such as Rafsanjani were willing to cooperate with the U.S. government. So it would be a mistake, some of the witnesses asserted, for the United States to decide that it should consistently oppose all forms of fundamentalism. Under some circumstances, the United States should be willing to negotiate with fundamentalists and attempt to find common ground. And there might well be times and places when it would make sense for the United States to accept fundamentalists' gaining control of particular nation-states. Some of the experts went so far as to say that when it became clear that the majority of a country's inhabitants were committed to moving their nation away from secular norms and toward Islamic ones, the United States should be willing to let the will of the people determine the direction in which that nation would move.[35] Given the dreadful fears that had been kindled by the rise of global fundamentalism, the witnesses gave remarkably level-headed advice. In fact, the overall tenor of the experts' testimony was surprisingly irenic. Few texts that were published in the mid-1980s exhibit comparable attempts to present evenhanded analyses of fundamentalism.

I certainly do not want to imply that most of the people involved in the hearings were apologists for fundamentalism. They weren't. The hearings were based on the assumption that fundamentalists were gaining influence throughout the Muslim world *and* that the rise of fundamentalism would create a set of problems that the US government should address. It was assumed that the existence of Islamic fundamentalism would make it more difficult for the United States to advance its interests in the Middle East and that fundamentalism posed a threat to global peace.[36] In the course of the hearings, fundamentalism was linked to kidnappings, hijackings, murders, and plots to assassinate the president of the Unites States and was described as mindless radicalism run amok.[37] Fundamentalists were said to be so full of hatred for the United States that no amount of "bargaining" with them could ever put an end to their hostility to the United States.[38] In addition, fundamentalists were not, it was said, reasonable men who could be placated by changes in U.S. foreign policy. Fundamentalists did not hate what the United States *did*; they hated what the United States *was*. They despised the fundamental values that Americans hold dear.[39]

Conclusion

Although the members of Congress who participated in the hearings had almost nothing to say about Jewish, Hindu, or Buddhist fundamentalism, we cannot be certain that all of them believed that fundamentalism was limited exclusively to Islam and Christianity. It is entirely possible that none of them believed that. By the time the hearings were held, a great many Americans had become convinced that expressions of fundamentalism could be found in all the world's great religious traditions. By 1985, the existence of global fundamentalism was well on its way to being regarded as a self-evident truth.

Shortly after the hearings concluded, the Library of Congress created a new classification number, BL238, under which books about global fundamentalism could be filed. Since 1985, books on global fundamentalism have appeared at a steady clip. In some libraries, simply leafing through all the books filed under BL238 can now take the better part of a week. Reading through them carefully would take months or years. And in the past three decades, many of the books filed in the reference section of the nation's libraries have been revised to make it clear that fundamentalism is not an exclusively Christian phenomenon. The article on fundamentalism in the current edition of the *Encyclopædia Britannica* notes, for instance, that although fundamentalism was once "used exclusively to refer to American Protestants," it is now used more broadly. "Many of the major religions of the world," the article asserts, "may be said to have fundamentalist movements."[40]

One can make a case for saying that the concept of global fundamentalism has now been so firmly lodged in our minds that we can no longer make a conscious choice about whether or not to rely on it. Peter van der Veer, a distinguished anthropologist, has argued that it is simply impossible to discard global fundamentalism. "A powerful language or discourse is not," he argues, "something one can choose to reject or accept; it can be critiqued or deconstructed, but that will not make it go away."[41] Van der Veer may well be right. But I am not entirely convinced that he is. In the past thirty years, a great many thoughtful women and men have concluded that far more is lost than gained when global fundamentalism is invoked. Some of the arguments against the concept of global fundamentalism are quite strong, and I think there is a good chance that those arguments will eventually win out. But it is impossible to know for sure.

We are on firmer ground when we talk about the past. It is not difficult to say what it was that people did with the concept of global fundamentalism after it was invented. They used it for many different purposes, chief of which was conjuring up a dangerous other. That conjuring and its consequences are explored in the next chapter and in the conclusion.

8

Zenith

The previous chapter looked at the history of antifundamentalism in the late 1960s, the 1970s, and the early 1980s, paying special attention to the period 1980 to 1985. Between 1965 and 1985 the concept of fundamentalism was reinvented; it was made far less specific and far more elastic and was transformed into a category that was broad enough to accommodate movements that could be found in many different religious traditions. Increasingly, fundamentalism was thought of as a global phenomenon rather than one that was limited to North American Protestantism. The present chapter, which focuses on the years between 1986 and 2006, examines some of the things that Americans did with the concept of fundamentalism in the two decades after it was reinvented.

One of those things was to use it as a way of trying to make sense of Islam. That is not surprising. After all, fundamentalism was reinvented in part in order to try to make sense of events such as the Iranian Revolution. Since the late 1970s, Americans had repeatedly suggested that Muslims were the sort of people who were particularly likely to succumb to the siren call of fundamentalism. This chapter begins with a consideration of Bernard Lewis's 1990 article, "The Roots of Muslim Rage."[1] It's a dazzling text that nicely encapsulates the arguments of a thinker who played an important role in shaping how Americans thought about Islamic fundamentalism.

But Americans also used the concept of fundamentalism to analyze Jews whom they thought of as zealots or fanatics. A book-length analysis of such Jews—Israel Shahak and Norton Mezvinsky's *Jewish Fundamentalism in Israel*—appeared in 1999.[2] Its interpretation of fundamentalism is examined in this chapter. So is the interpretation of fundamentalism that Bill Moyers presented in 2006 in "9/11 and God's Sport."[3] Moyers wanted his readers to consider the possibility that the very nature of monotheism guarantees that Judaism, Islam, and Christianity all predispose their adherents to violence. It is possible, Moyers's article implied, that violent fundamentalism is simply monotheism taken to its logical extreme. *Jewish Fundamentalism in Israel* and "9/11 and God's Sport" both present extremely dark interpretations of global fundamentalism. Both emphasize the threats fundamentalists pose to nonfundamentalists. Neither text is presented in a way that could possibly be construed as impartial or evenhanded, and neither text is especially scholarly. Thousands of similar discussions of fundamentalism appeared in the period 1986 to 2006.

A good many scholarly examinations of global fundamentalism made their way into print in those years. Indeed, a case could be made that the period 1989 to 1995 constituted a sort of golden age for the scholarly study of fundamentalism. The first major book-length scholarly analysis of global fundamentalism, Bruce Lawrence's *Defenders of God: The Fundamentalist Revolt against the Modern Age*, appeared in 1989. Two years later the University of Chicago Press published *Fundamentalisms Observed*, the first major publication produced by the Fundamentalism Project directed by Marty and Appleby. By the time the project drew to a close in 1995, four more mammoth explorations of global fundamentalism had been published. Each volume received a good deal of attention, much of it quite favorable. None of the scholarly publications on global fundamentalism that appeared after 1995 sparked as much commentary as those produced by the Fundamentalism Project, and there are some indications that scholars' enthusiasm for the concept of global fundamentalism had already begun to wane by the time the Fundamentalism Project came to a close. Nevertheless, although scholarly interest in global fundamentalism might well have begun to decline during the 1990s, it certainly did not disappear.

In this chapter I also explore two important scholarly articles on global fundamentalism: James Davison Hunter's "Fundamentalism in Its Global Contours," which was published in 1990, and Martin Riesebrodt's "Fundamentalism and the Resurgence of Religion," published in 2000.[4] Taken together, the two texts reveal some of the ways scholars used global fundamentalism during and just after the era when the scholarly study of global fundamentalism was at its zenith.

Responding to Humiliation

In 1990, the National Endowment for the Humanities gave Bernard Lewis, a professor emeritus of Near Eastern Studies at Princeton, one of the greatest honors the federal government can bestow: it invited him to deliver that year's Jefferson Lecture. A revised version of the lecture was published a few months later in *The Atlantic* under the title "The Roots of Muslim Rage." In the lecture, Lewis made a point of expressing his respect for Islam. He said that Islam had "brought comfort and peace to countless millions of men and women" and that it had "given dignity and meaning" to many people who had to live "drab and impoverished lives." Islam had also produced, in certain times and in certain places, a spirit of tolerance.[5] But it was also true, Lewis told his audience, that Islam sometimes produced feelings of hatred. That was what was happening in the contemporary era. The Muslim world was seething with hatred, and much of that hatred was directed at the West. Fundamentalism was a powerful expression of that rage. It gave "aim and form to the otherwise aimless and formless anger of the Muslim masses" and provided Muslims with a language they could use to protest against the forces that had "robbed them of their beliefs, aspirations, [and] dignity."[6]

Lewis told his audience that the fury of the Muslim people was not, in the final analysis, a rational reaction to the specific policies that the United States and the other Western powers had adopted. Muslim rage, Lewis argued, was rooted in a historic rivalry that stretched back to the seventh century. From that time through the present day, Muslims have believed that they are locked in a struggle against the West. That belief was far from groundless. There really was a sense in which the differences between the Muslim world and the West were profound and unbridgeable. It really was true that those huge differences had inevitably produced a titanic "clash of civilizations."[7]

One of the fundamental differences between Muslim civilization and Western civilization, Lewis said, had to do with the relationship between religion and politics. The West, Lewis argued, had been decisively shaped by Christians' sense that a distinction can be made between political institutions and religious ones. Christians had always recognized that it was possible in theory to separate the things that belonged to Caesar from the things that belonged to God. Christians believed that it was entirely possible to have two chains of authority—one ecclesiastical, the other civil—within a single locale. And in modern times Christians had embraced the idea that church and state ought to be separate and distinct. They had come to see the advantages of creating nation-states in which no ecclesiastical body received any special privileges. In the modern West people were free to join whatever religious community they wanted without incurring any penalty. Indeed, they were free to decide that they did not want to align themselves with any religious community whatsoever. The West had come to cherish religious freedom. The Muslim world, on the other hand, was profoundly hostile to it. Muslims tended to view religious freedom as it was understood in the West as a move away from the ideals of the Qur'an.[8] From the perspective of a Muslim fundamentalist, Lewis implied, religious freedom was not a sign of progress. It was a sign of moral decline.

As Lewis told the story, decline and humiliation were at the heart of fundamentalists' hatred of the West. In their early encounters with the West, Muslims had often triumphed. From the seventh century through the seventeenth, Muslims tended to be on the offensive and the West often seemed to be in decline. Since the eighteenth century, however, Muslim power had been on the wane. Westerners had won control of the Americas and were able to establish dominance in Africa and much of Asia. The West had eventually succeeded in bringing the whole world—including the entire Muslim world—"within its orbit." One of the results of the triumph of the West, Lewis said, was a widespread sense of "humiliation" in the Muslim world. The heirs of "an old, proud, and dominant civilization" sensed that they had been "overtaken, overborne, and overwhelmed by those whom they regarded as their inferiors."[9]

In order to dramatize this point, Lewis used a trope that suggested that all the Muslims in the world had had a similar set of experiences. "The Muslim," Lewis explained, had to give up on his dream of conquering the entire world. He had to watch as foreign ideas and laws invaded his country. And the Muslim had even found that "his mastery in his own house" was no longer secure. His power was challenged by "emancipated women and rebellious children." Without pausing to consider the complexities that might arise from the fact that not all Muslims are adult males, Lewis went on to assert that the Muslim found these challenges to his way of life to be unendurable. Forces that he could not understand had undercut the Muslim's dominance. The losses he had endured filled the Muslim with rage.[10]

The primary reason that Muslim fundamentalists hated the West, Lewis suggested, was quite straightforward. They experienced the triumph of the West as a personal humiliation. They were determined to find a way of striking back against a rival civilization, and their hostility to the West was the defining characteristic of the fundamentalists. Fundamentalism was, in some respects, simply one example of a much broader phenomenon: anti-Westernism. Lewis noted that the West was often said to have been complicit in all sorts of evil, such as racism, patriarchy, tyranny, exploitation, and imperialism. Lewis said that such charges contained a grain of truth. But it was simply wrong to conclude that Westerners ought to take special responsibility for such "heinous" behavior. All "members of the human race" were subject to such charges, and all were in some sense guilty. The West was not uniquely sinful. Indeed, in many respects the record of the West was quite good when measured against those of other world civilizations. Westerners had certainly been involved in imperialism, but so had Arabs, Mongols, and Ottomans. Westerners had been involved in slavery, but they were the first to realize that slavery was a moral evil and were the first to abolish it. The West was not especially wicked. It was, in fact, responsible for much of human progress.[11]

Given all that the West had accomplished, Lewis implied, fundamentalists' hostility to it was profoundly misguided. Fundamentalists were dangerous people. They had something in common with Communists and Nazis.[12]

Confronting Modernity

In the late 1980s and early 1990s, many Americans were struck by the magnitude of the fundamentalist threat. They believed that world events demonstrated that fundamentalism's influence was waxing rather than waning. In 1988, the Roman Catholic Church concluded that the actions taken by Marcel Lefebvre, an archbishop who fiercely opposed efforts to liberalize the Church, were so extreme that the Church had no choice but to excommunicate him. A year later, in Iran, Ayatollah Khomeini issued a fatwa against Salman Rushdie, who had written a novel that Khomeini judged blasphemous. Khomeini called for Rushdie's execution, and Rushdie went into hiding and remained there for nearly a decade. In 1991, a suicide bomber affiliated with the Tamil Tigers assassinated Rajiv Gandhi, a former prime minister of India. In 1993, terrorists planted a bomb in the garage underneath the World Trade Center in New York; the explosion killed six people and injured more than a thousand. That same year, in Waco, Texas, a conflict between governmental officials and leaders of a small Christian group called the Branch Davidians resulted in a fire that killed eighty of the group's members. In 1995, Israel's prime minister, Yitzhak Rabin, was assassinated by a young man named Yigal Amir. In the eyes of some Israelis, the assassin became a national hero.[13]

None of these events captured Americans' imaginations in quite the same way that the Iranian Revolution had. And none of them *had* to be interpreted as indications of the power of a single global phenomenon. Indeed, the connections between some of the events were rather tenuous. The motives of the assassin who killed Gandhi, for example, and those of the man who killed Rabin were worlds apart. Nevertheless, many Americans understood both assassinations to be indications of the power of global fundamentalism. Many of them believed that the Catholic Church's clampdown on Lefebvre and Rushdie's withdrawal from public life were reactions to the growing fundamentalist threat; many saw both the explosion at the World Trade Center and the conflagration in Waco as signs of fundamentalists' predilection to create violent confrontations between themselves and their opponents.

In the era when "The Roots of Muslim Rage" appeared, many Americans—including a good many politicians—were looking for expert advice on fundamentalism, and scholars such as Lewis were more than willing to provide it. In the late 1980s and early 1990s, scholars paid more attention to fundamentalism than they ever had before. Some of texts on global fundamentalism that scholars produced in those years were terribly weak; many others were mediocre. Nearly all of them were vulnerable to the sort of criticisms that I discussed in the first two chapters of this book. But a number of the texts that scholars produced in the late 1980s and early 1990s—including, of course, a good percentage of those produced by scholars connected with the Fundamentalism Project—were quite sound. And some of them were absolutely stellar.

James Davison Hunter's "Fundamentalism in Its Global Contours," which appeared in 1990, was one such text. It reminds us how useful a tool the concept of global fundamentalism could seem to be when wielded by first-rate scholars. When he wrote the article, Hunter was still a relatively young man. Although he was not nearly as famous as Lewis, he had already written two important sociological accounts of evangelical Protestantism and eventually would go on to become one of the nation's most highly respected sociologists of religion.

Hunter's article focused in large part on the relationship between fundamentalism and orthodoxy. He argued that all fundamentalists believed that the religious beliefs and practices to which they adhered were a "basic, unaltered orthodoxy." Hunter was sure that fundamentalists' self-understanding was simply erroneous. The differences between fundamentalism and orthodoxy were actually quite stark. Orthodoxy was a kind of consensus that had been arrived at over the course of much time. It was a cultural system whose authority and legitimacy derived from its "unfaltering continuity with truth as originally revealed—truth in its primitive and purest expression."[14]

Fundamentalism, Hunter wrote, was produced by orthodoxy's confrontation with—and transformation by—modernity. He argued that the coming of modernity had left religious groups with only three real options. One option was to revise inherited traditions in order to bring them into accord with modernity. (This often involved liberalization and desacralization.) Another option—the one groups such as the Amish pursued—was to withdraw insofar as was possible to "a closed total world" made up solely of the faithful. The third and final option—the one fundamentalists pursued—was to fight back against modernity.

As they fought that fight, fundamentalists relied heavily on literal readings of sacred texts. The Gush Emunim insisted on reading the Torah literally, and they were certain that such a reading demonstrated that their political and religious ideals had been sanctioned by God. Protestant fundamentalists maintained that the Christian scriptures were the inerrant Word of God and were deeply committed to a "hermeneutic of literalism." An insistence that the Qur'an was made up exclusively of "the literal dictations of the eternal thoughts of God" was one of the hallmarks of Islamic fundamentalism, Hunter wrote. And a literal reading of the Bhagavad Gita was a distinguishing characteristic of Hindu fundamentalism. Hindu fundamentalists—indeed, all fundamentalists—used a sacred text to establish "absolute standards of life and thought."[15]

Those standards, thus derived, enabled fundamentalists to escape—or at least to think that they had escaped—the ambiguities and complexities to which modernity and postmodernity had given rise. They also gave fundamentalists a very clear sense of the direction in which history *ought* to be moving. Fundamentalists all believed, Hunter said, either that history was not moving in the proper direction or that there was a real danger that it might start moving in the wrong direction in the very near future. Jewish fundamentalists, Hunter said, had been generally heartened by the recent course of history. They saw the hands of providence in both the establishment of the State of Israel and Israel's victory in the Six-Day War. But Jewish fundamentalists were also full of foreboding. They feared that in the coming years control of the West Bank might revert to Arabs, and they believed that such a reversion would thwart the will of God. Jewish fundamentalists were, Hunter said, motivated by a strong commitment to keeping history on track.[16]

Muslim fundamentalists believed that history had *already* gone terribly wrong. They were appalled by the West's triumph over Islam and believed that the power of the West made it difficult—even impossible, perhaps—for Muslims to control their own destiny. Islamic fundamentalists were determined to find a way to get history back on the proper path. Hindu fundamentalists also believed that history had gone terribly wrong, that previous generations of Hindus had failed to adhere to dharma, and that that failure had paved the way for Hindu subjugation. Hindu fundamentalists wanted to return to a pure form of Hindu culture; they were determined to make "history right again."[17]

Protestant fundamentalists in the United States, Hunter wrote, also believed that history had gone wrong. They were convinced that many Americans were no longer committed to the fundamental truths of the Christian gospel. They also were sure that American society exhibited a great many signs of moral decay: abortion was legal, public schools no longer encouraged students to engage in devotional activities, sex outside marriage was commonplace, and family life did not conform to the norms set forth in the Bible. Protestant fundamentalists in the United States believed that history "was going awry, and that it was up to the faithful followers of the gospel to make it right again." If the faithful succeeded in pushing history back into its proper course, then America might once again enjoy God's providential favor. The United States might once again become what God intended it to be.[18]

In Hunter's view, fundamentalists all believed that religion and politics should not be separate. Jewish fundamentalists hoped to transform the State of Israel into a theocracy. Hindu fundamentalists longed to take over the reins of power in India and then turn India into a nation that conformed to the norms of the Hindu religion. Muslim fundamentalists wanted to create societies in which political power and spiritual authority were both entrusted to a single person who occupied an office that was modeled after the leader of the caliphate. Christian fundamentalists longed for the day when the United States would be a Christian nation. They believed that it was completely appropriate to use the "machinery of the state" to suppress sinful behavior and promote righteousness.[19] Hunter asserted that there were strong links between fundamentalism and violence. The violent predilections of Protestant fundamentalists were, he said, largely a matter of rhetoric. Although Protestant fundamentalists often spoke about "spiritual warfare," they seldom resorted to the use of actual violence. But Hindu, Sikh, and Muslim fundamentalists were all quite willing to use literal violence to accomplish their ends. Those fundamentalists believed that believers ought to be willing to die—and to kill—in order to advance the interests of the godly. Jewish fundamentalists were likewise prone to violence. Indeed, some Jewish fundamentalists believed that God had commanded them to kill all Arabs—including women and children—who stood in the way of Israel's expansion to the borders that God had destined it to have.[20]

Hunter's analysis of global fundamentalism was not a comforting one. He argued that many fundamentalists were angry people who were not at all reluctant to resort to violence. Fundamentalists wanted to gain control of particular nation-states and use the power of those states to create societies that conformed to their own somewhat idiosyncratic notions of righteousness. Fundamentalists were also people who had failed to understand their relationship to the religious traditions to which they gave their loyalty. Fundamentalists thought they were staunch defenders of a timeless orthodox faith, but they were wrong. The faiths to which fundamentalists gave their allegiance were not immutable; they were forms of orthodoxy that been dramatically transformed by their encounter with modernity. Fundamentalists had thus convinced themselves that they were something they were not. Hunter's analysis seemed to suggest that fundamentalists were mistaken, belligerent, and determined to gain political power. They could not be trusted.

A Cultural Revolution

A particularly noteworthy aspect of "Fundamentalism in Its Global Contours" is Hunter's determination to present global fundamentalism as a hypothesis rather than as a fact. He noted that politicians, journalists, and pundits frequently used the term "fundamentalism" with considerable nonchalance. In popular discourse, the term was used to describe a remarkably heterogeneous collection of movements about which it was difficult to make any meaningful generalizations. Even if such generalizations were possible, there was good reason to doubt that calling those movements fundamentalist was the best way to make sense of them. Hunter noted that the concept of fundamentalism was deeply rooted in the particularities of American religious history and that it was entirely possible that scholars would eventually decide that it made no sense to call Muslims, Jews, Hindus, or Sikhs fundamentalists.[21]

In Hunter's view, although scholars who attempted to define and explore global fundamentalism were engaged in an experiment that might well fail, the experiment was nevertheless worth conducting. There really did seem to be some important similarities between Protestant fundamentalism in the United States and other religious movements throughout the world. The concept of global fundamentalism could perhaps prove to be the best way to make sense of those similarities. It might turn out to be the case that in spite of all the many problems associated with it, global fundamentalism might "actually have a certain utility."[22] Many other early scholarly explorations of global fundamentalism also presented the concept as a kind of experiment. Marty and Appleby, for instance, made a point of calling the conclusion to the first book to come out of the Fundamentalism Project "An Interim Report on a *Hypothetical* Family."[23]

Experiments can fail. Attempts to create new scientific theories can end up leading scholars into blind alleys, and I think that is what happened to the concept of global fundamentalism. For reasons that I considered in some detail in chapters 1 and 2, scholarly interest in exploring global fundamentalism seems to me to have declined steadily since 1995. Few genuinely novel ideas about global fundamentalism have been proposed since then. Fewer and fewer scholars have attempted to create coherent scholarly theories about the nature of global fundamentalism. Some scholars concluded that to search for such theories was "to fall prey to the rhetoric of anti-fundamentalists." To the people who adopted this perspective, it was clear that the rhetoric of politicians, religious leaders, and journalists who denounce fundamentalism could not be taken at face value. To them it seemed clear that the rhetoric of antifundamentalist discourse could not possibly produce material that could be used to build a general theory of fundamentalism. They concluded that the concept of global fundamentalism was based on partisan polemics and that it was naïve to believe that an objective, consistent, and convincing theory of fundamentalism could be constructed on such a foundation. Trying to construct such a theory was, they believed, a poor use of time.[24]

I am certainly not suggesting that scholarly interest in global fundamentalism has completely disappeared. It hasn't. Since the mid-1990s, a number of distinguished scholars—Gabriel Almond, R. Scott Appleby, Martin Riesebrodt, Malise Ruthven, and Emmanuel Sivan, for instance—have focused their attention on global fundamentalism. Some of the books and articles they have produced have been quite strong. Martin Riesebrodt's 2000 essay "Fundamentalism and the Resurgence of Religion" is a case in point. Riesebrodt, a highly respected sociologist of religion, presented an unusually thoughtful analysis of global fundamentalism and the people who joined fundamentalist movements. His account of global fundamentalism, like Hunter's, is an example of the scholarly study of global fundamentalism at its very best. Riesebrodt argued that fundamentalism ought to be regarded as a set of religious revitalization movements that had emerged in the wake of profound social changes. Those movements did not spring up in traditional societies; they developed in societies that had been transformed by secularization, professionalization, bureaucratization, industrialization, urbanization, and the growth of the market economy. Fundamentalist movements drew many of their adherents from the ranks of those who believed that those processes had produced social decline and moral decay. These movements had a special appeal for men and women who felt they had lost their cultural dominance. But, Riesebrodt argued, fundamentalism was by no means simply the religion of the dispossessed and the marginalized; it also had considerable appeal for people who were highly educated and economically secure.[25]

Riesebrodt said that a casual observer might conclude that the laymen and laywomen who joined fundamentalist movements were attaching themselves to a set of institutions and organizations that were dominated by clerics. Such a conclusion would be incorrect. Fundamentalism was not a top-down religion, nor was it an especially hierarchical one. Fundamentalist movements actually tended to shift power away from clergy and toward laypeople; indeed, fundamentalism's astounding ability to successfully mobilize lay energies accounted for a great deal of its vigor. Riesebrodt stated that a portion of the energy that was created by fundamentalism's mobilization of lay people flowed into political activity; fundamentalism sometimes made it possible for men and women who had previously been cut off from participation in political matters to exercise political agency. But it was very easy to overemphasize fundamentalists' interest in politics, Riesebrodt warned. He asserted that fundamentalism

> is not exclusively or even predominantly about political mobilization and influence. It is often much more centrally about the reshaping of the self through a pious life conduct and the development and cultivation of a specifically religious ethos. In other words, fundamentalist religiosity does not necessarily or primarily serve non-religious ends of economic betterment or political empowerment, but often defines ends which are pursued because of their believed inherent value, like being good, pious, or virtuous.[26]

Riesebrodt argued that fundamentalists' approach to living virtuous lives almost always involved a rejection of women's emancipation. Fundamentalists placed a very high value on the patriarchal family, believing that God had assigned women the role of raising children and that women's "natural sphere" was within the confines of domesticity. Fundamentalists also believed that the proper roles for men to play—protecting their families and providing the financial resources their wives and children required—had been fixed by God. Adhering to this divinely sanctioned gender dualism made it possible, fundamentalists believed, for women and men to live lives that honored God. But fundamentalist women who wanted to honor God did not have to passively accept inherited notions about how they ought to act. Women who became fundamentalists often ended up negotiating new social roles for themselves and tended to become more interested in political and religious matters. In some instances they even created what might be seen as a type of "indigenous religious feminism."[27]

Riesebrodt was well aware of the fact that fundamentalists often acted in ways that nonfundamentalists found irritating. And "Fundamentalism and the Resurgence of Religion" certainly left open the possibility that fundamentalists had a set of psychological proclivities—a tendency to see the world in Manichean terms, for instance—that were not especially helpful. But Riesebrodt's essay strongly suggests that he was genuinely impressed by some of the things that fundamentalists accomplished. They had fashioned modern communication networks that enabled them to disseminate a powerful critique of the modern world. They had established a formidable array of congregations, kindergartens, schools, and mutual aid societies. They had created vibrant communities that did not fully conform to the logic of the marketplace. Riesebrodt suggested that fundamentalists seemed to have successfully launched what might well turn out to be "a cultural revolution of great importance."[28]

Riesebrodt also implied that the revolution fundamentalists had launched was not necessarily destined to make the world a worse place in which to live. "Fundamentalism and the Resurgence of Religion" did not portray fundamentalist movements as especially odd or unusually dangerous. Instead, the essay consistently emphasized how much fundamentalist movements had in common with other religious revitalization movements. Riesebrodt's text presents fundamentalists as resourceful religious people living in the modern world who have a good deal in common with other resourceful religious people living in the modern world. It leaves the impression that Riesebrodt feels that joining a fundamentalist movement is not necessarily a bad thing to do and that some people who joined fundamentalist movements might well end up living better lives than they would have had they remained outside those movements. Riesebrodt's essay was by no means a thorough condemnation of fundamentalism.

Justifying Bloodshed

Riesebrodt's relatively upbeat assessment set him apart from the great majority of people who focused their attention on the concept of global fundamentalism. Since the concept was invented, global fundamentalism has been used most frequently to identify religious movements that were thought to pose a threat to something or someone. For the past three decades most people have expressed very little interest in talking about fundamentalists who they did not think of as dangerous; the whole point of drawing a line between fundamentalists and nonfundamentalists has been to draw a contrast between a set of people who were dangerous and another set of people who were not.

Religious Jews were the dangerous other upon whom Norton Mezvinsky, a professor who taught history at Central Connecticut State College, and Israel Shahak, a chemist who taught at Hebrew University, focused their attention. In *Jewish Fundamentalism in Israel*, which was published in 1999, Mezvinsky and Shahak painted an extraordinarily dark portrait of those men and women. Jewish fundamentalists, they said, had already inflicted a great deal of damage on the Middle East and were poised to inflict even more. Mezvinsky was not an especially prominent figure in Jewish circles, but Shahak certainly was, and a controversial figure at that. A good many Israelis regarded him as a crank. But Shahak, a survivor of the Holocaust who had made his way to Palestine while it was still under British control, also had a good many admirers in Israel and in the occupied territories. In the eyes of his supporters, he was a great spokesman for peace and a powerful advocate for human rights. Shahak's fame extended far beyond the Middle East: his admirers included journalists such as Christopher Hitchens, novelists such as Gore Vidal, and scholars such as Edward Said.

In Shahak and Mezvinsky's analysis, Jewish fundamentalism was a bloodthirsty religion. The act that best revealed its character was the assassination of Yitzhak Rabin. Jewish fundamentalism's violent proclivities also found expression in the massacre of Muslim worshippers in the Cave of the Patriarchs that Baruch Goldstein carried out in 1994 and in the willingness of Israelis to spill the blood of others over and over again to achieve their aims. These proclivities were also evident in the support a few Israeli rabbis voiced for executing men whose sexual practices did not conform to the standards set forth in the Torah.[29]

Shahak and Mezvinsky asserted that the violent tendencies of Jewish fundamentalism posed a terrible threat to a wide variety of groups in the Middle East. Fundamentalism's deleterious effects on the Palestinian people and on the inhabitants of Lebanon were obvious, they said. But it was also true that if fundamentalists were to gain control of the State of Israel, they would treat Israeli Jews who refused to embrace fundamentalism "worse" than they "would treat the Palestinians."[30] Shahak and Mezvinsky feared that such a fundamentalist regime might be established in Israel. They wrote out of a hope that by unmasking the real nature of Jewish fundamentalism, they could possibly help avert such a catastrophic turn of events.

In order to unmask Jewish fundamentalism, Shahak and Mezvinsky embarked on an exploration of Jewish history. They focused on what they called the third period of Jewish history—the period that stretched between the destruction of the Second Temple and the coming of modernity. As they understood it, that period was a "dark age," characterized as much by superstition and witchcraft as by deep spirituality. The typical Jews of that period did not practice a respectable religion. Instead, they passed their time looking at the planets and "attempting to perform magic rites." A cover-up had obscured the true nature of the Jewish dark ages, Shahak and Mezvinsky said: nearly all the English-language texts on that era of Jewish history were untrustworthy because they omitted anything that made Jews look superstitious—indeed, anything that made Jews look bad. They were actually a kind of propaganda, and the people who wrote them, such as Gershom Scholem, were "supreme hypocrites."[31]

When examined honestly, Shahak and Mezvinsky insisted, the third period of Jewish history was a shameful time. It was an era of authoritarianism, intolerance, violence, and persecution of Jews by other Jews. Only non-Jewish rulers' imposition of strict limits on Jewish autonomy checked those evils. Left to their own devices, Jews maimed and killed other Jews with astonishing avidity. That bloodshed was not an unintended by-product of the practices and beliefs of Judaism; it was one of Judaism's essential elements.[32] During the years between the destruction of the Temple and the coming of modernity, Judaism was fundamentalist and therefore evil.

Discovering these ugly truths about the nature of traditional Judaism, Shahak and Mezvinsky acknowledged, would make many readers uncomfortable; it would cause some readers real pain. They also emphasized that producing their analysis of Jewish history had brought them no pleasure, for criticizing one's own people is never easy. The kind of criticism they advanced was in a very real sense simply a family quarrel, they said. "As Jews," they said, "we understand that our own grandparents or great-grandparents probably believed in at least some of the views described in our book." Still, they said, an unflinching examination of historic Judaism had to be undertaken. "To oppose the current dangers posed by Jewish fundamentalism," one had to have a clear understanding of fundamentalism's "historical basis."[33] One had to look at the horrible truths about the history of the Jewish religion without blinking.

Adopting this rhetorical stance—we have to tell you the truth, although doing so has hurt us just as much as it will hurt you—enabled Shahak and Mezvinsky to present themselves as reluctant critics of Judaism. I am not sure this self-presentation was completely convincing. Their analysis of fundamentalism and its historical antecedents produced passages that seem almost gleefully anti-Judaic. *Jewish Fundamentalism in Israel* came very close to suggesting that most forms of traditional Judaism were expressions of Jewish fundamentalism and that Jewish fundamentalism was a loathsome phenomenon that always stood in opposition to freedom and progress. Shahak and Mezvinsky's book argued that it would be best for all concerned if traditional Judaism were relegated to the ash heap of history. Jewish fundamentalists were obstacles to peace and freedom, nothing less. And certainly nothing more.

Monotheistic Violence

The threat of Jewish fundamentalism was taken up in a talk the well-known progressive journalist Bill Moyers delivered in September 2005. In the lecture, titled "9/11 and God's Sport," Moyers asserted that Jewish fundamentalism was simply one expression of a logic that can be found in all monotheistic faiths. Moyers, who has deep roots in the Baptist Church, delivered his speech at Union Theological Seminary—the school where Harry Emerson Fosdick, the author of the first great antifundamentalist polemic, found his academic home. Moyers began by invoking the memory of some of the Christian thinkers who had been associated with Union, including Dietrich Bonhoeffer, Paul Tillich, and Reinhold Niebuhr. He then told his audience that he was convinced that America was in the midst of a great crisis and that it was imperative that the seminary pour its energy into responding to that crisis in ways that did justice to its great heritage. The crisis had been occasioned in large part by the recrudescence of fundamentalism. Moyers's speech almost made it sound like Fosdick's nightmare had come true: the fundamentalists had in fact won.

Moyers gave his speech just four days before the observance of the fourth anniversary of the attacks of 9/11, and he delivered it in a building just a few miles north of the site of the destroyed World Trade Center. His decision to devote a portion of his talk to the effects of those attacks was hardly surprising. Indeed, it would have been surprising if Moyers had avoided the topic. By the time he delivered his speech, many Americans had gotten into the habit of talking about 9/11 on public occasions. Invocations of those events had become routine; speakers often resorted to rather passionless, formulaic pronouncements. But Moyer's analysis of the events of 9/11 was passionate. It was almost poetic: "In the name of God they came. They came bent on murder and martyrdom. It was as if they rode to earth on the fierce breath of Allah himself, for the sacred scriptures that had nurtured these murderous young men are steeped in the images of a violent and vengeful God who wills life for the faithful and horrific torment for unbelievers."[34]

Moyers spoke of the effects of the attacks in highly personal terms. He talked about how he and his wife had worked to keep the New York television station that employed them on the air in the hours immediately after the attacks and about how close their son-in-law had come to being killed that day. Moyers also reflected on how his daughter had been influenced by the attacks: she was filled with anxiety when she wasn't able to contact her husband in the immediate aftermath and she feared that another attack that would injure or kill her children might be on its way.

Implanting such fears in the minds of Americans was precisely what the fundamentalists had hoped to accomplish, Moyers said.

In sharp contrast with Karen Armstrong (and with many other prominent public intellectuals), Moyers did not view the attacks of 9/11 as a betrayal of true Islam. He viewed them as an authentic embodiment of the ideals of the Qur'an. Moyers quoted four passages from the Qur'an, each of which, he asserted, could have been on the lips of Muslims who carried out the attacks of 9/11. He said that glorification of violence was at the heart of the Qur'an and that when the hijackers flew the planes into the World Trade Center, they were, in a sense, simply doing what their scriptures impelled them to do.[35]

As Moyers understood them, the ideals of Islam were not much different from those of Judaism and Christianity. Glorification of violence was embedded in the DNA of all of the monotheistic faiths. Finding passages in the Christian scriptures that glorified violence was just as easy as locating such passages in the Qur'an. The Bible, like the Qur'an, urged the men and women who read it to wage war to carry out God's will. Both books portrayed God as a tyrant who took great delight in the destruction of human bodies. Both asserted that human beings had a holy obligation to worship a God who loved the sight of human beings killing other human beings.[36]

Having presented an analysis of the Qur'an and the Bible that was not especially nuanced, Moyers paused for a moment to assure his readers that he realized that those texts were in fact shot through with complexity and contradiction. They included a good many admonitions to act mercifully and to avoid bloodshed whenever possible. It was possible, Moyers said, to interpret the Qur'an and the Bible in ways that minimized the damage they could inflict on human beings. It was something, Moyers said, that "all of us know." But fundamentalists—such as the men who flew the planes into the World Trade Center and the Pentagon and who crashed into the field in Shanksville, Pennsylvania—refused to read scriptures that way. Instead, they read those texts literally. They thus came to believe in a God who was "sadistic, brutal, vengeful, callow, cruel, and savage—a killer beyond reckoning." They were hell-bent on pleasing their God.[37]

After reflecting on the faith of the Muslim fundamentalists who carried out the attacks on 9/11, Moyers turned, somewhat abruptly, to the way that Christian fundamentalists living in the United States interpreted those attacks. While the ruins of the World Trade Center "were still smoldering," Moyers said, Jerry Falwell and Pat Robertson went on television to tell their followers why the attacks had occurred. Although many Americans found Falwell and Robertson's interpretation to be patently absurd, it was one that "millions of Christian fundamentalists" found quite plausible. Falwell and Robertson were, of course, outraged by the attacks, and they assumed that the men who carried them out were evil. But Falwell and Robertson also believed that the attacks would never have occurred had not God removed his protection from the American people. God had done that, Falwell and Robertson said, because the American government had allowed itself to be influenced by people who were ungodly. America was getting just what it deserved. Falwell and Robertson asserted that God was using the men who launched the attacks to give America a wake-up call. God wanted America to turn away from the evil ideas of "the pagans, and the abortionists, and the feminists, and the gays and the lesbians" and to "get right with God."[38]

As Moyers understood it, Falwell and Robertson were calling for a course of action that was in many ways simply a mirror image of what Osama bin Laden advocated. Reading the Qur'an, praying to God for guidance, preparing to do battle against the Jews and Christians who resisted God's will—that was bin Laden's plan. Reading the Bible, praying to God, and punishing Muslims for attacking America—that was the program Falwell and Robertson called on America to adopt.[39]

After 9/11, Moyers said, "we were immersed in the pathology of a 'holy war' as defined by fundamentalists on both sides." Muslim fundamentalists were waging war against the enemies of Allah; Christian fundamentalists were fighting a crusade against the enemies of Christ. Moyers did not go so far as to claim that the State Department and the Pentagon had been taken over by fundamentalists. Nor did he deny the obvious—that America's so-called war on terror was fervently supported by many men and women who were not Christian fundamentalists. Rather, Moyers portrayed the war on terror as one of the many expressions of the misguided policies of a government that had been captured by the radical right. He then went on to assert that the radical right would never have been able to capture the government without the fervent support of Christian fundamentalists.[40]

As Moyers interpreted it, Christian fundamentalism in America was a betrayal of the country's highest ideals. Fundamentalists were intolerant. They treated the courts, the press, reason, and science with contempt. Fundamentalists made alliances with unscrupulous politicians and greedy businessmen. They did all they could to prevent the American government from meeting the needs of the poor and the vulnerable. Instead, fundamentalists used the government to further the agenda of "crony capitalism." And fundamentalists were also determined—this was a matter Moyers was especially interested in—to tear down the wall that America's founding fathers had erected to separate church from state.[41]

Moyers's speech was truculent—far more truculent than Fosdick's "Shall the Fundamentalists Win?" had been. Unlike Fosdick, Moyers did not say that fundamentalists had some qualities he admired. He did not admit that some fundamentalists were virtuous. He did not say that some of them were sincere Christians. He did not say that there were many important points upon which he could find common ground with fundamentalists. Instead, Moyers described fundamentalists as America's "homegrown ayatollahs." They were "religious bullies," and trying to appease them would be a terrible mistake. Men and women of goodwill had to be willing to fight fundamentalists tooth and nail. What was at stake was nothing less than the future of the nation.[42]

On one level, Moyers's stirring calling for an uncompromising struggle against fundamentalists was simply an appeal for progressive Christians to do all they could to diminish the power of the new religious right. But there were passages in "9/11 and God's Sport" that implied that the new religious right was simply one manifestation of a much more basic problem. Moyers told his listeners time and time again that monotheism—unless it was very carefully reinterpreted—was a violent and genocidal ideology. The God of the Bible and the God of the Qur'an really were evil, according to Moyers. Implicit in his analysis of monotheists was the suggestion that all monotheists who had not found a way to reinterpret that ideology in ways that drew the poison out of the faith were in some sense fundamentalists. Moyers seemed to be suggesting that fundamentalists were not people who had misunderstood the essential message of monotheism. They were, rather, people who had correctly apprehended that message and chosen to follow it wholeheartedly. Fundamentalists did not demonstrate how monotheism could be misinterpreted; they showed, rather, what monotheism really is.[43]

During the early years of the twenty-first century, Bill Moyers looked at the relationships between religion, society, and politics over and over again. He was hardly alone. During that era a good many more Americans were certain that religion was worth examining than had been the case two decades earlier. In the early years of the twentieth century, it seemed clear that religion mattered. It mattered a lot. People who were unwilling to think about religion and about its political and social effects could not, it was generally assumed, ever really understand the world in which they lived. When Americans looked at religion in the early years of the twenty-first century they very often did so through the lens of global fundamentalism. To be sure, by 2006 there were some indications that the scholarly study of global fundamentalism was losing momentum. The Fundamentalism Project that Marty and Appleby had directed had come to an end in 1995, and none of the subsequent scholarly investigations of fundamentalism garnered as much attention and acclaim as it had. But less scholarly, more casual meditations on the nature of global fundamentalism continued to proliferate in the early twenty-first century. Those meditations were rarely reassuring. When Americans invoked fundamentalism, they used it to talk about theirs fears far more frequently than they used it to talk about their hopes. Fundamentalism was a concept Americans used to talk about what happened when religion turned toxic and about how dangerous religion could be once it had gone bad.

Conclusion

The Future of Fundamentalism

The Reluctant Fundamentalist, Mira Nair's thriller about the CIA, Pakistan, and the aftereffects of 9/11, premiered in 2013. The film, which starred Riz Ahmed, Kate Hudson, Liev Schreiber, and Kiefer Sutherland, was not a great financial success, and the reviews it received—unlike those received by the award-winning novel on which it was based—were decidedly mixed. Nevertheless, it is a noteworthy movie. Few American films—if any—have done a better job of capturing fundamentalism's allure.

The film's protagonist, Changez Khan (Riz Ahmed), comes from a Pakistani family with a long history of artistic and intellectual achievement. Khan moves to the Unites States to study at Princeton, lands a job working for a prestigious financial firm called Underwood Samson, and quickly wins the admiration of Jim Cross (Kiefer Sutherland), one of the firm's partners. Impressed by Khan's drive and intelligence, Cross goes out of his way to help Khan apprehend the company's approach to business. That approach involves ignoring matters of sentiment, disregarding mere hunches, and "creating value" by "focusing on the fundamentals."

Khan is a gifted student. He masters the principles Cross teaches him and applies those principles to brilliant effect. Khan seems destined for fame, success, and wealth.

But after 9/11, things begin to change. Although Cross continues to support Khan, many other Americans view him with suspicion. He is repeatedly subjected to humiliating demands that he demonstrate his loyalty to the United States. And in truth, Khan's views of America are quite complex. He has warm feelings toward many Americans—indeed, he has fallen in love with an American photographer—but he is also keenly aware of the hubristic tendencies of Americans. When the World Trade Center collapsed, Khan felt neither sadness nor rage; he felt awe. He marveled at the audacity of the attackers. Their demolition of the towers reminded him of David's victory over Goliath. As he gains a fuller understanding of what it is that Underwood Samson actually does, Khan becomes increasingly aware of the collateral damage its ruthless search for profits causes. He realizes that he and his colleagues are paid, in a sense, to expand the reach of heartless neoliberalism. He comes to believe that firms such as Underwood Samson are wreaking havoc throughout the world.

Eventually Khan gives up his job, makes his way to Pakistan, and takes up a position teaching at a university. His lectures are popular, highly intelligent, and somewhat inflammatory. His students, some of whom are quite radical, admire him deeply. The CIA begins keeping track of Khan's activities and subsequently comes to suspect that Khan is involved in the kidnapping of an American spy.

As the film moves toward its conclusion, it becomes clear that the CIA is wrong. A violent extremist named Mustafa Fazil has indeed asked Khan to join his movement. Khan is willing to hear what Fazil had to say and he thinks that a great deal of what he hears makes good sense. But during the course of their conversation, Fazil says something that stops Khan dead in his tracks. "Our only hope as a people," Fazil asserts, is "the fundamental truths given to us in the Qur'an." As soon as he hears those words, Khan experiences an epiphany. He realizes that Fazil and his fellow radicals are "engaged in their own valuation, just like Underwood Samson, moving human beings in and out of binary columns: worker, liability, American, Pakistani, martyr, infidel, alive, dead." They, just like the employees of Underwood Samson, take delight in "deciding . . . the fate of people [they] [do] not know." Khan sees that Fazil is not offering him a genuine alternative to Cross's fundamentalism; he is simply peddling a different version of that same basic approach to life. Khan decides to reject Fazil's invitation and to chart a different path—one that avoided the sort of Islamic fundamentalism Fazil proclaims and the market fundamentalism Cross preaches. The film ends with Khan giving an impassioned speech extolling the humanistic ideals he has embraced.

Unlike a great many movies, *The Reluctant Fundamentalist* did not encourage viewers to assume that religion is the realm of constraint and the secular world the realm of freedom. Instead, Nair skillfully deployed the concept of fundamentalism in ways that enabled her to critique a particular kind of secular regime: the kind associated with unfettered capitalism. In recent years, some writers (George Soros, Margaret Somers, and Fred Block, for example) have made similar moves. The critiques of market fundamentalism writers such as Soros, Somers, and Block have presented are few and far between and they do not attract a great deal of attention. But they are in one respect quite revealing: they highlight how consistently the concept of fundamentalism has been deployed in recent years to identify phenomena that are thought of as threatening. In *The Reluctant Fundamentalist*, people who have great faith in capitalism are presented as fundamentalists precisely because that faith is excessive and therefore dangerous. In the film the wise man is the one who rejects both a simpleminded faith in capitalism and a simpleminded faith in God. When the film concludes viewers know that Cross and Fazil are both villains. They understand that Khan, on other hand, is a genuine hero who really might end up making the world a better place. In this respect, *The Reluctant Fundamentalist* did not undercut the basic logic of the fundamentalist/nonfundamentalist binary: fundamentalists are bad, nonfundamentalists are good. Instead, it reinscribed it.[1]

An Array of Defects

Today, nearly all Americans believe that fundamentalists have something important in common, and nearly all of them believe that whatever it is they have in common is repellent. Americans have not, however, been able to agree on precisely what those problematic commonalities are. The defining characteristics of fundamentalists are shifting, unstable, and heterogeneous. One frequently consulted thesaurus suggests that fundamentalists are people who exhibit bigotry, dogmatism, dourness, hideboundness, inflexibility, obstinacy, precisianism, puritanicalism, rigidity, stiffness, strictness, unbendingness, or unrelentingness.[2] That is a rather long list of defects, but it is far from complete. Fundamentalists have also been called closed-minded, aggressive, and insufficiently cosmopolitan.[3] Frequently, fundamentalists have also been said to display an irrational hatred for the West. At other times, fundamentalists have been thought to be people who have failed to embrace the truths revealed by the European Enlightenment.[4] On other occasions, fundamentalists have been described as people who are trying to resist the changing role of women in modern societies.[5] And of course fundamentalists have been repeatedly presented as people waging a foolish crusade against modernity itself.[6]

According to some writers, fundamentalists are prone to legalism. William Loader has argued, for instance, that fundamentalists focus on the letter of the law rather than on its spirit. He says that fundamentalists are modern-day Pharisees.[7] And of course, fundamentalists are very often said to be people who read scriptures incorrectly. In *Burning to Read: English Fundamentalism and Its Reformation Opponents*, James Simpson referred to sixteenth-century Protestants such as William Tyndale as fundamentalists who interpreted the Christian scriptures in a way that was less sophisticated and more dangerous than the way their Catholic opponents read them. The publisher of *Burning to Read*, Harvard University Press, assured potential readers that even people with no special interest in early modern England could gain a better understanding of the roots of contemporary religious turmoil by reading Simpson's book. The rise of sixteenth-century Christian fundamentalism produced "150 years of violent upheaval," the press observed; now, as a second wave of violence is about to break over us, *Burning to Read* warns us of the dangers *we* confront. The publisher seems to be suggesting that people who want to understand fundamentalists such as Osama bin Laden would do well to learn more about fundamentalists such as William Tyndale.[8]

That brings us to what might well be the charge that has been leveled most frequently against fundamentalists: that they are people who possess a peculiar proclivity for violence. A poem by Marge Piercy, "The Fundamental Truth" exemplifies this idea of fundamentalism. It was written in the wake of the assassination of Yitzhak Rabin, the prime minister of Israel whose attempts to decrease the hostilities between Israelis and Palestinians earned him the Nobel Prize for Peace. Rabin was assassinated by a young Zionist named Yigal Amir, who was implacably opposed to the sorts of compromise that Rabin was willing to make to reach a peaceful conclusion to the conflict between Israel and Palestine. Amir was an orthodox Jew whose religious views were quite extreme from almost any perspective.

Piercy's poem can be seen as a polemic against people such as Amir who are willing to use violence in the service of religion. "The Jewish right bank settlers," "the Japanese sects" who bomb subways, "the Islamic Jihad," and "the Christian right," she wrote, all hate one another. But those groups also had a great deal in common. They were "braggarts of hatred" whose faith was built on the "death of others" and for whom everyone was other. They experience the holy not through meditation or study but through violence. They were devoid of "humility" and "self-doubt," sure that God had given them "a license to kill." The scriptures they read were "splattered in letters of blood."[9]

Piercy wanted to allow those zealots to exercise that license. She imagined a universe in which all the world's religious zealots had been exiled from the earth and transported to "a barren moon with artificial atmosphere." Their departure would enable the rest of humanity to live more secure lives. And there was a sense, Piercy suggested, in which the zealots themselves desired a separate existence. On their barren moon they would be closer to their gods and they would have many opportunities to confront the enemies they most detested. The zealots could murder one another with great glee until only one man was left standing. Their eradication would be virtually complete and the universe would be a better place.

The rage Piercy's poem expresses seems almost genocidal. Piercy was unwilling to ask her nonfundamentalist sisters and brothers to take up arms to smite the fundamentalists hip and thigh. But she was willing to fantasize about the conditions under which the fundamentalists could be made to disappear from the face of the earth without nonfundamentalists themselves having to commit any overtly violent acts. The fundamentalists would simply be rounded up, somehow transported to their own moon, and allowed to exterminate themselves. Piercy did not specify the means that would be used to round them up or how they would be transported into outer space. Would all the fundamentalists of the world somehow volunteer to leave their homes and make their way into the killing fields? Was that what Piercy was envisaging? Possibly. Or perhaps she longed for a universe in which some supernatural force would intervene in human history to wipe out the fundamentalist threat. In any case, it was clear that Piercy longed for a world that had somehow been cleansed of fundamentalism.

A portion of Piercy's poem was cast in the future tense. That is a grammatical construction that historians generally shy away from. We know that we are better at looking back than ahead. When we talk about the past there are landmarks to guide us. When we talk about the future we have to rely on guesswork. We like to believe that some of our guesses about what lies ahead are educated rather than preposterous, but we know that they are guesses nevertheless. Still, I am prepared to say (with a little trepidation) that I believe that the scholarly study of global fundamentalism is probably not going to be reinvigorated anytime soon. Scholars have been endeavoring to turn the concept of global fundamentalism into an objective, value-free category with a stable, clear-cut meaning for several decades. They have not succeeded. The glory days of scholarly investigations of global fundamentalism are probably behind us. It seems to me that the serious study of global fundamentalism reached its high point in the 1990s and that it has been in decline ever since. I would be surprised if future scholars devoted as much energy to investigating global fundamentalism as scholars did in the past.

I would be surprised, too, if the number of people in the world who call themselves fundamentalists increased dramatically in the next few decades. For the past thirty years or so, the number of people who are willing to label themselves fundamentalists has been steadily declining. To be sure, some polygamists who think of themselves as the true spiritual heirs of Joseph Smith and Brigham Young continue to call themselves fundamentalists. Doing so is a convenient way for them to distinguish themselves from the millions of people who belong to the Church of Jesus Christ of Latter-day Saints—the dominant form of Mormonism and the form that does not practice polygamy. The Fundamentalist Church of Jesus Christ of Latter-Day Saints is often in the news, but it does not have many members—perhaps only 10,000 or so.

It is clear that only a small number of American Protestants think that identifying themselves as fundamentalists is the best way of telling people what their religious beliefs are: national surveys suggest that the figure may well be no more than 100,000.[10] Of course, a good many more might be willing to accept "fundamentalist" as a secondary or tertiary description: something like "I am a Presbyterian, an evangelical, and a fundamentalist." Some evangelical Protestants continue to call themselves fundamentalists as a way of indicating that their theological views are more conservative than those of evangelicals, moderates, and liberals. But the number of people who do that is decreasing. And a substantial number of people who by almost any measure have every right to call themselves fundamentalists are making a determined effort to describe themselves in other ways.

Bob Jones III, for instance, certainly has cause to call himself a fundamentalist. He is deeply committed to the fundamentals of the Christian faith as they were defined by the fundamentalists of the 1920s and 1930s, and he is a biological and spiritual descendant of a prominent leader of the fundamentalist movement. But Jones has come to believe that a Christian who calls himself a fundamentalist can no longer be sure that the people he is talking to will know the true meaning of the term. He has concluded that people may well think that a fundamentalist is, by definition, a dangerous man with radical ideas and a predilection for violence. Jones suspects that people who share his religious commitments should perhaps stop calling themselves fundamentalists and begin to call themselves preservationists instead.[11]

The people who maintain the website of Bob Jones University also seem to be aware of fundamentalism's negative connotations. The website does not highlight the institution's fundamentalist credentials and presents the school as a Christian university that is dedicated to fostering "Christlike character that is scripturally disciplined, others-serving, [and] Godloving."[12] The website of Liberty University, which was founded by Jerry Falwell in 1971, contains almost no references to concepts such as "fundamentalist," "fundamentalists," and "fundamentalism." Although Falwell wore the fundamentalist label as a badge of honor, Liberty's website now says that the university is an "evangelical liberal arts institution."[13] And the words "fundamentalists" and "fundamentalism" are difficult to find on the website of the organization that was founded in 1930 as the Independent Fundamental Churches of America. In the late 1990s, the organization changed its name to IFCA-International. The website's recounting of the history of the organization almost never uses the title Independent Fundamental Churches of America. Instead, it proceeds as if the name of the organization has never indicated that it was a fundamentalist institution. I don't want to make too much of this anachronism; the people who maintain the website are probably not professional historians. But it does seem as if the website of the IFCA now presents a portrait of the organization in which nearly all traces of fundamentalism have been made to vanish; fundamentalism has nearly disappeared from the history of this particular fundamentalist organization. It almost seems as if fundamentalism is treated like an uncle whose eccentricities have made him an embarrassment and who has therefore been hidden away in a back room. Or perhaps even in the attic.[14]

So it seems unlikely that we are moving toward a world that contains an overabundance of people who refer to *themselves* as fundamentalists. But we are not moving toward the sort of world Piercy envisioned: a world that does not include any of the people whom *others* label as fundamentalists. Those so-called fundamentalists probably will not end up dominating the world to the extent that their opponents have sometimes prophesied. (Theocratic caliphates are probably not going to conquer all the lands where Muslims live. India, Israel, and the United States are probably not going to be transformed into impregnable theocracies). But there is no reason to believe that the so-called fundamentalists are going to simply vanish. That is not in the cards.

Is Fundamentalism Now Completely Useless?

If the concepts of fundamentalists and fundamentalism are as deeply flawed as I have suggested, then it is worth considering what would happen if we simply stopped using them. If the concepts disappeared completely, what would be lost? A little, I think, but not much. The concepts really do come in handy when we are discussing the fundamentalists of the 1920s and 1930s. They are also useful when we are talking about the very conservative Protestants of the 1940s and 1950s—Carl McIntire, for instance—or about many of the people—Jerry Falwell, for instance—associated with the New Christian Right. Those Protestant Christians called themselves fundamentalists and there is no good reason for us to call them something else. As I have already suggested, there are a good many people in the world who continue to describe themselves as fundamentalists. In discussions of those people, it makes good sense to rely on the concepts of fundamentalism and fundamentalists.

I believe, however, that the farther we move from twentieth- and twenty-first-century American Protestantism, the more problematic the concepts of fundamentalists and fundamentalism become. I think that the category of global fundamentalism is rotten to its core. Of course, I can certainly see why thoughtful people might want to rely on it. It offers us a tool that we can use to contest ways of looking at the world that are both prevalent and inaccurate. One of these has to do with the relationship between people who are religious and people who are secular. According to this view, nearly all the people in the world who are religious are irrational and nearly all of them stand in the way of progress. From this perspective, rational, progressive people can be found only among those who have embraced secularism. Religion is almost always bad and the secular is almost always good. The religion-is-bad/secular-is-good binary provides a poor starting point for thinking about the role religion plays in the contemporary world. It prevents us from seeing that progressive social movements are sometimes fueled by religious devotion. It closes off the possibility of cooperation between religious progressives and secular progressives to serve the common good. Part of what Marty was trying to do in his influential 1980 article was to open that space up. It is not difficult to see why he would want to do that.

The concepts of fundamentalism and fundamentalists can also be used to challenge the claim that "Islam" and "the West" are two distinct and irreconcilable civilizations whose relations must always be adversarial. Karen Armstrong has used them to make just that point, insisting that the Islamic religion is no more dangerous than Christianity or Judaism. Muslims, Christians, and Jews, she said, do terrible things. They also do beautiful things. Demonizing Muslims is hazardous and silly. Armstrong argues that it makes no sense to say that the attacks on the World Trade Center and the Pentagon prove that all Muslims are full of rage, or that the attacks were a product of some grand clash of civilizations, as some Americans have asserted. They were rooted, rather, in a terrible perversion of Islam: fundamentalism. For Armstrong, people who claim that the problem confronting the West is not Islamic fundamentalism but Islam are simply wrong. Muslim fundamentalism is, in fact, exactly what people who are trying to prevent terrorists from carrying out more attacks on the West are up against. Fundamentalism, she said, is not a purely Islamic phenomenon; Judaism has its fundamentalist adherents, as does Christianity. So do many other of the world's religions. The men who carried out the attacks of 9/11 were religious fanatics whose hearts were full of hate, but the hatred was rooted in fundamentalism, not in Islam.[15] Armstrong believes that invoking the fundamentalist/nonfundamentalist distinction provides a way of counteracting anti-Muslim propaganda. She has a point, and her determination to fight back against that kind of polemic is admirable.

I have a great deal of sympathy for the aims of people such as Armstrong and Marty. But many writers—William E. Arnal, Richard W. Bulliet, Timothy Fitzgerald, Janet Jakobsen, Saba Mahmood, Ann Pellegrini, and Russell McCutcheon, to name but a few—have found ways of interrogating the binaries of religious/secular and of Islam/the West that do not rely on the concept of global fundamentalism. We don't have to invoke that concept in order to interrogate those binaries. People who claim that there are no alternative ways of doing the work that global fundamentalism is supposed to do are simply incorrect.[16]

The Risks We Run

The fundamentalist/nonfundamentalist binary is not, of course, much more sophisticated than the binaries it has been used to contest. A good many of the assumptions the concept of global fundamentalism rests upon now seem highly questionable. The concept makes the most sense if we assume that the European Enlightenment uncovered certain universal truths that everyone in the world ought to embrace, that it is not especially difficult to define the nature of modernity, that it is perverse to focus on the problems that seem to be associated with modernity instead of on the benefits it supposedly bestows, that there is a simple way to differentiate between political matters and religious ones, and that religious matters ought to be confined, whenever and wherever possible, to the private sphere. But even in Talcott Parsons's heyday, those assumptions were not universally accepted. In recent decades they have been subjected to withering critique. It is fair to say, I think, that a very large proportion of the best recent work in the humanities has been produced by scholars who question the assumptions on which the concept of global fundamentalism is built. When we speak and write as though those assumptions are not in dispute, we run the risk of making ourselves laughingstocks. Those assumptions may possibly be true, but they are also fiercely contested and it is entirely possible that they are simply false. If we ignore that possibility, we risk cutting ourselves off from some of the most interesting conversations that are taking place today.

That is not the only risk we run when we rely on the fundamentalist/nonfundamentalist binary. Relying on the concept can lull us into thinking that the people who join Al Qaeda, the West Bank settlers, and students at Bob Jones University simply represent three different expressions of a single worldwide impulse. Habitual reliance also predisposes us to assume that the distinction is natural rather than invented and makes it difficult for us to see that there is a sense in which the worldviews of both fundamentalists and nonfundamentalists are parochial and idiosyncratic. Our attachment to that distinction can make it difficult for us to remember that neither fundamentalists nor nonfundamentalists stand on an Archimedean point from which the totality of human history can be inspected objectively. It can persuade us that the people we call fundamentalists are struggling with problems that nonfundamentalists have solved and that fundamentalists always swim against the flow of history while nonfundamentalists always swim with it.

Those of us who are not fundamentalists sometimes overstate the amount of violence that is currently deployed in the service of fundamentalism, even as we understate the degree to which those of us with other cultural commitments—liberalism and patriotism, for example—are willing to use violence and the threat of violence to achieve our aims.[17] We sometimes speak, for example, as though fundamentalist governments are willing to use force and coercion in order to exercise control over women's bodies while secular governments are not. But the situation is more complicated than that. Controlling bodies is something that all governments do. Women who want to cross a border in order to work or live within the boundaries of a fundamentalist regime have to show their passports. So do those who want to enter a space controlled by a secular liberal state. Governmental officials in some countries are willing to use coercion to make sure that women wear garments that conceal their face and hair;

officials in other countries are willing to use coercion to make sure that women do not wear such garments.[18] Coercion exercised in the name of progress is no less coercive than coercion for the sake of modesty.

The fundamentalist/nonfundamentalist binary reinforces our tendency to divide the world into heroes and villains. Saying that not all religious people are bad guys and then asserting that the real bad guys are fundamentalists does not get us all that far from where we started. The logic of the message is still pretty much the same. There are people out there who are not like us. We are better than they are. They wish us ill. They are dangerous. Life would be better if they were to simply disappear.

At this point, I need to guard against a possible misunderstanding. When I am talking about the problems associated with fundamentalism, people sometimes think that what I am asking for are words to replace "fundamentalist," "fundamentalists," and "fundamentalism." Sometimes they even ask me to suggest a substitute. "All right," they say, "if you don't want us to call those people fundamentalists, then what do you want us to call them?" Whenever I am asked that question, I realize that I have failed to make my position clear.

Getting rid of the words "fundamentalist," "fundamentalists," and "fundamentalism" will not solve the problem. The problem is not with the words. The problem is with the assumptions, hopes, and habits of mind upon which they rest. Simply coming up with new names without rethinking those assumptions, hopes, and habits of mind does us no good whatsoever. If tomorrow everyone in the world were to stop talking about fundamentalism and begin talking about something like "reactionary religious groups" or "bad religion" or "Falwellianism" or "Qutbism," we'd have made no progress. The problem is not with the term per se but with the category itself and with the desire to name a dangerous other. It is about the wish to pretend that we know the direction history is moving in and what it means to stand in the way of progress. It is about a desire to sort humanity into two groups: those who are virtuous and those who are not. It is, in other words, about our desire to separate the sheep from the goats.

The image of dividing the sheep from the goats is, of course, an ancient one, from the Gospel of Matthew. Creating simple moral binaries into which people can be sorted is something that human beings have been doing for thousands of years. Humans love to create us/them dichotomies and to think that the group of which they are a part is morally superior to the other one. We are better than they are. We are the children of light; they are the children of darkness. They worship idols; we worship the true God. They are barbaric; we are civilized. We are progressive; they are reactionaries. They have false consciousness; we have correctly understood the nature of the universe. The particular categories into which people are sorted are transitory, but the logic upon which the division rests is remarkably stable.

Dividing the human race into people like us who are good and people not like us who are bad is a comforting thing to do, and such a division often contains a grain of truth. The people who are not like us sometimes do evil things; our group sometimes does behave quite admirably. But such a simple division rarely captures the complexity of a situation. It seems to rule out of consideration the possibility that scoundrels can be found among both the people like us and the people who are not like us.[19] It blinds us to the possibility that people like us sometimes do a great deal of harm.

And the "we are good and they are bad" scheme, when carried to its logical extreme, can push us to regard the dangerous other against whom we define ourselves as bestial—so dissimilar to us as to belong to another species altogether. As Piercy's "The Fundamental Truth" reminds us, relying on the concept of global fundamentalism can lead us to think of fundamentalists as somehow not fully human and somehow not deserving of the rights and privileges accorded to beings who are unambiguously human. The concept of global fundamentalism focuses our attention on attitudes and actions that we find especially destabilizing, frightening, and dangerous. In so doing, it opens up the possibility that we ought to do whatever it takes to keep the fundamentalists in their proper—that is, subordinated—place. The concept can even justify schemes that would lead to all the fundamentalists being wiped off the face of the earth. As we battle the monsters conjured up by the concept of global fundamentalism, we might consider courses of action that would be unthinkable if our opponents were actual human beings. Because we know that fundamentalists are more prone than we are to resort to violence, we can entertain with equanimity the possibility of killing them before they kill us. In point of fact, some of the people we label as fundamentalists are willing to use violence to accomplish their ends. But eradicating fundamentalism would not lead to world peace. Indeed, attempts to eradicate fundamentalists will probably do more harm than good.

Chronology of Events

This chart lists some of the events observers have connected to the creation and expansion of global fundamentalism. It should be noted, however, that many of these events have no connection whatsoever with the history of Protestant fundamentalism.

1910 The booklets in the series *The Fundamentals: A Testimony to the Truth* begin to appear.
1919 The World's Christian Fundamentals Association is founded in Philadelphia.
1920 Curtis Lee Laws invents the word "fundamentalists."
1925 In Dayton, Tennessee, John Scopes is convicted of teaching evolution and fined $100.
1928 Hasan al-Banna founds the Muslim Brotherhood.
1941 Carl McIntire launches the American Council of Christian Churches.
1942 The National Association of Evangelicals is created.

1948 In New Delhi, a Hindu nationalist assassinates Mahatma Gandhi.
1951 Sayyid Qutb publishes "The America I Have Seen."
1956 *Christianity Today* is founded by Carl F. H. Henry and Billy Graham. It goes on to become one of the most prominent Christian magazines in the United States.
1966 Sayyid Qutb is executed.
1968 A group of orthodox Jews establish Kiryat Arba, one of the first settlements in the occupied territories.
1974 In the wake of the Yom Kippur War, Gush Emunim is created.
1976 Jimmy Carter, who describes himself as a born-again Christian, is elected to the U.S. presidency.
1979 Ayatollah Ruhollah Khomeini returns to Tehran.
1979 Jerry Falwell founds the Moral Majority.
1980 Hindu nationalists organize the Bharatiya Janata Party.
1981 Members of the Egyptian Islamic Jihad assassinate Anwar Sadat.
1987 Hamas is founded.
1993 A bomb is detonated in the parking garage of the World Trade Center.
1995 Yitzhak Rabin is killed.
2001 The World Trade Center and the Pentagon are attacked.
2003 The United States invades Afghanistan.
2006 Hamas decisively defeats Fatah in parliamentary elections in Palestine.
2012 Mohamed Morsi is elected president of Egypt.
2013 A military coup removes Morsi from power.

Chronology of Interpretations

This chronology lists some of the most noteworthy interpretations of fundamentalism that were created between 1922 and the present.

1922 Harry Emerson Fosdick, "Shall the Fundamentalists Win?"
1925 Kirsopp Lake, Religion of Yesterday and To-morrow
1931 Frederick Lewis Allen, Only Yesterday
1940 Talcott Parsons, "Memorandum: The Development of Groups and Organizations Amenable to Use against American Institutions and Foreign Policy"
1947 Carl F. H. Henry, The Uneasy Conscience of Modern Fundamentalism
1954 Norman F. Furniss, The Fundamentalist Controversy
1960 Stanley Kramer, Inherit the Wind
1963 Richard Hofstadter, Anti-Intellectualism in American Life
1970 Ernest Sandeen, The Roots of Fundamentalism
1980 Martin E. Marty, "Fundamentalism Reborn: Faith and Fanaticism"

1982 Flo Conway and Jim Siegelman, Holy Terror
1988 Martin E. Marty, "Fundamentalism as a Social Phenomenon"
1990 Bernard Lewis, "The Roots of Muslim Rage"
1991 Martin Marty and R. Scott Appleby, Fundamentalisms Observed
1994 Karen McCarthy Brown, "Fundamentalism and the Control of Women"
1994 Jay Harris, "'Fundamentalism': Objections from a Modern Jewish Historian"
1995 Martin Marty and R. Scott Appleby, Fundamentalisms Comprehended
1995 Henry Munson Jr., "Not All Crustaceans Are Crabs: Reflections on the Comparative Study of Fundamentalism and Politics"
1996 Martin Marty, "Too Bad We Are So Relevant"
1997 Bobby Sayyid, A Fundamental Fear
1999 Haideh Moghissi, Feminism and Islamic Fundamentalism
1999 Israel Shahak and Norton Mezvinsky, Jewish Fundamentalism in Israel
2000 Martin Riesebrodt, "Fundamentalism and the Resurgence of Religion"
2001 Brenda Brasher, Encyclopedia of Fundamentalism
2002 Karen Armstrong, "Is a Holy War Inevitable?"
2003 Gabriel Almond, R. Scott Appleby, and Emmanuel Sivan, Strong Religion
2006 Bill Moyers, "9/11 and God's Sport"
2007 Rebecca Joyce Frey, Fundamentalism
2012 Mira Nair, The Reluctant Fundamentalist

Notes

Preface

1. Salim Chowdhury is a pseudonym.

2. Jamaat-e-Islami does not define itself as a political party pure and simple. It sees itself as "a complete Islamic movement" that is concerned with spiritual issues as well as political ones and that is deeply committed to thoroughgoing social reform. Bangladesh Jamaat-e-Islami, "About Us," http://jamaat-e-islami.org/en/aboutus.php, accessed May 11, 2016. Since 2006, Jamaat-e-Islami has fallen on hard times. It suffered disastrous losses in the 2008 parliamentary elections, and as of this writing it is not a part of the coalition that governs Bangladesh. Several of its leaders, including the man herein referred to as Salim Chowdhury, have been hanged.

3. Bashir Khan is a pseudonym.

4. Jamaat-e-Islami, "Parliamentary Elections 2001: Bangladesh Jamaat-e-Islami, Constitutional and Legal Reforms," www.bangla2000.com/Election_2001/Manifesto_Jamaat-e-Islami.shtm, accessed March 28, 2016.

5. For a passionate critique of Jamaat-e-Islami, see Hiranmay Karlekar, *Bangladesh: The Next Afghanistan?* (New Delhi: Sage, 2005). A less alarmist and more scholarly analysis of Jamaat-e-Islami can be found in Ali Riaz, *God Willing: The Politics of Islamism in Bangladesh* (Lanham, MD: Rowman & Littlefield, 2004).

6. See, for example, Haideh Moghissi, *Feminism and Islamic Fundamentalism: The Limits of Postmodern Analysis* (London: Zed Books, 1999), 70–73 and Gabriel A. Almond,

R. Scott Appleby, and Emmanuel Sivan, *Strong Religion: The Rise of Fundamentalisms around the World* (Chicago: University of Chicago Press, 2003), 17.

7. *Webster's New International Dictionary of the English Language* (Springfield, MA: G. & C. Merriam, 1954).

8. Barack Obama, "Preface to the 2004 Edition," in *Dreams from My Father: A Story of Race and Inheritance* (New York: Three Rivers Press, 2004), xi.

9. Lisa Leff, "World Still Dangerous, Quayle Tells Midshipman," *Washington Post*, May 31, 1990.

10. U.S. Congress, House Committee on Foreign Affairs, *Islamic Fundamentalism in Africa and Implications for US Policy: Hearings before the Subcommittee on Africa of the Committee on Foreign Affairs, House of Representatives, 102nd Congress, 2nd Session, May 20, 1992* (Washington, DC: U.S. Government Printing Office, 1993), 41.

11. Khaled Elgindy, "AIPAC 1995: Politics and Priorities," *Journal of Palestine Studies* 24, no. 4 (1995): 86.

12. Bill Clinton, "Interview with the French Media in Paris," June 7, 1994, in *Public Papers of the Presidents of the United States: William J. Clinton, 1994*, Book 1, *January 1 to July 31, 1994* (Washington, DC: U.S. Government Printing Office, 1995), 1056.

Introduction

1. Karen Armstrong, *The Battle for God* (New York: Knopf, 2000); Karen Armstrong, *A History of God: The 4000-Year Quest of Judaism, Christianity, and Islam* (New York: Knopf, 1993).

2. Karen Armstrong, "Is a Holy War Inevitable?" *GQ*, January 2002, 96–101, 122–123.

3. Morgan Norval, *Triumph of Disorder: Islamic Fundamentalism, the New Face of War* (Indian Wells, CA: McKenna), 9.

4. Armstrong, "Is a Holy War Inevitable?" 99, 101, 123.

5. The role the Fundamentalism Project played in shaping Armstrong's ideas about fundamentalism is particularly evident in the introduction to and the endnotes for Armstrong, *The Battle for God*.

6. Martin E. Marty, "Fundamentalism Reborn: Faith and Fanaticism," *Saturday Review*, May 1980, 37–42.

7. R. Scott Appleby, "But All Crabs Are Crabby: Valid and Less Valid Criticisms of the Fundamentalism Project," *Contention* 4, no. 3 (1995): 196–197.

8. "Fundamentalisms around the World," *Bulletin of the American Academy of Arts and Sciences* 41 (March 1988): 9–12.

9. Martin E. Marty, "Fundamentalism as a Social Phenomenon," *Bulletin of the American Academy of Arts and Sciences* 42 (November 1988): 25–26.

10. Ibid., 16–17.

11. Ibid., 20–23.

12. "The Fundamentalism Project," *American Academy of Arts and Sciences*, https://www.amacad.org/content/Research/researchproject.aspx?d=246, accessed March 28, 2016.

13. Martin E. Marty, "Just Desserts," *The Christian Century* 110, no. 7 (Mar. 1993), 255.

14. Martin E. Marty and R. Scott Appleby, "Introduction," in *Fundamentalisms Comprehended*, ed. Martin E. Marty and R. Scott Appleby (Chicago: University of Chicago Press, 1995), 6.

15. Martin E. Marty and R. Scott Appleby, *The Glory and the Power: The Fundamentalist Challenge to the Modern World* (Boston: Beacon, 1992).

16. James Piscatori, ed., *Islamic Fundamentalisms and the Gulf Crisis* (Chicago: Fundamentalism Project, American Academy of Arts and Sciences, 1991).

17. Martin E. Marty, "Too Bad We Are So Relevant: The Fundamentalism Project Projected," *Bulletin of the American Academy of Arts and Sciences* 49, no. 6 (1996): 34.

18. "Fundamentalism Project Honored," *Bulletin of the American Academy of Arts and Sciences* 50, no. 2 (1996): 47.

19. Susan Harding, "Imaging the Last Days: The Politics of Apocalyptic Language," in *Accounting for Fundamentalisms*, ed. Martin E. Marty and R. Scott Appleby (Chicago: University of Chicago Press, 1994), 57–78; Mumantz Ahmad, "Islamic Fundamentalism in South Asia: The Jamaat-i-Islami and Tablighi Jamaat," in *Fundamentalisms Observed*, ed. Martin E. Marty and R. Scott Appleby (Chicago: University of Chicago Press, 1991), 457–530; and D. Michael Quinn, "Plural Marriage and Mormon Fundamentalism," in *Fundamentalisms and Society*, ed. Martin E. Marty and R. Scott Appleby (Chicago: University of Chicago Press, 1991), 240–293.

20. Marty, "Too Bad We Are So Relevant," 37; "Transcript for Martin Marty—America's Changing Religious Landscape," *On Being*, November 2, 2006, http://www.onbeing.org/program/america039s-changing-religious-landscape-conversation-martin-marty/transcript/603, accessed April 26, 2016; Martin E. Marty and R. Scott Appleby, "Conclusion," in *Fundamentalisms and the State*, ed. Martin E. Marty and R. Scott Appleby (Chicago: University of Chicago Press, 1993), 640–641.

21. Writing in the introduction to *Fundamentalisms and Society*, the directors of the Fundamentalism Project said: "The fact that nonfundamentalists do the writing guarantees that this volume, and the entire project, will reflect a particular orientation to foundational questions and will produce conclusions in keeping with that orientation." Martin E. Marty and R. Scott Appleby, "Introduction," in *Fundamentalisms and Society* (Chicago: University of Chicago Press, 1991), 17. In 1993, Samuel Heilman, one of the participants in the Fundamentalism Project, noted that "the project did not succeed in integrating fundamentalist representatives themselves in its work." Peter Steinfels, "Fundamentalism: The 20th Century's Last Ideology," *New York Times*, April 6, 1993. For a discussion of the Fundamentalism Project's failure to publish any essays written by fundamentalists, see Marty, "Too Bad We Are So Relevant," 33.

22. See, for example, Jorge E. Maldonado, "Building 'Fundamentalism' from the Family in Latin America," in *Fundamentalisms and Society*, ed. Martin E. Marty and R. Scott Appleby (Chicago: University of Chicago Press, 1993), 214–215.

23. On this point, see Martin E. Marty and R. Scott Appleby, "Introduction," in *Accounting for Fundamentalisms*, ed. Martin E. Marty and R. Scott Appleby (Chicago: University of Chicago Press, 1994), 8–9.

24. Martin E. Marty and R. Scott Appleby, "Introduction," in *Fundamentalisms Comprehended*, ed. Martin E. Marty and R. Scott Appleby (Chicago: University of Chicago Press, 1995), 6–7.

25. Marty, "Too Bad We Are So Relevant," 27–28.

26. Juan Eduardo Campo quoted Ramadan in "Hegemonic Discourse and the Islamic Question in Egypt," *Contention* 4, no. 3 (1995): 182.

27. Ibid., 182.

1. Skeptics

1. Kenneth D. Wald, "Accounting for Jewish Fundamentalisms: Dynamic Movements, Static Frameworks?" *Review of Religious Research* 37 (1996): 365; Laurence R. Iannaccone, "Toward an Economic Theory of 'Fundamentalism,'" *Journal of Institutional and Theoretical Economics* 153, no. 1 (1997): 100–101.

2. Khalid Yahya Blankinship, "Muslim 'Fundamentalism,' Salafism, Sufism, and Other Trends," in *Fundamentalism: Perspectives on a Contested History*, ed. Simon A. Wood and David Harrington Watt (Columbia: University of South Carolina Press, 2014), 149–150, 157–158.

3. Alvin Plantinga, *Warranted Christian Belief* (New York: Oxford University Press, 2000), 244–245.

4. Blankinship, "Muslim 'Fundamentalism.'"

5. Martin E. Marty, "Fundamentalism Reborn: Faith and Fanaticism," *Saturday Review*, May 1980, 37–38.

6. Jay M. Harris, "'Fundamentalism': Objections from a Modern Jewish Historian," in *Fundamentalism and Gender*, ed. John Stratton Hawley (New York: Oxford University Press, 1994), 137.

7. David Landau, *Piety and Power: The World of Jewish Fundamentalism* (New York: Hill and Wang, 1993), 155–156.

8. Ira M. Lapidus, *A History of Islamic Societies*, 2nd ed. (Cambridge: Cambridge University Press, 2002), 823.

9. Blankinship, "Muslim 'Fundamentalism.'"

10. Iannaccone, "Toward an Economic Theory of 'Fundamentalism,'" 103–104.

11. Saba Mahmood, *Politics of Piety: The Islamic Revival and the Feminist Subject* (Princeton, NJ: Princeton University Press, 2005), 1–4, 41–43.

12. Bobby S. Sayyid, *A Fundamental Fear: Eurocentrism and the Emergence of Islamism* (London: Zed Books, 1997), 8–11. One of the many works that emphasizes fundamentalists' attempts to control women and their bodies is Gita Sahgal and Nira Yuval-Davis, eds., *Refusing Holy Orders: Women and Fundamentalism in Britain* (London: Virago, 1992).

13. Harris, "'Fundamentalism,'" 157–160.

14. Malise Ruthven, *Fundamentalism: The Search for Meaning* (Oxford: Oxford University Press, 2004), 5–6.

15. For an example of this sort of approach to defining fundamentalism, see Johannes J. G. Jansen, *The Dual Nature of Islamic Fundamentalism* (Ithaca, NY: Cornell University Press, 1997). For a criticism of it, see Vinay Lal, "Hindu 'Fundamentalism' Revisited," *Contention* 4, no. 2 (1995): 170.

16. Sayyid, *A Fundamental Fear*, 14–15.

17. Saba Mahmood, "Islamism and Fundamentalism," *Middle East Report* no. 191 (November–December 1994): 30.

18. Sayyid, *A Fundamental Fear*, 3–4.

19. For a useful discussion of the complexities related to modernity, see Dipesh Chakrabarty, "The Muddle of Modernity," *American Historical Review* 116, no. 3 (2011): 663–675.

20. Henry Munson Jr., "Not All Crustaceans Are Crabs: Reflections on the Comparative Study of Fundamentalism and Politics," *Contention* 4, no. 3 (1995): 162–163.

21. Blankinship, "Muslim 'Fundamentalism.'"

22. Mark Juergensmeyer, "Antifundamentalism," in *Fundamentalisms Comprehended*, ed. Martin E. Marty and R. Scott Appleby (Chicago: University of Chicago Press, 1995), 353–359.

23. Ibid., 354.

24. Mahmood, "Islamism and Fundamentalism," 30.

25. John H. Simpson, review of *Fundamentalisms and the State*, edited by Martin E. Marty and Scott Appleby, *Journal for the Scientific Study of Religion* 33, no. 4 (1994): 388–389.

26. Iannaccone, "Toward an Economic Theory of 'Fundamentalism,'" 101, italics in the original.

27. Ibid., 114.

28. Sayyid, *A Fundamental Fear*, 4.

29. Gabriele Marranci, *Understanding Muslim Identity: Rethinking Fundamentalism* (Basingstoke: Palgrave Macmillan, 2009), 48–49.

30. Edward W. Said, *Culture and Imperialism* (New York: Knopf, 1993).

31. Edward W. Said, *Orientalism* (New York: Vintage Books, 1979); Dipesh Chakrabarty, *Provincializing Europe: Postcolonial Thought and Historical Difference* (Princeton, NJ: Princeton University Press, 2000).

32. Said, *Culture and Imperialism*, 310.

33. Simpson, review of *Fundamentalisms and the State*, 388.

2. Defenders

1. Steve Bruce, *Fundamentalism* (Cambridge: Polity, 2000), 125–126.

2. Minoo Moallem, *Between Warrior Brother and Veiled Sister: Islamic Fundamentalism and the Politics of Patriarchy in Iran* (Berkeley: University of California Press, 2005), 10.

3. Brenda E. Brasher, ed., *Encyclopedia of Fundamentalism* (New York: Routledge, 2001), xvii.

4. Karen Armstrong, *The Battle for God* (New York: Knopf, 2000), x–xi.

5. Martin E. Marty, "The Fundamentals of Fundamentalism," in *Fundamentalism in Comparative Perspective*, ed. Lawrence Kaplan (Amherst: University of Massachusetts Press, 1992), 17. In the original, the passage I quote here was printed in all capital letters.

6. Tessa J. Bartholomeusz and Chandra R. de Silva, "Buddhist Fundamentalism and Identity in Sri Lanka," in *Buddhist Fundamentalism and Minority Identities in Sri Lanka*, ed. Tessa J. Bartholomeusz and Chandra R. de Silva (Albany: State University of New York Press, 1998), 2; R. Scott Appleby, "Fundamentalism," in *The Encyclopedia of Politics and Religion*, ed. Robert Wuthnow (Washington, DC: Congressional Quarterly, 1998), 280–288.

7. Bruce B. Lawrence, *Defenders of God: The Fundamentalist Revolt against the Modern Age* (Columbia: University of South Carolina Press, 1995), xxi.

8. R. Scott Appleby, "But All Crabs Are Crabby: Valid and Less Valid Criticisms of the Fundamentalism Project," *Contention* 4, no. 3 (1995): 196–199.

9. Haideh Moghissi, *Feminism and Islamic Fundamentalism: The Limits of Postmodern Analysis* (New York: Zed Books, 1999), 65–66; Sadik J. al-Azm, "Islamic Fundamentalism Reconsidered: A Critical Outline of Problems, Ideas, and Approaches, Part 1," *South Asia Bulletin* 13 (1993): 95.

10. Marty, "The Fundamentals of Fundamentalism," 17; Martin E. Marty, "Comparing Fundamentalisms," *Contention* 4, no. 2 (1995): 19–20. Cf. William James, *Varieties of Religious Experience: A Study in Human Nature* (New York: Longmans, Green, & Co, 1902), 9.

11. Marty, "Comparing Fundamentalisms," 19–25.

12. Marty, "The Fundamentals of Fundamentalism," 17.

13. Lawrence, *Defenders of God*, 27.

14. Moallem, *Between Warrior Brother and Veiled Sister*, 10.

15. Martin E. Marty and R. Scott Appleby, "Conclusion: An Interim Report on a Hypothetical Family," in *Fundamentalisms Observed*, ed. Martin E. Marty and R. Scott Appleby (Chicago: University of Chicago Press, 1991), 835.

16. Martin E. Marty and R. Scott Appleby, *The Glory and the Power: The Fundamentalist Challenge to the Modern World* (Boston: Beacon, 1992), 198.

17. Lawrence, *Defenders of God*, xiii.

18. Henry Munson Jr., "Not All Crustaceans Are Crabs: Reflections on the Comparative Study of Fundamentalism and Politics," *Contention* 4, no. 3 (1995): 161–162.

19. Appleby, "But All Crabs Are Crabby," 198.

20. Ibid., 196, 199.

21. Marty, "Comparing Fundamentalisms," 28.

22. Gabriel A. Almond, R. Scott Appleby, and Emmanuel Sivan, *Strong Religion: The Rise of Fundamentalisms around the World* (Chicago: University of Chicago Press, 2003), 16–17.

23. Moghissi, *Feminism and Islamic Fundamentalism*, 47–63.

24. Juan Eduardo Campo, "Hegemonic Discourse and the Islamic Question in Egypt," *Contention* 4, no. 3 (1995): 189.

25. Munson, "Not All Crustaceans Are Crabs," 153.

26. Marty, "Comparing Fundamentalisms," 19.

27. Campo, "Hegemonic Discourse and the Islamic Question in Egypt," 189.

28. Appleby, "But All Crabs Are Crabby," 196–197.

29. Johannes J. G. Jansen, *The Dual Nature of Islamic Fundamentalism* (Ithaca, NY: Cornell University Press, 1997), xiv–xvi, 177–180; Henry Munson Jr., "Western Academia and Islamic Fundamentalism," *Contention* 5, no. 3 (1996): 99–117.

30. "Fundamentalisms around the World," *Bulletin of the American Academy of Arts and Sciences* 41 (March 1988): 16, emphasis added. The project's focus on public policy is also emphasized in Martin E. Marty, "Too Bad We Are So Relevant: The Fundamentalism Project Projected," *Bulletin of the American Academy of Arts and Sciences* 49, no. 6 (1996): 22.

31. Martin E. Marty, "The Future of World Fundamentalisms," *Proceedings of the American Philosophical Society* 142, no. 3 (1998): 372–373. The project's interest in policy questions is particularly evident in James Piscatori, ed., *Islamic Fundamentalisms and the Gulf Crisis* (Chicago: Fundamentalism Project, American Academy of Arts and Sciences, 1991).

32. Ernest Gellner, *Postmodernism, Reason, and Religion* (London: Routledge, 1991), 80.

33. Roxanne L. Euben, *Enemy in the Mirror: Islamic Fundamentalism and the Limits of Modern Rationalism* (Princeton, NJ: Princeton University Press, 1999), xi; Daniel T. Rodgers, *Age of Fracture* (Cambridge, MA: Harvard University Press, 2011), 155–164, 173–176.

34. Almond, Appleby, and Sivan, *Strong Religion*, 15–16.

35. Ibid., 16.

3. The First Fundamentalists

1. Lyman's brother Milton also contributed money to support *The Fundamentals*, but it is clear that Lyman was the driving force behind the booklets. Ernest R. Sandeen, *The Roots of Fundamentalism* (Chicago: University of Chicago Press, 1970), 188–198.

2. James Orr, "Holy Scripture and Modern Negations," in *The Fundamentals: A Testimony to the Truth*, ed. R. A. Torrey, A. C. Dixon, and Louis Meyer (1910–1915; repr., Grand Rapids, MI: Baker, 2000), 1:94 and 108.

3. C. Allyn Russell, *Voices of American Fundamentalism: Seven Biographical Studies* (Philadelphia: Westminster, 1976), 98.

4. World Conference on Christian Fundamentals, *God Hath Spoken: Twenty-Five Addresses Delivered at the World Conference on Christian Fundamentals, May 25–June 1, 1919*, ed. Joel A. Carpenter (1919; repr., New York: Garland, 1988), 11–12.

5. W. B. Riley, "The Menace of Modernism," in *Conservative Call to Arms*, ed. Joel A. Carpenter (1917; repr., New York: Garland, 1988), 35. Riley was the driving force behind the creation of the WCFA.

6. Curtis Lee Laws, "Convention Side Lights," *Watchman-Examiner*, July 1, 1920, 834.

7. For a highly intelligent critique of what I take to be the current scholarly consensus on Christian fundamentalism, see Michael S. Hamilton, "The Interdenominational Evangelicalism of D. L. Moody and the Problem of Fundamentalism," in *American Evangelicalism: George Marsden and the State of American Religious History*, ed. Darren Dochuk, Thomas S.

Kidd, and Kurt W. Peterson (South Bend, IN: University of Notre Dame Press, 2014), 230–280.

8. Norman F. Furniss, *The Fundamentalist Controversy, 1918–1931* (New Haven, CT: Yale University Press, 1954); Richard Hofstadter, *Anti-Intellectualism in American Life* (New York: Knopf, 1963).

9. Particularly helpful analyses of fundamentalism can be found in Margaret Lamberts Bendroth, *Fundamentalists in the City: Conflict and Division in Boston's Churches, 1885–1950* (New York: Oxford University Press, 2005); Virginia Lieson Brereton, *Training God's Army: The American Bible School, 1880–1940* (Bloomington: Indiana University Press, 1990); Joel A. Carpenter, *Revive Us Again: The Reawakening of American Fundamentalism* (New York: Oxford University Press, 1997); Betty A. DeBerg, *Ungodly Women: Gender and the First Wave of American Fundamentalism* (Minneapolis, MN: Fortress Press, 1990); Timothy E. W. Gloege, *Guaranteed Pure: The Moody Bible Institute, Business, and the Making of Modern Evangelicalism* (Chapel Hill: University of North Carolina Press, 2015); D. G. Hart, *Defending the Faith: J. Gresham Machen and the Crisis of Conservative Protestantism in Modern America* (Baltimore, MD: Johns Hopkins University Press, 1994); George M. Marsden, *Fundamentalism and American Culture*, 2nd ed. (New York: Oxford University Press, 2006); Mary Beth Swetnam Mathews, *Rethinking Zion: How the Print Media Placed Fundamentalism in the South* (Knoxville: University of Tennessee Press, 2006); B. M. Pietsch, *Dispensational Modernism* (New York: Oxford University Press, 2015); Matthew Avery Sutton, *American Apocalypse: A History of Modern Evangelicalism* (Cambridge, MA: The Belknap Press of Harvard University Press, 2014); William Vance Trollinger, *God's Empire: William Bell Riley and Midwestern Fundamentalism* (Madison: University of Wisconsin Press, 1990); and Timothy P. Weber, *Living in the Shadow of the Second Coming: American Premillennialism, 1875–1925* (New York: Oxford University Press, 1979). Fundamentalism is also analyzed in David Harrington Watt, *A Transforming Faith: Explorations of Twentieth-Century American Evangelicalism* (New Brunswick, NJ: Rutgers University Press, 1991).

10. Carpenter, *Revive Us Again*, 4–5.

11. Although American fundamentalists had a number of connections to conservative Protestants in Great Britain and there were a good many fundamentalists in Canada, fundamentalism proper was firmly rooted in the United States. For a particularly lucid analysis of this issue, see Marsden, *Fundamentalism and American Culture*, 179–180, 221–228.

12. William R. Hutchison, *Religious Pluralism in America: The Contentious History of A Founding Ideal* (New Haven, CT: Yale University Press, 2003), 148, notes that some lists of the fundamentals contained five points and that others listed as many as fourteen. Such discrepancies, Hutchison notes, gave some observers the impressions that fundamentalists could not agree on exactly what it was they believed to be fundamental.

13. World Conference on Christian Fundamentals, *God Hath Spoken*, 12.

14. A very fine analysis of the role Bible institutes played in shaping fundamentalism in the United States can be found in Brereton, *Training God's Army.*

15. Bob Jones College, which was founded in 1926, did not become Bob Jones University until 1947.

16. Carpenter, *Revive Us Again*, 25–28.

17. Many fundamentalists looked to Machen for intellectual leadership, and Machen acknowledged that he was a fundamentalist, according to some definitions of the term. But he generally avoided using that term to describe himself, and he declined an invitation to join the WCFA. J. Gresham Machen to R. S. Kellerman, October 7, 1924, J. Gresham Machen Papers, Montgomery Memorial Library, Westminster Theological Seminary, Glenside, PA; Hart, *Defending the Faith*, 61–65.

18. Edward J. Larson, *Summer for the Gods: The Scopes Trial and America's Continuing Debate over Science and Religion* (New York: Basic Books, 1997), 230–231.

19. Joel A. Carpenter, "Fundamentalist Institutions and the Rise of Evangelical Protestantism," *Church History* 49, no. 1 (1980): 74–75.

20. Robert Elwood Wenger, "Social Thought in American Fundamentalism, 1918–1933" (PhD diss., University of Nebraska, 1973).

21. Daniel W. Draney, *When Streams Diverge: John Murdoch MacInnis and the Origins of Protestant Fundamentalism in Los Angeles* (Eugene, OR: Wipf and Stock, 2008); Bendroth, *Fundamentalists in the City*; Trollinger, *God's Empire*; and Carpenter, "Fundamentalist Institutions and the Rise of Evangelical Protestantism," 62–63.

22. Brereton, *Training God's Army*, 29.

23. Jeffrey P. Moran, "The Scopes Trial and Southern Fundamentalism in Black and White: Race, Region, and Religion," *Journal of Southern History* 70, no. 1 (2004): 115.

24. Barbara Diane Savage, *Your Spirits Walk Beside Us: The Politics of Black Religion* (Cambridge, MA: Harvard University Press, 2008), 124; Carl Abrams, e-mail message to the author, October 11, 2009.

25. Moran, "The Scopes Trial and Southern Fundamentalism," 118–120; Jeffrey P. Moran, "Reading Race into the Scopes Trial: African American Elites, Science, and Fundamentalism," *Journal of American History* 90, no. 3 (2003): 896–899.

26. Ann Braude, "Women's History *Is* American Religious History," in *Retelling U.S. Religious History*, ed. Thomas A. Tweed (Berkeley: University of California Press, 1997), 87–107; Bendroth, *Fundamentalists in the City*, 166.

27. Margaret Lamberts Bendroth, "The New Evangelical History," paper presented at the Annual Meeting of the American Academy of Religion, Montreal, Canada, November 9, 2009.

28. Margaret Lamberts Bendroth, *Fundamentalism and Gender, 1875 to the Present* (New Haven, CT: Yale University Press, 1993), 81–89.

29. Brereton, *Training God's Army*, 26–29. Brereton notes that advertisements that appeared in fundamentalist magazines suggest that many fundamentalists wanted to improve their command of the English language in order to improve their social standing and their economic condition.

30. For a discussion of fundamentalists' willingness to pour their energy into serving God, see Brereton, *Training God's Army*, 114–115.

31. A chart drawn by one of the fundamentalists' spiritual ancestors that illustrates this point is reproduced in Marsden, *Fundamentalism and American Culture*, 69.

32. Carpenter, *Revive Us Again*, 76–80.

33. Larson, *Summer for the Gods*, 188–189.

34. Carpenter, *Revive Us Again*, 89–109.

35. Brereton, *Training God's Army*, 29; Carpenter, *Revive Us Again*, 63–64, 107.

36. George M. Marsden, "Fundamentalism," in *Encyclopedia of the American Religious Experience*, ed. Charles H. Lippy and Peter W. Williams (New York: Scribner, 1988), 956.

37. Ibid., 949.

38. Ibid.

39. Douglas Carl Abrams, *Selling the Old-Time Religion: American Fundamentalists and Mass Culture, 1920–1940* (Athens: University of Georgia Press, 2001), 21.

40. Elizabeth Knauss, *The Conflict: A Narrative Based on the Fundamentalist Movement* (Los Angeles: Bible Institute of Los Angeles, 1923).

41. Arno Clemens Gaebelein, *The Conflict of the Ages* (New York: Our Hope, 1933), 150.

42. J. Gresham Machen, *Christianity and Liberalism* (New York: Macmillan, 1923), 52.

43. J. Gresham Machen, *What Is Faith?* (New York: Macmillan, 1925), 102.

44. Hart, *Defending the Faith*, 69–71.

45. Machen, *Christianity and Liberalism*, 110, 117.

46. Ibid., 157–180. Machen did not argue, however, that church membership should be limited to people who were wholeheartedly committed to the central doctrines of the Christian faith. He wanted there to be room in the church for laymen who were beset by doubt but who were also engaged in an honest search for truth. On this point, see ibid., 163–164.

47. The Machen Archives at Westminster Theological Seminary contain a good many letters in which Machen respectfully addresses people with whom he had deep disagreements. See, for example, J. Gresham Machen to John W. Milton, May 27, 1923; J. Gresham Machen to Arthur E. Whatham, January 14, 1924; and J. Gresham Machen to Charles J. Wood, December 31, 1924, J. Gresham Machen Papers, Montgomery Memorial Library, Westminster Theological Seminary, Glenside, PA.

48. Machen, *Christianity and Liberalism*, 8.

49. Ibid., 160.

50. William R. Hutchison, *The Modernist Impulse in American Protestantism* (Cambridge, MA: Harvard University Press, 1976), 264, 267.

51. Russell, *Voices of American Fundamentalism*, 65–66.

52. Gaebelein, *The Conflict of the Ages*, 135.

53. Bendroth, *Fundamentalism and Gender*, 66.

54. W. B. Riley, *Inspiration or Evolution*, 2nd ed. (Cleveland: Union Gospel Press, 1926), 5.

55. For an analysis of a struggle that did involve actual violence, see Barry Hankins, *God's Rascal: J. Frank Norris and the Beginnings of Southern Fundamentalism* (Lexington: University Press of Kentucky, 1996), 118–120.

4. Invention

1. Harry Emerson Fosdick, "A Spiritual Autobiography," unpublished ms., n.d., p. 2, Series 3B, Box 1, Folder 2, Harry Emerson Fosdick Papers, Burke Library, Union Theological Seminary, New York, NY.

2. For a fine analysis of Rockefeller's religiosity and his support of Fosdick's work, see Robert Moats Miller, *Harry Emerson Fosdick: Preacher, Pastor, Prophet* (New York: Oxford University Press, 1985), 159–169, 464–469. Although Fosdick's stands on economic issues sometimes puzzled Rockefeller, the two men were able to forge a deep friendship.

3. Ibid., 5, 99–100. The kind of Quakerism that Fosdick found most congenial was a mystical, liberal version of Quakerism espoused by one of his mentors, Rufus Jones.

4. Ibid., 115–117.

5. Harry Emerson Fosdick, "Shall the Fundamentalists Win?" in *American Sermons: The Pilgrims to Martin Luther King, Jr.*, ed. Michael Warner (New York: Library of America, 1999), 776.

6. Ibid., 777, 786.

7. Miller, *Harry Emerson Fosdick*, 158.

8. Fosdick, "Shall the Fundamentalists Win?" 775.

9. Ibid., 780.

10. Ibid., 780–781.

11. Malachi, one of the books of the middle section of the Tanakh, appears at the very end of the Protestant Old Testament.

12. Fosdick, "Shall the Fundamentalists Win?" 775–776.

13. Ibid., 783.

14. Information about Lake's life can be found in Gerald K. Lake, "Biographical Note," in *Quantulacumque: Studies Presented to Kirsopp Lake by Pupils, Colleagues, and Friends*,

ed. Robert P. Casey, Silva Lake, and Agnes K. Lake (London: Christophers, 1937), vii–viii; and in the *Dictionary of American Biography*, s.v. "Lake, Kirsopp."

15. Morton S. Enslin, "A Notable Contribution to Acts," *Journal of Biblical Literature* 52, no. 4 (1933): 230–238; Margaret Hope Bacon, *Let This Life Speak* (Philadelphia: University of Pennsylvania Press, 1987), 56, 70.

16. Kirsopp Lake, *The Religion of Yesterday and To-morrow* (London: Christophers, 1925), 9.

17. Ibid., 78, 106–107, 113, 154–155.

18. Ibid., 68, 70, 132, 161–163.

19. Ibid., 60–62, 69–70, 159–161.

20. Ibid., 62, 69, 112.

21. Ibid., 61, 69, 145. The phrase "God's Word written" comes from the Thirty-Nine Articles of Religion of the Church of England.

22. Lake, *The Religion of Yesterday and To-morrow*, 62, 87, 102, 132.

23. Ibid., 61, 119.

24. Darwin Payne, *The Man of Only Yesterday* (New York: Harper and Row, 1975), 99–105.

25. Ibid., 95.

26. Frederick Lewis Allen, *Only Yesterday: An Informal History of the Nineteen-Twenties* (New York: Harper and Brothers, 1931), 195–197.

27. Ibid., 220.

28. Ibid., 199.

29. Ibid., 202.

30. Ibid., 152.

31. Ibid., 204–206.

32. Edwin W. Hullinger, "Islam's Ties of Unity Are Loosening," *New York Times*, July 18, 1926.

33. William Jourdan Rapp, "Islam Fundamentalists Fight Modernist Trend," *New York Times*, September 20, 1925.

34. Another group of Muslims were referred to as "Islamic fundamentalists" in Roswell Locke Band Jr., "Ahmed Called Disturber of the Peace in Near East," *New York Times*, August 23, 1925.

35. The Google Books Ngram Viewer, an imperfect but useful online research tool, produces a graph like the one described above.

5. Ratification

1. "Rev. H. Richard Niebuhr Dead; Authority on Christian Ethics," *New York Times*, July 6, 1962.

2. Jon Diefenthaler, *H. Richard Niebuhr: A Lifetime of Reflection on the Church and the World* (Macon, GA: Mercer University Press, 1986), 7–8.

3. Niebuhr was also willing to assert that it was dangerous for a Christian to make Jesus Christ "the absolute center of confidence and loyalty." See H. Richard Niebuhr, *Radical Monotheism and Western Culture, with Supplementary Essays* (New York: Harper, 1960), 59.

4. Niebuhr's definition of provincialism was quite broad. He believed that analyses of the universe that privileged the human beings who lived on Earth were provincial and therefore inadequate. H. Richard Niebuhr, "Planetary Provincialism," manuscript, bMS695/6 (38), Series III: Addresses, Sermons, and Chapel Talks, H. Richard Niebuhr Papers, Andover-Harvard Theological Library, Harvard Divinity School, Cambridge, MA.

5. Diefenthaler, *H. Richard Niebuhr*, 5.

6. H. Richard Niebuhr to the Board of Directors of Eden Theological Seminary, June 13, 1929, H. Richard Niebuhr Papers, Andover-Harvard Theological Library, Harvard Divinity School, Cambridge, MA; Walter Brueggemann, *Ethos and Ecumenism, an Evangelical Blend: A History of Eden Theological Seminary, 1925–1975* (St. Louis, MO: Eden, 1975), 13–20.

7. Diefenthaler, *H. Richard Niebuhr*, 36–37.

8. H. Richard Niebuhr, "Fundamentalism," in *Encyclopedia of the Social Sciences*, vol. 6 (New York: Macmillan, 1931), 526–527.

9. Ibid., 527.

10. Ibid. On the similarities between magical practices and the religious practices of rural America, see H. Richard Niebuhr, *The Social Sources of Denominationalism* (New York: Holt, 1929), 184–185.

11. Niebuhr, "Fundamentalism," 527.

12. Niebuhr, *The Social Sources of Denominationalism*, 186–187.

13. Mike F. Keen, "No One above Suspicion: Talcott Parsons under Surveillance," *The American Sociologist* 24, no. 3/4 (1993): 37.

14. Scholars who highlight and critique Parsons's teleological assumptions are right, I think, to do so. Parsons often did seem to write as though history had a telos toward which it ought to be moving. Parsons did not, however, believe that modernization and rationalization were inevitable; he regarded them as vulnerable, hard-won achievements. On this point see Uta Gerhardt, *Talcott Parsons: An Intellectual Biography* (Cambridge: Cambridge University Press, 2002), 174–175, 268–270.

15. Jesse R. Pitts, "Talcott Parsons: The Sociologist as the Last Puritan," August 1979, Papers of Talcott Parsons, Harvard University Archives, Cambridge, MA.

16. Parsons was not an avid churchgoer. See Charles Parsons, "Some Remarks on Talcott Parsons's Family," *American Sociologist* 35, no. 4 (2004): 17. But he was deeply interested in religion, and some of his contemporaries believed that he was "a deeply religious man." See Willy De Craemer, "Prayer at Memorial Service for Professor Talcott Parsons," May 18, 1979, Papers of Talcott Parsons, Harvard University Archives, Cambridge, MA.

17. For a note about Parsons's mother and her ancestors, see the captions to the photographs that precede chapter 3 of Gerhardt, *Talcott Parsons*.

18. Talcott Parsons, *Social Systems and the Evolution of Action Theory* (New York: Free Press, 1977), 29.

19. Gerhardt, *Talcott Parsons*, 273.

20. Ibid., 74–75.

21. That text is now stored in the Parsons papers in the Harvard University Archives. The published version of the essay is Talcott Parsons, "Memorandum: The Development of Groups and Organizations Amenable to Use against American Institutions and Foreign Policy," in *Talcott Parsons on National Socialism*, ed. Uta Gerhardt (New York: Aldine De Gruyter, 1993), 101–130. The page references that follow all refer to the published version of the paper.

22. Ibid., 101.

23. For a note about Parsons's love of newspapers in general and the *New York Times* in particular, see the captions to the photographs that precede chapter 3 of Gerhardt, *Talcott Parsons*.

24. Parsons, "Memorandum: The Development of Groups and Organizations Amenable to Use against American Institutions and Foreign Policy," 103–104.

25. Writing in 2004, Talcott Parsons's son said that although many people knew of his father's "New England ancestry," some did not realize "how pure this ancestry was." One of Talcott Parsons's ancestors probably came to New England on the *Mayflower*. Up until the middle decades of the twentieth century, the Parsons family was made up very largely of New

Englanders and almost exclusively of white Anglo-Saxon Protestants. Parsons, "Some Remarks on Talcott Parsons's Family," 4 and 17.

26. Parsons, "Memorandum: The Development of Groups and Organizations Amenable to Use against American Institutions and Foreign Policy," 107.

27. Parsons put special emphasis on the possibility that immigrants from Ireland might sympathize with the Nazis. See ibid., 105–107.

28. Ibid., 106–107.

29. John T. McGreevy, *Catholicism and American Freedom: A History* (New York: Norton, 2003).

30. Talcott Parsons, *Essays in Sociological Theory* (Glencoe, IL: Free Press, 1954), 138.

31. Parsons, "Memorandum: The Development of Groups and Organizations Amenable to Use against American Institutions and Foreign Policy," 110–111.

32. Parsons, *Essays in Sociological Theory*, 123.

33. Parsons, "Memorandum: The Development of Groups and Organizations Amenable to Use against American Institutions and Foreign Policy," 110–111, 116–117.

34. Joel Carpenter, *Revive Us Again: The Reawakening of American Fundamentalism* (New York: Oxford University Press, 1997), 162–171. The fervent nationalism that pervaded the fundamentalist subculture during World War II is portrayed beautifully in Shirley Nelson's novel *The Last Year of the War* (New York: Harper and Row, 1978).

35. Heather Hendershot, *What's Fair on the Air? Cold War Right-Wing Broadcasting and the Public Interest* (Chicago: University of Chicago Press, 2011), 113; and Tona J. Hangen, *Redeeming the Dial: Radio, Religion and Popular Culture in America* (Chapel Hill: University of North Carolina Press, 2002), 23–26.

36. Carpenter, *Revive Us Again*, 145–151.

37. Ibid., 150–152; and Garth M. Rosell, *The Surprising Work of God: Harold John Ockenga, Billy Graham, and the Rebirth of Evangelicalism* (Grand Rapids, MI: Baker Academic, 2008), 73–106.

38. Carl F. H. Henry, *Confessions of a Theologian: An Autobiography* (Waco, TX: Word Books, 1986), 105–106, 115, 147.

39. Laurie Goldstein, "Rev. Dr. Carl F. H. Henry, 90, Brain of Evangelical Movement," *New York Times*, December 13, 2003. Useful analyses of Henry's life and thought can be found in Carpenter, *Revive Us Again*, 191–209; and Bob E. Patterson, *Carl F. H. Henry* (Waco, TX: Word Books, 1983).

40. Carl F. H. Henry, *The Uneasy Conscience of Modern Fundamentalism* (Grand Rapids, MI: Eerdmans, 1947), 16.

41. Carl F. H. Henry, "The Vigor of the New Evangelicalism [Part Three]," *Christian Life*, April 1948, 69.

42. Henry, *The Uneasy Conscience of Modern Fundamentalism*, 62.

43. Ibid., 39.

44. Ibid., 60–61.

45. Ibid., 10, 51.

46. Ibid., 26–27, 44–45.

47. Isaac Asimov, one of America's best-known writers of science fiction, used the concept of fundamentalism in a similar fashion. In *I, Robot* (Garden City, NY: Doubleday, 1950), Asimov labeled people who failed to adapt to the new social realities created by modern technology as fundamentalists.

48. Martin E. Marty, "Fundamentalism Reborn: Faith and Fanaticism," *Saturday Review*, May 1980, 42.

6. The Dustbin of History

1. Flannery O'Connor, *Wise Blood* (New York: Harcourt, Brace, 1952), chapter 14. For a different take on this matter, see David Harrington Watt, *Bible-Carrying Christians: Conservative Protestants and Social Power* (New York: Oxford University Press, 2002), 118.

2. For a recent appraisal of the importance of Sandeen's work, see Matthew Avery Sutton, *American Apocalypse: A History of Modern Evangelicalism* (Cambridge, MA: The Belknap Press of Harvard University Press, 2014), xi–xii.

3. Norman F. Furniss, *The Fundamentalist Controversy, 1918–1931* (New Haven, CT: Yale University Press, 1954).

4. Luther A. Weigle, Review of *The Fundamentalist Controversy*, by Norman Furniss, *Church History* 25, no. 1 (March 1956): 92; Irvin G. Wyllie, Review of *The Fundamentalist Controversy*, by Norman Furniss, *Journal of Southern History*, 20, no. 4 (November 1954), 565–567; Edward A. White, Review of *The Fundamentalist Controversy*, by Norman Furniss, *Mississippi Valley Historical Review* 42, no. 1 (June 1955), 146.

5. Furniss, *The Fundamentalist Controversy*, 14.

6. Ibid., 23.

7. Ibid., 179.

8. Ibid., 178–179.

9. Ibid., 179–180.

10. Wyllie, review of *The Fundamentalist Controversy*, 567.

11. Young was, in fact, blacklisted. When he wrote the screenplay for *Inherit the Wind*, he used the pen name Nathan E. Douglas.

12. John Thomas Scopes and James Presley, *Center of the Storm: Memoirs of John T. Scopes* (New York: Holt, Rinehart, and Winston, 1967), 267–268.

13. *Inherit the Wind*, dir. Stanley Kramer, 1960, DVD, GM/UA Home Video, Culver City, CA, 2001.

14. David S. Brown, *Richard Hofstadter: An Intellectual Biography* (Chicago: University of Chicago Press, 2007), 37, 40, 47–49. Brown's many insights into Hofstadter's work deeply influenced my understanding of Hofstadter's analysis of fundamentalism.

15. Ibid., 50, 65–71, 73–74, 215.

16. Ibid., 207–221.

17. Richard Hofstadter, *Anti-Intellectualism in American Life* (New York: Knopf, 1963), 3–5.

18. Ibid., 27–28.

19. Ibid., 19.

20. Ibid., 29.

21. Ibid., 58–59.

22. Ibid., 118–120.

23. Ibid., 117, 121.

24. Ibid., 125.

25. Ibid., 126–127.

26. Ibid., 133–134.

27. Ibid., 122.

28. Ibid., 135.

29. Ibid., 119.

30. Ibid., 121.

31. Ibid., 131.

32. Brown, *Richard Hofstadter*, 131.

33. Brown, *Richard Hofstadter*, 138–140; Rush Welter, Review of *Anti-Intellectualism in American Life*, by Richard Hofstadter, *Journal of American History* 51, no. 3 (1964), 482–483; Cushing Strout, Review of *Anti-Intellectualism in American Life*, by Richard Hofstadter, *Journal of Southern History* 29, no. 4 (1963), 544–545; Arthur Bestor, Review of *Anti-Intellectualism in American Life*, by Richard Hofstadter, *American Historical Review* 70, no. 4 (1965), 1118–1120; Philip Gleason, Review of *Anti-Intellectualism in American Life*, by Richard Hofstadter, *Review of Politics* 28, no. 2 (1966), 238–242; Daniel J. Boorstin, Review of *Anti-Intellectualism in American Life*, by Richard Hofstadter, *Saturday Review* (June 1, 1963), 19; Kenneth S. Lynn, "Elitism on the Left," Review of *Anti-Intellectualism in American Life*, by Richard Hofstadter, *The Reporter* (July 4, 1963), 37–39.

34. Quoted in Brown, *Richard Hofstadter*, 138.

35. Ibid., 124.

36. Ibid., 124–125.

37. William R. Hutchison, Review of *The Roots of Fundamentalism: British and American Millenarianism, 1830–1930*, by Ernest R. Sandeen, *Journal of American History* 58, no. 1 (1971): 159–160; George M. Marsden, "Defining Fundamentalism," *Christian Scholars Review* 1, no. 2 (1971): 142.

38. Ernest R. Sandeen, "Fundamentalism and American Identity," *Annals of the American Academy of Political and Social Science* 387, no. 1 (1970): 57.

39. Ernest R. Sandeen, "Toward a Historical Interpretation of the Origins of Fundamentalism," *Church History* 36, no. 1 (1967): 83.

40. Ernest R. Sandeen, "Defining Fundamentalism: A Response to Professor Marsden," *Christian Scholars Review* 1, no. 3 (1971): 228.

41. Ernest R. Sandeen, *The Roots of Fundamentalism: British and American Millenarianism, 1800–1930* (1970; repr., Grand Rapids, MI: Baker, 1978), 114–131.

42. Sandeen, "Fundamentalism and American Identity," 57; Sandeen, "Toward a Historical Interpretation," 67.

43. Benjamin B. Warfield, *The Inspiration and Authority of the Bible* (Philadelphia, PA: Presbyterian and Reformed Publishing Co., 1948), 112. See also Sandeen, *Roots of Fundamentalism*, 123.

44. Cyrus Ingerson Scofield, ed., *The Scofield Reference Bible: The Holy Bible Containing the Old and the New Testaments* (New York: Oxford University Press, 1909), was a particularly effective vehicle for broadcasting the ideas Sandeen analyzed. Paul Boyer concludes that from 1909 to 1967, Oxford University Press may well have sold more than ten million copies of the *Scofield Reference Bible*. Sales certainly exceeded five million. Paul Boyer, *When Time Shall Be No More: Prophecy Belief in Modern American Culture* (Cambridge, MA: Belknap Press, 1992), 97–98.

7. Reinvention

1. See, for example, "The CIA at Harvard," *Boston Globe*, November 29, 1985.

2. Charles R. Babcock, "Harvard Unaware CIA Funded Book, Seminar," *Washington Post*, October 12, 1985; "Harvard Allows Professor to Use $50,000 Grant from C.I.A. for Conference on Islam," *New York Times*, October 12, 1985.

3. A.J. Toynbee, *A Journey to China or Things Which Are Seen* (London: Constable, 1931), 117; H.A.R. Gibb, *Modern Trends in Islam* (Chicago: University of Chicago Press, 1947); H.A.R. Gibb, *Mohammedanism: An Historical Survey* (New York: Oxford University Press, 1949); and Leonard Binder, *Religion and Politics in Pakistan* (Berkeley: University of California Press, 1961). For a pathbreaking analysis of the early history of the concept of

Islamic fundamentalism, see Rosemary R. Corbett, "Islamic 'Fundamentalism': The Mission Creep of an American Religious Metaphor," *Journal of the American Academy of Religion* 83, no. 4 (2015): 977–1004.

4. In 1985, people were talking about fundamentalism a good deal more frequently—perhaps two or three times more frequently, in fact—than they were in 1965. (This estimate is based on a search using Google's Ngram Viewer. The line on the Ngram graph is fairly flat from 1963 to 1977. It begins to climb upward in 1978. In 1985 it was still going up quite dramatically.)

5. Martin E. Marty, "Fundamentalism Reborn: Faith and Fanaticism," *Saturday Review*, May 1980, 37–42; Flo Conway and Jim Siegelman, *Holy Terror: The Fundamentalist War on America's Freedoms in Religion, Politics, and Our Private Lives* (Garden City, NY: Doubleday, 1982); U.S. Congress, House Committee on Foreign Affairs, *Islamic Fundamentalism and Islamic Radicalism: Hearings before the Subcommittee on Europe and the Middle East of the Committee on Foreign Affairs, House of Representatives, 99th Cong., 1st session, June 24, July 15, and September 30, 1985* (Washington, DC: U.S. Government Printing Office, 1985).

6. David Martin, "Towards Eliminating the Concept of Secularization," in *Penguin Survey of the Social Sciences*, ed. Julius Gould (Baltimore: Penguin, 1965), 169–182; Robert N. Bellah, "Confessions of a Former Establishment Fundamentalist," *Bulletin of the Council on the Study of Religion* 1, no. 3 (1970): 3–6; and Andrew M. Greeley, *Unsecular Man: The Persistence of Religion* (New York: Schocken Books, 1974), 7.

7. Sol W. Sanders, "The First Domino of Central America," *Business Week*, July 23, 1979, 81.

8. Dean M. Kelley, *Why Conservative Churches Are Growing: A Study in Sociology of Religion* (New York: Harper and Row, 1972), 1–33.

9. Ibid., 35.

10. See, for example, Ernest R. Sandeen, "Fundamentalism and American Identity," *Annals of the American Academy of Political and Social Science* 387, no. 1 (1970): 56; "Explo '72: 'Holler for Jesus,'" *New York Times*, June 18, 1972.

11. Grant Wacker, *America's Pastor: Billy Graham and the Shaping of a Nation* (Cambridge, MA: Harvard University Press, 2014), 68–101.

12. Helpful analyses of the New Christian Right can be found in Daniel K. Williams, *God's Own Party: The Making of the Christian Right* (New York: Oxford University Press, 2010), 105–212; Randall Balmer, *God in the White House: A History* (New York: HarperOne), 92–124; and Matthew Avery Sutton, *American Apocalypse: A History of Modern Evangelicalism* (Cambridge, MA: Harvard University Press, 2014). For a succinct statement of the political and social ideals of one of the more prominent leaders of the New Christian Right, see Jerry Falwell, *America Can Be Saved!* (Murfreesboro, TN: Sword of the Lord Publishers, 1979).

13. For an expression of alarm over the power of the Protestant fundamentalist radical right, see Gary K. Clabaugh, *Thunder on the Right: The Protestant Fundamentalists* (Chicago: Nelson-Hall, 1974). By the early 1980s, some observers seem to have begun to suspect that the fundamentalists and their allies were "subversives" who were plotting to impose a fascist regime on the United States. See Daniel C. Maguire, *The New Subversives: The Anti-Americanism of the Religious Right* (New York: Continuum, 1982).

14. Marty, "Fundamentalism Reborn," 37.

15. Ibid., 38.

16. Ibid., 37.

17. Ibid., 38.

18. Ibid., 37–38.

19. Ibid., 37.
20. Ibid., 42.
21. Ibid., 38, 42.
22. Conway and Siegelman, *Holy Terror*, 32.
23. Ibid., 208–215.
24. Ibid., 207.
25. Ibid., 10.
26. Ibid., 263–271.
27. Ibid., 340.
28. Ibid., 301.
29. Ibid., 310–314.
30. U.S. Congress, House Committee on Foreign Affairs, *Islamic Fundamentalism and Islamic Radicalism*, 81, 87, 154, 156, 164–166, 270.
31. Ibid., 40–43.
32. Ibid., 2, 3, 84.
33. Ibid., 107.
34. Ibid., 5, 87, 123, 168.
35. Ibid., 86–87, 93, 96–99, 122.
36. Ibid., 1.
37. Ibid., 25, 72, 77.
38. Ibid., 170.
39. Ibid., 149–150.
40. *Encyclopædia Britannica Online*, s. v. "fundamentalism," accessed March 30, 2015.
41. Peter van der Veer, "Religious Nationalism in India and Global Fundamentalism," in *Globalizations and Social Movements: Culture, Power, and the Transnational Public Sphere*, ed. John A. Guidry, Michael D. Kennedy, and Mayer N. Zald (Ann Arbor: University of Michigan Press, 2000), 316.

8. Zenith

1. Bernard Lewis, "The Roots of Muslim Rage," *Atlantic Monthly*, September 1990, 47–60.
2. Israel Shahak and Norton Mezvinsky, *Jewish Fundamentalism in Israel* (Sterling, VA: Pluto Press, 1999).
3. Bill Moyers, "9/11 and God's Sport," *CrossCurrents* 55 (2006): 442–455.
4. James Davison Hunter, "Fundamentalism in Its Global Contours," in *The Fundamentalist Phenomenon: A View from Within; A Response from Without*, ed. Norman J. Cohen (Grand Rapids, MI: Eerdmans, 1990), 38–55; Martin Riesebrodt, "Fundamentalism and the Resurgence of Religion," *Numen* 47, no. 3 (2000): 266–287.
5. Lewis, "The Roots of Muslim Rage,"48, 59.
6. Ibid., 59.
7. Ibid., 60.
8. Ibid., 47–49, 56.
9. Ibid., 49, 59.
10. Ibid., 49.
11. Ibid., 53–54.
12. Ibid., 52.
13. Rebecca Joyce Frey, *Fundamentalism* (New York: Facts on File, 2007), 364–366.
14. Hunter, "Fundamentalism in Its Global Contours," 57.
15. Ibid., 67–69.

16. Ibid., 58–59, 62.
17. Ibid., 60–62.
18. Ibid., 59.
19. Ibid., 65–67.
20. Ibid., 63–65.
21. Ibid., 56–57.
22. Ibid., 57.
23. Martin E. Marty and R. Scott Appleby, "Conclusion: An Interim Report on a Hypothetical Family," in *Fundamentalisms Observed*, ed. Martin E. Marty and R. Scott Appleby (Chicago: University of Chicago Press, 1991), 814–842, my italics.
24. Laurence R. Iannaccone, "Toward an Economic Theory of 'Fundamentalism,'" *Journal of Institutional and Theoretical Economics* 153, no. 1 (1997): 114.
25. Riesebrodt, "Fundamentalism and the Resurgence of Religion," 271, 276–278, 283.
26. Ibid., 281–282.
27. Ibid., 279–280.
28. Ibid., 266–267, 276–278, 282, 286.
29. Shahak and Mezvinsky, *Jewish Fundamentalism in Israel*, vii, ix, 96, 153–154.
30. Ibid., 149.
31. Ibid., 157.
32. Ibid., 113–149.
33. Ibid., 160.
34. Moyers, "9/11 and God's Sport," 444.
35. Ibid., 444–445.
36. Ibid., 447–449.
37. Ibid., 449.
38. Ibid., 449.
39. Ibid., 449.
40. Ibid., 449–450.
41. Ibid., 450–453.
42. Ibid., 450, 455.
43. Ibid., 447–449.

Conclusion

1. *The Reluctant Fundamentalist*, directed by Mira Nair, DVD, IFC Films, distributed by MPI Home Video, Chicago, 2013; George Soros, *Crisis of Global Capitalism* (New York: Public Affairs, 1998), 126–128; Fred Block and Margaret R. Somers, *The Power of Market Fundamentalism: Karl Polanyi's Critique* (Cambridge, MA: Harvard University Press, 2014), 150–192.
2. *Babylon 10 Thesaurus*, s.v. "Fundamentalism," http://thesaurus.babylon.com, accessed July 9, 2015.
3. Terry H. Wallace, "Misunderstanding Quaker Faith and Practice," *Friends Journal*, January 2007, 6–8, 44; Sallie B. King, *A Quaker Response to Christian Fundamentalism: A Curriculum for Friends* (Sandy Spring, MD: Baltimore Yearly Meeting, Religious Education Committee, 2007), 1; Anthony Giddens, *Runaway World* (New York: Routledge, 2000), 22–23.
4. David Brooks, "Drafting Hitler," *New York Times*, February 9, 2006.
5. Susan D. Rose, "Antifeminism," in *Encyclopedia of Fundamentalism*, ed. Brenda Brasher (New York: Routledge, 2001), 16–18.
6. Steve Bruce, *Fundamentalism* (Cambridge: Polity, 2000), 16–39, 118–123.

7. William R. G. Loader, *Jesus and the Fundamentalism of His Day* (Grand Rapids, MI: Eerdmans, 2001), 27.

8. James Simpson, *Burning to Read: English Fundamentalism and Its Reformation Opponents* (Cambridge, MA: Belknap Press of Harvard University Press, 2007); Harvard University Press, "Burning to Read: English Fundamentalism and Its Reformation Opponents," http://www.hup.harvard.edu/catalog, accessed September 24, 2010.

9. Marge Piercy, "The Fundamental Truth," *Tikkun*, January/February 1996, inside front cover.

10. Barry A. Kosmin, Egon Mayer, and Ariela Keysar, *American Religious Identification Survey* (New York: Graduate Center of the City University of New York, 2001), 12.

11. Ted Olsen, "The End of Christian Fundamentalism?" *Christianity Today*, March 1, 2002, http://www.christianitytoday.com/ct/2002/marchweb-only/3-11-53.0.html, accessed March 24, 2016.

12. "University Creed and Mission," *Bob Jones University*, http://www.bju.edu/about/mission-statement.php, accessed March 24, 2016.

13. "About Liberty," *Liberty University*, http://www.liberty.edu/aboutliberty/, accessed March 24, 2016.

14. A systematic comparison of the relationship between the role fundamentalists play in American culture with the role Quakers play might prove instructive. Fundamentalism is often seen as religion at its worst: intolerant, reactionary, cruel, and belligerent. Quakerism, on the other hand, is often viewed as religion at its best: tolerant, progressive, kindhearted, and peaceful. For a very fine analysis of the role Quakerism has historically played in Americans' imaginations, see James Emmett Ryan, *Imaginary Friends: Representing Quakers in American Culture, 1650–1950* (Madison: University of Wisconsin Press, 2009).

15. Karen Armstrong, "Is a Holy War Inevitable?" *GQ*, January 2002, 97–98. Cf. Samuel Huntington, *The Clash of Civilizations and the Remaking of World Order* (New York: Simon and Schuster, 1996), 217: "The underlying problem for the West is not Islamic fundamentalism. It is Islam."

16. William E. Arnal and Russell T. McCutcheon, *The Sacred Is the Profane: The Political Nature of "Religion"* (New York: Oxford University Press, 2013); Richard W. Bulliet, *The Case for Islamo-Christian Civilization* (New York: Columbia University Press, 2004); Timothy Fitzgerald, *Discourse on Civility and Barbarity: A Critical History of Religion and Related Categories* (New York: Oxford University Press, 2007); Janet R. Jakobsen and Ann Pellegrini, eds., *Secularisms* (Durham, NC: Duke University Press, 2008); Saba Mahmood, *Politics of Piety: The Islamic Revival and the Feminist Subject* (Princeton, NJ: Princeton University Press, 2005).

17. On this point, see Wendy Brown, *Regulating Aversion: Tolerance in the Age of Identity and Empire* (Princeton, NJ: Princeton University Press, 2006).

18. For a particularly clearheaded discussion of this issue, see Bobby S. Sayyid, *A Fundamental Fear: Eurocentrism and the Emergence of Islamism* (London: Zed, 1997), 8–11.

19. See Talal Asad, *Genealogies of Religion: Discipline and Reasons of Power in Christianity and Islam* (Baltimore, MD: Johns Hopkins University Press, 1993), 236.

Select Bibliography

Manuscript Collections

General Manuscript Collection. Rare Book and Manuscript Library. Columbia University, New York, NY.

Harry Emerson Fosdick Papers. Burke Library. Union Theological Seminary. New York, NY.

H. Richard Niebuhr Papers. Andover-Harvard Theological Library. Harvard Divinity School, Cambridge, MA

J. Gresham Machen Papers. Montgomery Memorial Library. Westminster Theological Seminary, Glenside, PA.

Papers of Talcott Parsons. Harvard University Archives. Cambridge, MA.

Richard Hofstadter Papers. Rare Book and Manuscript Library. Columbia University, New York, NY.

Films

Inherit the Wind. 1960. Dir. Stanley Kramer. United Artists. DVD distributed by GM/UA Home Video, Culver City, CA.

The Reluctant Fundamentalist. 2013. Dir. Mira Nair. IFC Films. DVD distributed by MPI Home Video, Chicago.

Published Sources

Abrams, Douglas Carl. *Selling the Old-Time Religion: American Fundamentalists and Mass Culture, 1920–1940*. Athens: University of Georgia Press, 2001.

Ahmad, Mumantz. "Islamic Fundamentalism in South Asia: The Jamaat-i-Islami and Tablighi Jamaat." In *Fundamentalisms Observed*, ed. Martin E. Marty and R. Scott Appleby, 457–530. Chicago: University of Chicago Press, 1991.

al-Azm, Sadik J. "Islamic Fundamentalism Reconsidered: A Critical Outline of Problems, Ideas, and Approaches, Part 1." *South Asia Bulletin* 13 (1993): 93–121.

——. "Islamic Fundamentalism Reconsidered: A Critical Outline of Problems, Ideas, and Approaches, Part 2." *South Asia Bulletin* 14 (1994): 73–98.

Ali, Tariq. *The Clash of Fundamentalisms: Crusades, Jihads and Modernity*. London: Verso, 2002.

Allen, Frederick Lewis. *Only Yesterday: An Informal History of the Nineteen-Twenties*. New York: Harper and Brothers, 1931.

Almond, Gabriel A., R. Scott Appleby, and Emmanuel Sivan. *Strong Religion: The Rise of Fundamentalisms around the World*. Chicago: University of Chicago Press, 2003.

Ammerman, Nancy Tatom. *Bible Believers: Fundamentalists in the Modern World*. New Brunswick, NJ: Rutgers University Press, 1987.

Anidjar, Gil. *The Jew, the Arab: A History of the Enemy*. Stanford, CA: Stanford University Press, 2003.

Antoun, Richard T. *Understanding Fundamentalism: Christian, Islamic, and Jewish Movements*. Walnut Creek, CA: AltaMira Press, 2001.

Appleby, R. Scott. "But All Crabs Are Crabby: Valid and Less Valid Criticisms of the Fundamentalism Project." *Contention* 4 (1995): 195–202.

——. "Fundamentalism." In *The Encyclopedia of Politics and Religion*, ed. Robert Wuthnow. Washington, DC: Congressional Quarterly, 1998.

Armstrong, Karen. *The Battle for God*. New York: Knopf, 2000.

——. *A History of God: The 4000-Year Quest of Judaism, Christianity, and Islam*. New York: Knopf, 1993.

——. "Is a Holy War Inevitable?" *GQ*, January 2002, 97–101, 122–123.

Arnal, William E., and Russell T. McCutcheon. *The Sacred Is the Profane: The Political Nature of "Religion."* New York: Oxford University Press, 2013.

Asad, Talal. *Formations of the Secular*. Stanford, CA: Stanford University Press, 2003.

——. *Genealogies of Religion: Discipline and Reasons of Power in Christianity and Islam*. Baltimore, MD: Johns Hopkins University Press, 1993.

Atwood, Margaret. *The Handmaid's Tale*. Boston: Houghton Mifflin, 1986.

Bacon, Margaret Hope. *Let This Life Speak*. Philadelphia: University of Pennsylvania Press, 1987.

Baker, Susan Stout. *Radical Beginnings: Richard Hofstadter and the 1930s*. Westport, CT: Greenwood Press, 1985.

Balmer, Randall. *God in the White House: A History*. New York: HarperOne, 2008.
Band, Roswell Locke, Jr. "Ahmed Called Disturber of Peace in Near East." *New York Times*, August 23, 1925.
Bartholomeusz, Tessa J., and Chandra R. de Silva. *Buddhist Fundamentalism and Minority Identities in Sri Lanka*. Albany: State University of New York Press, 1998.
Bellah, Robert N. "Religious Evolution." *American Sociological Review* 29, no. 3 (1964): 358–374.
——. "Confessions of a Former Establishment Fundamentalist." *Bulletin of the Council on the Study of Religion* 1, no. 3 (1970): 3–6.
Bendroth, Margaret Lamberts. *Fundamentalism and Gender, 1875 to the Present*. New Haven, CT: Yale University Press, 1993.
——. *Fundamentalists in the City: Conflict and Division in Boston's Churches, 1885–1950*. New York: Oxford University Press, 2005.
——. "The New Evangelical History." Paper presented at the Annual Meeting of the American Academy of Religion, Montreal, Canada, November 9, 2009.
Berger, Peter L., ed. *The Desecularization of the World: Resurgent Religion and World Politics*. Washington, DC: Ethics and Public Policy Center, 1999.
——. *Between Relativism and Fundamentalism*. Grand Rapids, MI: Eerdmans, 2010.
Blankinship, Khalid Yahya. "Muslim 'Fundamentalism,' Salafism, Sufism, and Other Trends." In *Fundamentalism: Perspectives on a Contested History*, ed. Simon A. Wood and David Harrington Watt, 144–162. Columbia: University of South Carolina Press, 2014.
Blanshard, Paul. *Communism, Democracy, and Catholic Power*. Boston: Beacon Press, 1951.
Block, Fred, and Margaret R. Somers. *The Power of Market Fundamentalism: Karl Polanyi's Critique*. Cambridge, MA: Harvard University Press, 2014.
Boer, Roland. "Fundamentalism." In *New Keywords: A Revised Vocabulary of Culture and Society*, ed. Tony Bennett, Lawrence Grossberg, and Meaghan Morris, 134–137. Malden, MA: Blackwell, 2005.
Boyer, Paul. *When Time Shall Be No More: Prophecy Belief in Modern American Culture*. Cambridge, MA: Belknap Press, 1992.
Brasher, Brenda, ed. *Encyclopedia of Fundamentalism*. New York: Routledge, 2001.
Braude, Ann. "Women's History *Is* American Religious History." In *Retelling U.S. Religious History*, ed. Thomas A. Tweed, 87–107. Berkeley: University of California Press, 1997.
Brekke, Torkel. *Fundamentalism: Prophecy and Protest in an Age of Globalization*. New York: Cambridge University Press, 2012.
Brereton, Virginia Lieson. *Training God's Army: The American Bible School, 1880–1940*. Bloomington: Indiana University Press, 1990.
Brink, Judy, and Joan Mencher, eds. *Mixed Blessings: Gender and Religious Fundamentalism Cross Culturally*. New York: Routledge, 1997.
Brooks, David. "Drafting Hitler." *New York Times*, February 9, 2006.
Brouwer, Steve, Paul Gifford, and Susan D. Rose. *Exporting the American Gospel: Global Christian Fundamentalism*. New York: Routledge, 1996.
Brown, David S. *Richard Hofstadter: An Intellectual Biography*. Chicago: University of Chicago Press, 2007.

Brown, Karen McCarthy. "Fundamentalism and the Control of Women." In *Fundamentalism and Gender*, ed. John Stratton Hawley, 175–201. New York: Oxford University Press, 1994.

Brown, Wendy. *Regulating Aversion: Tolerance in the Age of Identity and Empire*. Princeton, NJ: Princeton University Press, 2006.

Bruce, Steve. *Fundamentalism*. Cambridge: Polity, 2000.

Brueggemann, Walter. *Ethos and Ecumenism, an Evangelical Blend: A History of Eden Theological Seminary, 1925–1975*. St. Louis, MO: Eden, 1975.

Bulliet, Richard W. *The Case for Islamo-Christian Civilization*. New York: Columbia University Press, 2004.

Campo, Juan Eduardo. "Hegemonic Discourse and the Islamic Question in Egypt." *Contention* 4 (1995): 167–194.

Caplan, Lionel, ed. *Studies in Religious Fundamentalism*. Albany: State University of New York Press, 1987.

Carpenter, Joel A. "Fundamentalist Institutions and the Rise of Evangelical Protestantism." *Church History* 49 (1980): 62–75.

——. *Revive Us Again: The Reawakening of American Fundamentalism*. New York: Oxford University Press, 1997.

Cavanaugh, William T. *The Myth of Religious Violence: Secular Ideology and the Roots of Modern Conflict*. Oxford: Oxford University Press, 2009.

Chakrabarty, Dipesh. "The Muddle of Modernity." *American Historical Review* 116, no. 3 (2011): 663–675.

——. *Provincializing Europe: Postcolonial Thought and Historical Difference*. Princeton, NJ: Princeton University Press, 2000.

Clabaugh, Gary K. *Thunder on the Right: The Protestant Fundamentalists*. Chicago: Nelson-Hall, 1974.

Cohen, Norman J., ed. *The Fundamentalist Phenomenon: A View from Within; A Response from Without*. Grand Rapids, MI: Eerdmans, 1990.

Conway, Flo, and Jim Siegelman. *Holy Terror: The Fundamentalist War on America's Freedoms in Religion, Politics, and Our Private Lives*. Garden City, NY: Doubleday, 1982.

Corbett, Rosemary R. "Islamic 'Fundamentalism': The Mission Creep of an American Religious Metaphor." *Journal of the American Academy of Religion* 83, no. 4 (2015): 977–1004.

Crapanzano, Vincent. *Serving the Word: Literalism in America from the Pulpit to the Bench*. New York: New Press, 2000.

Davidson, Lawrence. *Islamic Fundamentalism*. Westport, CT: Greenwood Press, 1998.

DeBerg, Betty A. *Ungodly Women: Gender and the First Wave of American Fundamentalism*. Minneapolis: Fortress Press, 1990.

Diefenthaler, Jon. *H. Richard Niebuhr: A Lifetime of Reflections on the Church and the World*. Macon, GA: Mercer University Press, 1986.

Draney, Daniel W. *When Streams Diverge: John Murdoch MacInnis and the Origins of Protestant Fundamentalism in Los Angeles*. Eugene, OR: Wipf and Stock, 2008.

Eisenstadt, S.N. *Tradition, Change and Modernity*. New York: Wiley, 1973.

El-Or, Tamar. *Educated and Ignorant: Ultraorthodox Jewish Women and Their World*. Trans. Haim Watzman. Boulder, CO: Lynne Rienner, 1994.

Emerson, Michael O., and David Hartman. "The Rise of Religious Fundamentalism." *Annual Review of Sociology* 32 (2006): 127–144.

Enslin, Morton S. "A Notable Contribution to Acts." *Journal of Biblical Literature* 52, no. 4 (1933): 230–238.

Euben, Roxanne Leslie. *Enemy in the Mirror: Islamic Fundamentalism and the Limits of Modern Rationalism*. Princeton, NJ: Princeton University Press, 1999.

Falwell, Jerry. *America Can Be Saved!* Murfreesboro, TN: Sword of the Lord, 1979.

——. *Listen America!* New York: Bantam, 1981.

——, ed. *The Fundamentalist Phenomenon: The Resurgence of Conservative Christianity*. Garden City, NY: Doubleday, 1981.

Fields, Echo E. "Understanding Activist Fundamentalism: Capitalist Crisis and the 'Colonization of Lifeworld.'" *Sociological Analysis* 52, no. 2 (1991): 175–190.

Fitzgerald, Timothy. *Discourse on Civility and Barbarity: A Critical History of Religion and Related Categories*. New York: Oxford University Press, 2007.

Fosdick, Harry Emerson. *As I See Religion*. New York: Harper and Brothers, 1932.

——. *The Living of These Days: An Autobiography*. New York: Harper and Brothers, 1956.

——. "Shall the Fundamentalists Win?" In *American Sermons: The Pilgrims to Martin Luther King, Jr*., ed. Michael Warner, 775–786. New York: Library of America, 1999.

Frey, Rebecca Joyce. *Fundamentalism*. New York: Facts on File, 2007.

"Fundamentalisms around the World." *Bulletin of the American Academy of Arts and Sciences* 41 (March 1988): 9–19.

"The Fundamentalism Project." *American Academy of Arts and Sciences*. https://www.amacad.org/content/Research/researchproject.aspx?d=246. Accessed March 28, 2016.

"Fundamentalism Project Honored." *Bulletin of the American Academy of Arts and Sciences* 50 (1996): 47.

Furniss, Norman F. *The Fundamentalist Controversy, 1918–1931*. New Haven, CT: Yale University Press, 1954.

Gaebelein, Arno Clemens. *The Conflict of the Ages*. New York: Our Hope, 1933.

Gellner, Ernest. *Postmodernism, Reason and Religion*. London: Routledge, 1992.

Gerhardt, Uta. *Talcott Parsons: An Intellectual Biography*. Cambridge: Cambridge University Press, 2002.

Gibb, H. A. R. *Modern Trends in Islam*. Chicago: University of Chicago Press, 1947.

——. *Mohammedanism: An Historical Survey*. New York: Oxford University Press, 1949.

Giddens, Anthony. *Runaway World*. New York: Routledge, 2000.

Gloege, Timothy E. W. *Guaranteed Pure: The Moody Bible Institute, Business, and the Making of Modern Evangelicalism*. Chapel Hill: University of North Carolina Press, 2015.

Goldstein, Laurie. "Rev. Dr. Carl F. H. Henry, 90, Brain of Evangelical Movement." *New York Times*, December 13, 2003.

Grace, Alexander M. *Holy War: A Novel*. Arlington, VA: Vandamere Press, 1998.

Greeley, Andrew M. *Unsecular Man: The Persistence of Religion*. New York: Schocken Books, 1974.

Hamid, Mohsin. *The Reluctant Fundamentalist*. Orlando, FL: Harcourt, 2007.

Hamilton, Michael S. "The Interdenominational Evangelicalism of D.L. Moody and the Problem of Fundamentalism." In *American Evangelicalism: George Marsden and the State of American Religious History*, ed. Kurt Peterson, Thomas Kidd and Darren Dochuk, 230–280. South Bend, IN: University of Notre Dame Press, 2014.

Hangen, Tona J. *Redeeming the Dial: Radio, Religion and Popular Culture in America*. Chapel Hill: University of North Carolina Press, 2002.

Hankins, Barry. *God's Rascal: J. Frank Norris and the Beginnings of Southern Fundamentalism*. Lexington: University Press of Kentucky, 1996.

Harding, Susan Friend. *The Book of Jerry Falwell: Fundamentalist Language and Politics*. Princeton, NJ: Princeton University Press, 2000.

——. "Imaging the Last Days: The Politics of Apocalyptic Language." In *Accounting for Fundamentalisms: The Dynamic Character of Movements*, ed. Martin E. Marty and R. Scott Appleby, 57–78. Chicago: University of Chicago Press, 1994.

Harris, Jay M. "'Fundamentalism': Objections from a Modern Jewish Historian." In *Fundamentalism and Gender*, ed. John Stratton Hawley, 137–173. New York: Oxford University Press, 1994.

Hart, D.G. *Defending the Faith: J. Gresham Machen and the Crisis of Conservative Protestantism in Modern America*. Baltimore, MD: Johns Hopkins University Press, 1994.

Hassan, Riffat. "The Burgeoning of Islamic Fundamentalism." In *The Fundamentalist Phenomenon: A View from Within; a Response from Without*, ed. Norman J. Cohen, 151–171. Grand Rapids, MI: Eerdmans, 1990.

Hawley, John Stratton, ed. *Fundamentalism and Gender*. New York: Oxford University Press, 1994.

Hedges, Chris. *When Atheism Becomes Religion: America's New Fundamentalists*. New York: Free Press, 2009.

Hendershot, Heather. *What's Fair on the Air? Cold War Right-Wing Broadcasting and the Public Interest*. Chicago: University of Chicago Press, 2011.

Henry, Carl F. H. *Confessions of a Theologian: An Autobiography*. Waco, TX: Word Books, 1986.

——. *The Uneasy Conscience of Modern Fundamentalism*. Grand Rapids, MI: Eerdmans, 1947.

——. "The Vigor of the New Evangelicalism [Part Three]." *Christian Life*, April 1948, 32–35, 65–69.

Hirschkind, Charles, and Saba Mahmood. "Feminism, the Taliban, and Politics of Counter-Insurgency." *Anthropological Quarterly* 75, no. 2 (2002): 339–354.

Hofstadter, Richard. *Anti-Intellectualism in American Life*. New York: Knopf, 1963.

Hullinger, Edwin W. "Islam's Ties of Unity Are Loosening." *New York Times*, July 18, 1926.

Hunter, James Davison. "Fundamentalism in Its Global Contours." In *The Fundamentalist Phenomenon: A View from Within; a Response from Without*, ed. Norman J. Cohen, 38–55. Grand Rapids, MI: Eerdmans, 1990.

Huntington, Samuel. *The Clash of Civilizations and the Remaking of World Order.* New York: Simon and Schuster, 1996.

Hutchison, William R. *The Modernist Impulse in American Protestantism.* Cambridge, MA: Harvard University Press, 1976.

——. *Religious Pluralism in America: The Contentious History of a Founding Ideal.* New Haven, CT: Yale University Press, 2003.

——. Review of *The Roots of Fundamentalism: British and American Millenarianism, 1830–1930,* by Ernest R. Sandeen. *Journal of American History* 58, no. 1 (1971): 159–160.

Iannaccone, Laurence R. "Toward an Economic Theory of 'Fundamentalism.'" *Journal of Institutional and Theoretical Economics* 153, no. 1 (1997): 100–116.

Jakobsen, Janet R., and Ann Pellegrini, eds. *Secularisms.* Durham, NC: Duke University Press, 2008.

James, William. *Varieties of Religious Experience: A Study in Human Nature.* New York: Longmans, Green, & Co, 1902.

Jansen, Johannes J. G. *The Dual Nature of Islamic Fundamentalism.* Ithaca, NY: Cornell University Press, 1997.

Jorstad, Erling. *The Politics of the Doomsday: Fundamentalists of the Far Right.* Nashville, TN: Abingdon Press, 1970.

Juergensmeyer, Mark. "Antifundamentalism." In *Fundamentalisms Comprehended,* ed. Martin E. Marty and R. Scott Appleby, 353–366. Chicago: University of Chicago Press, 1995.

——. "The Debate over Hindu Nationalism." *Contention* 4, no. 3 (1995): 211–221.

Kaplan, Lawrence, ed. *Fundamentalism in Comparative Perspective.* Amherst: University of Massachusetts Press, 1992.

Karlekar, Hiranmay. *Bangladesh: The Next Afghanistan?* New Delhi: Sage, 2005.

Keddie, Nikki R. "The New Religious Politics: Where, When and Why Do 'Fundamentalisms' Appear?" *Comparative Studies in Society and History* 40 (October 1998): 696–723.

Kelley, Dean M. *Why Conservative Churches Are Growing; A Study in Sociology of Religion.* New York: Harper and Row, 1972.

King, Sallie B. *A Quaker Response to Christian Fundamentalism: A Curriculum for Friends.* Sandy Spring, MD: Baltimore Yearly Meeting, Religious Education Committee, 2007.

Keen, Mike F. "No One above Suspicion: Talcott Parsons under Surveillance." *The American Sociologist* 24, no. 3/4 (1993): 37–54.

Knauss, Elizabeth. *The Conflict: A Narrative Based on the Fundamentalist Movement.* Los Angeles: Bible Institute of Los Angeles, 1923.

Kosmin, Barry, Egon Mayer, and Ariela Keysar. *American Religious Identification Survey.* New York: Graduate Center of the City University of New York, 2001.

Kramer, Martin. "Coming to Terms: Fundamentalists or Islamists?" *Middle East Quarterly* 10, no. 2 (2003): 65–77.

Lake, Gerald K. "Biographical Note." In *Quantulacumque: Studies Presented to Kirsopp Lake by Pupils, Colleagues, and Friends,* ed. Robert P. Casey, Silva Lake, and Agnes K. Lake, vii–viii. London: Christophers, 1937.

Lake, Kirsopp. *The Religion of Yesterday and To-morrow.* London: Christophers, 1925.

Landau, David. *Piety and Power: The World of Jewish Fundamentalism*. New York: Hill and Wang, 1993.
Lapidus, Ira M. *A History of Islamic Societies*. 2nd ed. Cambridge: Cambridge University Press, 2002.
Larsen, Stephen. *The Fundamentalist Mind: How Polarized Thinking Imperils Us All.* Wheaton, IL: Quest Books/Theosophical Publishing House, 2007.
Larson, Edward J. *Summer for the Gods: The Scopes Trial and America's Continuing Debate over Science and Religion*. New York: Basic Books, 1997.
Lasch, Christopher. *The True and Only Heaven: Progress and Its Critics*. New York: Norton, 1991.
Lawrence, Bruce B. *Defenders of God: The Fundamentalist Revolt against the Modern Age*. 1989; repr., Columbia: University of South Carolina Press, 1995.
Lawrence, Jerome, and Robert E. Lee. *Inherit the Wind*. New York: Random House, 1955.
[Laws, Curtis Lee]. "Convention Side Lights." *Watchman-Examiner*, July 1, 1920, 834–835.
Lewis, Bernard. "The Roots of Muslim Rage." *Atlantic Monthly*, September 1990, 47–60.
Lincoln, Bruce. *Holy Terrors: Thinking about Religion after September 11*. Chicago: University of Chicago Press, 2003.
Loader, William. *Jesus and the Fundamentalism of His Day*. Grand Rapids, MI: Eerdmans, 2001.
Long, Douglas. *Fundamentalists and Extremists*. New York: Facts on File, 2002.
Lustic, Ian S. *For the Land and the Lord: Jewish Fundamentalism in Israel*. New York: Council on Foreign Relations Press, 1988.
——. "Jewish Fundamentalism and the Israeli-Palestinian Impasse." In *Jewish Fundamentalism in Comparative Perspective: Religion, Ideology and the Crisis of Modernity*, ed. Laurence J. Silberstein, 104–116. New York: New York University Press, 1993.
Machen, J. Gresham. *Christianity and Liberalism*. New York: Macmillan, 1923.
——. *What Is Faith?* New York: Macmillan, 1925.
Maguire, Daniel C. The New Subversives: The Anti-Americanism of the Religious Right. New York: Continuum, 1982.
Mahmood, Saba. "Islamism and Fundamentalism." *Middle East Report* no. 191 (November–December 1994): 29–30.
——. *Politics of Piety: The Islamic Revival and the Feminist Subject*. Princeton: Princeton University Press, 2005.
Maldonado, Jorge E. "Building 'Fundamentalism' from the Family in Latin America." In *Fundamentalisms and Society*, ed. Martin E. Marty and R. Scott Appleby, 214–240. Chicago: University of Chicago Press, 1993.
Maley, William, ed. *Fundamentalism Reborn? Afghanistan and the Taliban*. New York: New York University Press, 1998.
Marranci, Gabriele. *Understanding Muslim Identity: Rethinking Fundamentalism*. Basingstoke: Palgrave Macmillan, 2009.
Marsden, George M. "Defining Fundamentalism." *Christian Scholars Review* 1, no. 2 (1971): 141–151.

——. "Fundamentalism." In *Encyclopedia of the American Religious Experience*, ed. Charles H. Lippy and Peter W. Williams, 956. New York: Scribner, 1988.
——. *Fundamentalism and American Culture: The Shaping of Twentieth-Century Evangelicalism, 1870–1925*. 2nd ed. New York: Oxford University Press, 2006.
——. "Fundamentalism as an American Phenomenon, A Comparison with English Evangelicalism." *Church History* 46, no. 2 (1977): 215–232.
——. *Reforming Fundamentalism: Fuller Seminary and the New Evangelicalism*. Grand Rapids, MI: Eerdmans, 1987.
Martin, David. "Towards Eliminating the Concept of Secularization." In *Penguin Survey of the Social Sciences*, ed. Julius Gould, 169–182. Baltimore: Penguin, 1965.
Marty, Martin E. "Comparing Fundamentalisms." *Contention* 4 (1995): 19–39.
——. "The Fundamentals of Fundamentalism." In *Fundamentalism in Comparative Perspective*, ed. Lawrence Kaplan, 15–23. Amherst: University of Massachusetts Press, 1992.
——. "Fundamentalism Reborn: Faith and Fanaticism." *Saturday Review*, May 1980, 37–42.
——. "Fundamentalism as a Social Phenomenon." *Bulletin of the American Academy of Arts and Sciences* 42 (November 1988): 15–29.
——. "The Future of World Fundamentalisms." *Proceedings of the American Philosophical Society* 1998 (142): 367–377.
——. "The Logic of Fundamentalism: Comparing Movements after September 11." *Boisi Center for Religion and American Public Life*, October 31, 2001. http://www.bc.edu/centers/boisi/publicevents/f01/martin-marty.html. Accessed July 19, 2016.
——. "Too Bad We Are So Relevant: The Fundamentalism Project Projected." *Bulletin of the American Academy of Arts and Sciences* 49, no. 6 (1996): 22–38.
Marty, Martin E., and R. Scott Appleby. "Conclusion: An Interim Report on a Hypothetical Family." In *Fundamentalisms Observed*, ed. Martin E. Marty and R. Scott Appleby, 814–842. Chicago: University of Chicago Press, 1991.
——. *The Glory and the Power: The Fundamentalist Challenge to the Modern World*. Boston: Beacon, 1992.
Marty, Martin E., and R. Scott Appleby, eds. *Accounting for Fundamentalisms: The Dynamic Character of Movements*. Vol. 4 of *Fundamentalism Project*. Chicago: University of Chicago Press, 1994.
——. *Fundamentalisms Comprehended*. Vol. 5 of *Fundamentalism Project*. Chicago: University of Chicago Press, 1995.
——. *Fundamentalisms Observed*. Vol. 1 of *Fundamentalism Project*. Chicago: University of Chicago Press, 1991.
——. *Fundamentalisms and Society: Reclaiming the Sciences, the Family, and Education*. Vol. 2 of *Fundamentalism Project*. Chicago: University of Chicago Press, 1993.
——. *Fundamentalisms and the State: Remaking Polities, Economies, and Militance*. Vol. 3 of *Fundamentalism Project*. Chicago: University of Chicago Press, 1993.
Marty, Martin E., and R. Scott Appleby. "Introduction." In *Accounting for Fundamentalisms*, ed. Martin E. Marty and R. Scott Appleby, 1–12. Chicago: University of Chicago Press, 1994.
——. "Introduction." In *Fundamentalisms Comprehended*, ed. Martin E. Marty and R. Scott Appleby, 1-7. Chicago: University of Chicago Press, 1995.

——. "Introduction." In *Fundamentalisms and Society*, ed. Martin E. Marty and R. Scott Appleby, 1–22. Chicago: University of Chicago Press, 1991.

Masuzawa, Tomoko. *The Invention of World Religions*. Chicago: University of Chicago Press, 2005.

Mathews, Mary Beth Swetnam. *Rethinking Zion: How the Print Media Placed Fundamentalism in the South*. Knoxville: University of Tennessee Press, 2006.

McAlister, Melani. *Epic Encounters: Culture, Media, and U.S. Interests in the Middle East, 1945–2000*. Berkeley: University of California Press, 2001.

Miller, Robert Moats. *Harry Emerson Fosdick: Preacher, Pastor, Prophet*. New York: Oxford University Press, 1985.

Moallem, Minoo. *Between Warrior Brother and Veiled Sister: Islamic Fundamentalism and the Politics of Patriarchy in Iran*. Berkeley: University of California Press, 2005.

Moghadam, Valentine M. "Feminism and Islamic Fundamentalism: A Secularist Interpretation." *Journal of Women's History* 13, no. 1 (2001): 42–45.

Moghissi, Haidah. *Feminism and Islamic Fundamentalism: The Limits of Postmodern Analysis*. New York: Zed Books, 1999.

Moore, LeRoy, Jr. "Another Look at Fundamentalism: A Response to Ernest R. Sandeen." *Church History* 37, no. 2 (1968): 195–202.

Moran, Jeffrey P. "Reading Race into the Scopes Trial: African American Elites, Science, and Fundamentalism." *Journal of American History* 90, no. 3 (2003): 891–911.

——. "The Scopes Trial and Southern Fundamentalism in Black and White: Race, Region, and Religion." *Journal of Southern History* 70, no. 1 (2004): 95–120.

Moyers, Bill. "9/11 and God's Sport." *CrossCurrents* 55 (2006): 442–455.

Munson, Henry, Jr. "Not All Crustaceans Are Crabs: Reflections on the Comparative Study of Fundamentalism and Politics." *Contention* 4 (1995): 151–166.

——. "Western Academia and Islamic Fundamentalism." *Contention* 5 (1996): 99–113.

Niebuhr, H. Richard. "Fundamentalism." *Encyclopedia of the Social Sciences*. New York: Macmillan, 1931.

——. *Radical Monotheism and Western Culture, with Supplementary Essays*. New York: Harper, 1960.

——. *The Social Sources of Denominationalism*. New York: Holt, 1929.

Nelson, Shirley. *The Last Year of the War*. New York: Harper and Row, 1978.

Nirenberg, David. *Anti-Judaism: The Western Tradition*. New York: Knopf, 2013.

Nongbri, Brent. *Before Religion: A History of a Modern Concept*. New Haven, CT: Yale University Press, 2013.

Norval, Morgan. *Triumph of Disorder: Islamic Fundamentalism, the New Face of War*. Indian Wells, CA: McKenna, 2001.

Olsen, Ted. "The End of Christian Fundamentalism?" *Christianity Today*, March 1, 2002. http://www.christianitytoday.com/ct/2002/marchweb-only/3-11-53.0.html. Accessed March 24, 2016.

Orr, James. "Holy Scripture and Modern Negations." In *The Fundamentals: A Testimony to the Truth*, edited by R.A. Torrey, A.C. Dixon, and Louis Meyer, 1:92–110. 1910–1915; repr., Grand Rapids, MI: Baker, 2000.

Parsons, Talcott. *Essays in Sociological Theory*. Glencoe, IL: Free Press, 1954.

——. "Memorandum: The Development of Groups and Organizations Amenable to Use against American Institutions and Foreign Policy." In *Talcott Parsons on National Socialism*, ed. Uta Gerhardt, 101–130. New York: Aldine De Gruyter, 1993.
——. *Social Systems and the Evolution of Action Theory*. New York: Free Press, 1977.
Patterson, Bob E. *Carl F. H. Henry*. Waco, TX: Word Books, 1983.
Payne, Darwin. *The Man of Only Yesterday*. New York: Harper and Row, 1975.
Peshkin, Alan. *God's Choice: The Total World of a Fundamentalist Christian School*. Chicago: University of Chicago Press, 1986.
Piercy, Marge. "The Fundamental Truth." *Tikkun*, January/February 1996, inside front cover.
Pietsch, B. M. *Dispensational Modernism*. New York: Oxford University Press, 2015.
Pipes, Daniel. *Militant Islam Reaches America*. New York: Norton, 2002.
Piscatori, James, ed. *Islamic Fundamentalisms and the Gulf Crisis*. Chicago: Fundamentalism Project, American Academy of Arts and Sciences, 1991.
Plantinga, Alvin. *Warranted Christian Belief*. New York: Oxford University Press, 2000.
Quinn, D. Michael. "Plural Marriage and Mormon Fundamentalism." In *Fundamentalisms and Society*, ed. Martin E. Marty and R. Scott Appleby, 240–293. Chicago: University of Chicago Press, 1991.
Ramadan, Abdel Azim. "Fundamentalist Influence in Egypt: The Strategies of the Muslim Brotherhood and the Takfir Groups." In *Fundamentalisms and the State*, ed. Martin E. Marty and R. Scott Appleby, 152–183. Chicago: University of Chicago Press, 1993.
Rapp, William Jourdan. "Islam Fundamentalists Fight Modernist Trend." *New York Times*, September 20, 1925.
"Rev. H. Richard Niebuhr Dead: Authority on Christian Ethics," *New York Times*, July 6, 1962.
Ribuffo, Leo. "American Fundamentalism to the 1950s: A Guide for New Yorkers." In *Fundamentalism in Comparative Perspective*, ed. Lawrence Kaplan, 24–37. Amherst: University of Massachusetts Press, 1992.
Riesebrodt, Martin. *Pious Passion: The Emergence of Modern Fundamentalism in the United States and Iran*. Berkeley: University of California, 1993.
——. "Fundamentalism and the Resurgence of Religion." *Numen* 47, no. 3 (2000): 266–287.
Riley, W. B. *Inspiration or Evolution*, 2nd ed. Cleveland: Union Gospel Press, 1926.
——. "The Menace of Modernism." In *Conservative Call to Arms*, ed. Joel A. Carpenter, 1–181. 1917; repr., New York: Garland, 1988.
Rodgers, Daniel T. *Age of Fracture*. Cambridge, MA: Harvard University Press, 2011.
Rose, Susan D. "Antifeminism." In *Encyclopedia of Fundamentalism*, ed. Brenda Brasher, 16–18. New York: Routledge, 2001.
Rosell, Garth. *The Surprising Work of God: Harold John Ockenga, Billy Graham, and the Rebirth of Evangelicalism*. Grand Rapids, MI: Baker Academic, 2008.
Russell, C. Allyn. *Voices of American Fundamentalism*. Philadelphia: Westminster, 1976.
Ruthven, Malise. *Fundamentalism: The Search for Meaning*. Oxford: Oxford University Press, 2004.

Ryan, James Emmett. *Imaginary Friends: Representing Quakers in American Culture, 1650–1950.* Madison: University of Wisconsin Press, 2009.

Sahgal, Gita, and Nira Yuval-Davis, eds. *Refusing Holy Orders: Women and Fundamentalism in Britain.* London: Virago, 1992.

Said, Edward W. *Culture and Imperialism.* New York: Knopf, 1993.

——. *Orientalism.* New York: Vintage Books, 1979.

Sandeen, Ernest R. "Defining Fundamentalism: A Response to Professor Marsden." *Christian Scholars Review* 1, no. 3 (1971): 227–233.

——. "Fundamentalism and American Identity." *Annals of the American Academy of Political and Social Science* 387 (1970): 56–65.

——. *The Roots of Fundamentalism: British and American Millenarianism, 1800–1930.* 1970; repr. Grand Rapids, MI: Baker, 1978.

——. "Toward a Historical Interpretation of the Origins of Fundamentalism." *Church History* 36, no. 1 (1967): 66–83.

Sanders, Sol W. "The First Domino of Central America." *Business Week*, July 23, 1979.

——. "The Broader Crisis beyond the Hostages." *Business Week*, December 10, 1979.

Savage, Barbara Diane. *Your Spirits Walk Beside Us: The Politics of Black Religion.* Cambridge, MA: Harvard University Press, 2008.

Sayyid, Bobby S. *A Fundamental Fear: Eurocentrism and the Emergence of Islamism.* London: Zed Books, 1997.

Scopes, John Thomas. *The World's Most Famous Court Trial: A Word-for-Word Report of the Famous Court Test of the Tennessee Anti-Evolution Act at Dayton, July 10 to 21, 1925.* Cincinnati: National Book Company, 1925.

Scopes, John Thomas, and James Presley. *Center of the Storm: Memoirs of John T. Scopes.* New York: Holt, Rinehart and Winston, 1967.

Shahak, Israel, and Norton Mezvinsky. *Jewish Fundamentalism in Israel.* Sterling, VA: Pluto Press, 1999.

Sharlet, Jeff. *The Family: The Secret Fundamentalism at the Heart of American Power.* New York: HarperCollins, 2008.

Silberstein, Laurence J., ed. *Jewish Fundamentalism in Comparative Perspective: Religion, Ideology and the Crisis of Modernity.* New York: New York University Press, 1993.

Simpson, James. *Burning to Read: English Fundamentalism and Its Reformation Opponents.* Cambridge, MA: Belknap Press of Harvard University Press, 2007.

Simpson, John H. Review of *Fundamentalisms and the State*, edited by Martin E. Marty and Scott Appleby. *Journal for the Scientific Study of Religion* 33, no. 4 (1994): 388–389.

Smith, Jonathan Z. "Religion, Religions, Religious." In *Critical Terms for Religious Studies*, ed. Mark C. Taylor, 269–284. Chicago: University of Chicago Press, 1998.

Spencer, William. *Islamic Fundamentalism in the Modern World.* Brookfield, CT: Millbrook Press, 1995.

Stadler, Nurit. *Yeshiva Fundamentalism: Piety, Gender, and Resistance in the Ultra-Orthodox World.* New York: New York University Press, 2009.

Steinfels, Peter. "Fundamentalism: The 20th Century's Last Ideology." *New York Times*, April 6, 1993.

Strozier, Charles B., David M. Terman, James William Jones, and Katharine Boyd. *The Fundamentalist Mindset: Psychological Perspectives on Religion, Violence, and History*. New York: Oxford University Press, 2010.

Stump, Roger W. *Boundaries of Faith: Geographical Perspectives on Religious Fundamentalism*. Lanham, MD: Rowman and Littlefield, 2000.

Sullivan, Andrew. "This *Is* a Religious War." *New York Times Magazine*, October 7, 2001.

Sullivan, Winnifred Fallers. *The Impossibility of Religious Freedom*. Princeton, NJ: Princeton University Press, 2005.

Sutton, Matthew Avery. *American Apocalypse: A History of Modern Evangelicalism*. Cambridge, MA: The Belknap Press of Harvard University Press, 2014.

Taylor, Charles. *A Secular Age*. Cambridge, MA: Belknap Press of Harvard University Press, 2007.

Tibbi, Bassam. *The Challenge of Fundamentalism: Political Islam and the New World Disorder*. Updated ed. Berkeley: University of California Press, 2002.

Torrey, R. A., A. C. Dixon, and Louis Meyer, eds. *The Fundamentals: A Testimony to the Truth*. 4 vols. 1910–1915; repr., Grand Rapids, MI: Baker, 2000.

Toynbee, A. J. *A Journey to China or Things Which Are Seen*. London: Constable, 1931.

"Transcript for Martin Marty—America's Changing Religious Landscape." *On Being*, November 2, 2006. http://www.onbeing.org/program/america039s-changing-religious-landscape-conversation-martin-marty/transcript/603. Accessed April 26, 2016.

Trollinger, William Vance. *God's Empire: William Bell Riley and Midwestern Fundamentalism*. Madison: University of Wisconsin Press, 1990.

U.S. Congress. House Committee on Foreign Affairs. *Islamic Fundamentalism and Islamic Radicalism: Hearings before the Subcommittee on Europe and the Middle East of the Committee on Foreign Affairs, House of Representatives, 99th Congress, 1st Session, June 24, July 15, and September 30, 1985*. Washington, DC: U.S. Government Printing Office, 1985.

——. *Islamic Fundamentalism in Africa and Implications for US Policy: Hearings before the Subcommittee on Africa of the Committee on Foreign Affairs, House of Representatives, 102nd Congress, 2nd Session, May 20, 1992*. Washington, DC: U.S. Government Printing Office, 1993.

van der Veer, Peter. "Religious Nationalism in India and Global Fundamentalism." In *Globalizations and Social Movements: Culture, Power, and the Transnational Public Sphere*, ed. John A. Guidry, Michael D. Kennedy, and Mayer N. Zald, 315–336. Ann Arbor: University of Michigan Press, 2000.

Vecsey, Christopher. *Following 9/11: Religion Coverage in the New York Times*. Syracuse, NY: Syracuse University Press, 2011.

Wacker, Grant. *America's Pastor: Billy Graham and the Shaping of a Nation*. Cambridge, MA: Harvard University Press, 2014.

Wald, Kenneth D. "Accounting for Jewish Fundamentalisms: Dynamic Movements, Static Frameworks?" *Review of Religious Research* 37 (1996): 362-365.

Wallace, Terry H. "Misunderstanding Quaker Faith and Practice." *Friends Journal*, January 2007, 6–8, 44.

Warfield, Benjamin B. *The Inspiration and Authority of the Bible*. Philadelphia, PA: Presbyterian and Reformed Publishing Co., 1948.

Watt, David Harrington. *Bible-Carrying Christians*. New York: Oxford University Press, 2002.

——. "Jews, Fundamentalism and Supersessionism." *Fides et Historia* 40 (Winter/Spring 2008): 1–23.

——. "The Meaning and End of Fundamentalism." *Religious Studies Review* 30 (October 2004): 271–274.

——. "Muslims, Fundamentalists, and the Fear of the Dangerous Other in American Culture." *Journal of Religion & Society* 12 (Summer 2010): 1–14.

——. *A Transforming Faith*. New Brunswick, NJ: Rutgers University Press, 1991.

Waugh, Earle H. "Fundamentalism: Harbinger of Academic Revisionism?" *Journal of the American Academy of Religion* 65, no. 1 (1997): 161–168.

Weber, Timothy P. *Living in the Shadow of the Second Coming: American Premillennialism, 1875–1925*. New York: Oxford University Press, 1979.

Webber, Jonathan. "Rethinking Fundamentalism." In *Studies in Religious Fundamentalism*, ed. Lionel Caplan, 95–121. Albany: State University of New York Press, 1987.

Wenger, Robert Elwood. "Social Thought in American Fundamentalism, 1918–1933." PhD diss., University of Nebraska, 1973.

Williams, Daniel K. *God's Own Party: The Making of the Christian Right*. New York: Oxford University Press, 2010.

Wills, Gary. "The Day the Enlightenment Went Out." *New York Times*, November 4, 2004.

Wood, Simon A. *Christian Criticisms, Islamic Proofs: Rashid Rida's Modernist Defence of Islam*. Oxford: Oneworld, 2008.

Wood, Simon A., and David Harrington Watt, eds. *Fundamentalism: Perspectives on a Contested History*. Columbia: University of South Carolina Press, 2014.

Woolf, Alex. *Fundamentalism*. Chicago: Raintree, 2004.

World Conference on Christian Fundamentals. *God Hath Spoken: Twenty-Five Addresses Delivered at the World Conference on Christian Fundamentals, May 25–June 1, 1919*. Ed. Joel A. Carpenter. 1919; repr., New York: Garland, 1988.

Wyllie, Irvin G. Review of *The Fundamentalist Controversy, 1918–1931*, by Norman F. Furniss. *Journal of Southern History* 20, no. 4 (1954): 567.

Index